Critical Questions

Jacques Barzun

Critical Questions

On Music and Letters
Culture and Biography
1940-1980

Selected, Edited, and Introduced by
Bea Friedland

The University of Chicago Press
Chicago and London

Jacques Barzun
is University Professor Emeritus
at Columbia University.

The University of Chicago Press, Chicago 60637
The University of Chicago Press, Ltd., London

© 1982 by The University of Chicago
All rights reserved. Published 1982
Printed in the United States of America
89 88 87 86 85 84 83 82   1 2 3 4 5

Library of Congress Cataloging in Publication Data

Barzun, Jacques, 1907–
Critical questions on music and letters, culture and
biography, 1940–1980.

1. Music—Addresses, essays, lectures. 2. Arts—
Addresses, essays, lectures. 3. Berlioz, Hector,
1803–1869. I. Friedland, Bea. II. Title.
ML60.B278   780   81–22023
ISBN 0–226–03863–7   AACR2

Contents

Culture and History

Introduction

This collection of essays and other short writings offers a glimpse of Jacques Barzun's intellect at work in certain strategic areas of cultural inquiry: music and musical life, and the broader cultural domain that takes in esthetics, biography, criticism, and social commentary. The pieces I have selected span four decades, but the point is not the length of time Barzun has concerned himself with vital themes of culture and civilization, rather it is the variety of contexts he finds appropriate and serviceable as a forum for evidence and opinion—the different literary and colloquial environments where, he has demonstrated, ideas can be sown, take root, and flourish.

During his half-century at Columbia, Jacques Barzun played a prominent role in both the academic community and the larger world of arts and letters; since his retirement from the university in 1975, he continues to make his views known and his influence felt through writing and lecturing. The breadth of his interests—the arts, history, criticism, the philosophy and craft of teaching—and the staggering quantity of his writings (twenty-three pages of Barzun bibliography, in the *Festschrift* marking his departure from Columbia!)[1] disclose, however, not simply the proverbial Renaissance man, a man of parts, but one whose "parts" are often paradoxical. The complexity and unorthodoxy of his intellectual disposition, its hospitality to seemingly antipodal currents, tend to

1. *From Parnassus: Essays in Honor of Jacques Barzun*, ed. Dora B. Weiner and William R. Keylor (New York: Harper and Row, 1976).

make Barzun a controversial figure very much in the public eye; at the same time, the richness and originality of his thought and its resistance to easy categorizing have no doubt caused him to be more widely known than deeply understood.

He has been designated "elitist" by some commentators, a popularizer by others. Compounding the confusion, the spectrum of intended meaning for each of these terms ranges from roundly censorious or mildly dismissive to warmly approving. Barzun's own books encompass erudite contributions to cultural history and critical thought as well as surprising titles like *A Catalogue of Crime* (1971), revealing his penchant for detective fiction, and a delightful—often hilarious—writing manual (*Simple and Direct* [1975]) "to help restore the power of using words intelligibly."

Hence the present anthology. I have tried to show the underlying order, the internal consistency of Jacques Barzun's thought by means of a collection exhibiting surface diversity. The individual items, most of them no longer easily available, vary in form, subject matter, weight, and purpose. Scholarly journals and widely circulated weeklies, formal lectures and informal conversations, letters and reviews—all have proved congenial to Barzun's freewheeling mode of defining and dealing with Critical Questions. Moreover, presumed antitheses like elitism and popularization, ordinarily irreconcilable, fuse by some magical Barzunian dialectic into a unity *sui generis*. Not given to using disparate styles tailored, as need, for laymen or specialists, he speaks with one voice, thereby charging all his utterances with unimpeachable authenticity.

Above all, Barzun's occasional pieces are uniformly insightful, provocative, and a pleasure to read—reason alone, perhaps, for bringing them together here.

In his book-length writings on music our author has successfully tackled such dissimilar projects as a comparative study of Richard Wagner and his two great contemporaries, Darwin and Marx, and an examination of all the elements and intricacies of musical culture in American society today.[2] Here, for this segment of the collection in hand, I have chosen some of his best shorter pieces on musical subjects.

"Music Into Words," a lecture delivered at the Library of Congress in 1951, manifests two distinctive features—one formal, the other substantive—of Barzun's discourse. Making the most of his evening-long stint on the podium, he develops his argument unhurriedly, step by step, with seamless, logical connections, building inexorably to the conclusion hinted at in the beginning—altogether a virtuoso feat of cohesive (one might say symphonic) organization. The content embodies themes familiar to Barzun-watchers: the cherished belief that art is not hermetic but genuinely accessible to the nonspecialist public; furthermore, music can be talked about in plain language, for it is "surely the equivalent of a lived experience" and its resident meaning can be distilled and rendered by "informed, sensitive, and . . . explicit criticism."

A consummate professional in the best sense (signifying rigorous preparation, total engagement, precision and elegance of expression), Jacques Barzun understands and treasures the amateur—again in the original, honorific essence of the word. "The Indispensable Amateur" (1949) shows how the nonprofessional devotee of the arts functions as a corrective to the guildsman syndrome—the amateur's openness, nonconformity, and diffidence contrasted with the clubbiness, orthodoxy, and self-congratulation of the professional fraternity.

The Barzun book review is a miniature art form. Unlike the dissertation-length displays of erudition favored in some

---

2. *Darwin, Marx, Wagner: Critique of a Heritage* (Boston: Atlantic–Little, Brown, 1941; rev. ed., Chicago: University of Chicago Press, 1981) and *Music in American Life* (New York: Doubleday, 1956; Bloomington, Ind.: Indiana University Press, Midland Books, 1958).

literary quarters, his commentaries are gems of wit, con-
cision, sound judgment, and unobtrusive learning. Of the
several reviews included in this anthology, I will mention just
one here. In discussing the *Life of Rossini* Barzun seizes the
moment to illuminate the "other" Stendhal—not the sophisticated social critic of the two major novels but Stendhal *in*
society, unguarded, feeling and thinking and drinking in
sensations—Stendhal brought alive through the *Rossini,* and
the reader's appetite whetted for "this astonishing stream of
consciousness about art."

Generous in contributing prefaces to books he admires,
Barzun is here, as always, his own man. Arthur Loesser's
Men, Women, and Pianos (1954)—its seductive title conjuring
up advertising copy rather than library stacks, its author a
"mere" performer without scholarly credentials—might not
seem a likely candidate for attention (let alone accolades)
from academia. But Loesser's depth and originality as a
thinker plus his lucidity and verve as a writer combined to
produce a sparkling social document whose importance Barzun quickly recognized—alone, at that time, among cultural
historians.

The memorial tribute to Erich Kleiber (1956) is a touching
personal reminiscence and an enlightened recognition of a
conductor then relatively unknown to Americans of the Toscanini generation. But this eulogy goes beyond conventional
praise for an accomplished musician; it squarely confronts the
uncomfortable question of Kleiber's alleged Nazi sympathies. Barzun sorts out the issues and gives a fair statement
of Kleiber's point of view—not the only or even the ideal
position, to be sure, but ethically grounded and artistically
consistent.

Always an interested and sympathetic observer of new developments in the arts, Jacques Barzun has sought to de-
mystify "modern" music and liberate its secrets to a broader
public. His remarks before the audience at the inaugural con-

certs of the Columbia-Princeton Electronic Music Center (1961) can still stand as an ideal eye- and ear-opener for skeptical or hostile listeners bewildered (if not angry) at the phenomenon of electronic music. He does not harangue, but rather nudges the hearer into new perceptions by analogy, common sense, and good humor.

Barzun's receptiveness to experimentation in sound materials has attracted him strongly to the innovations of Edgard Varèse and Harry Partch. Indeed, he delivers the judgment (in his introduction to *The Sense behind the Sound* [1971]) that the "truly new directions . . . are two and only two: electronic music and the 43-tone works and instruments of Harry Partch." To place one's bets so decisively on these as the only viable new paths in music (and declaring such latter-day classics as Stravinsky, Webern, et al. "a terminus, not a fresh start") bespeaks an independent spirit unconcerned with current academic orthodoxies, musical fashions, or critical chic.

In the important article, "The Meaning of Meaning in Music" (1980), Barzun ponders a vexing problem of music esthetics and comes up with stimulating ideas—buttressed with close reasoning—on such elusive concepts as "meaning," "expressiveness," and that notorious bugbear, "intention." To cite out of context would do an injustice to the rhythm and integrity of the argument, but I will call the reader's attention to one specially memorable passage: a deceptively simple but most evocative illustration, using Mendelssohn's *Hebrides* overture and a few revealing words from the composer's correspondence, to spark a sudden, intuitive apprehension of "the meaning of meaning in music."

Virtually single-handed, Jacques Barzun accomplished a musical miracle in rehabilitating Hector Berlioz—a composer of the first rank dismissed, patronized, and all but unknown in our era until the extraordinary reappraisal set in motion by *Berlioz and the Romantic Century*, first published in 1950. This monumental study fostered a basic change in attitudes not only in regard to the composer but also to the Romantic movement itself. The second segment of the present anthology offers a cross section of shorter pieces written between 1950 and 1980, as appropriate occasions have arisen, on one or another aspect of Berlioz or his music.

Barzun's twin strengths as a critic—his openness to the byways of the creative spirit and his impatience with the "caked wisdom" of the Beckmesser reflex—stand out clearly in the centenary essay (1970). Analyzing the reasons for the longtime misunderstanding of Berlioz, he summarizes: "The important point is to recognize the given object for what it is, and not take it for a defective form of some other object." And in a lighter vein is his eyewitness account of an event rarely shared by outsiders: the practical business of recording an opera. A guest at a *Benvenuto Cellini* recording session that turned into a three-week marathon, Barzun tasted the delights and experienced the tensions along with Sir Colin Davis and company—discovering, in the process, new wonders in this remarkable Berlioz score.

I have included in the collection two short letters, each demonstrating our author's view of the critic's role as extending beyond the customary channels of expression. Another unusual item is the *Lélio* essay, reconstructed for this volume from his notes for a talk given at a City College (New York) performance of the piece in 1955. An eccentric and controversial work, *Lélio* becomes less inscrutable as Barzun discusses this early Berlioz oddity in light of the unusual circumstances of its composition and Paris debut.

Of the various biographical entries Jacques Barzun has prepared for encyclopedias and other reference books, the two in this anthology, on Berlioz and Delacroix, seem to me to epitomize his gift for imparting knowledge with cogency, freshness, and charm. In a relaxed manner without a trace of pedantry, he provides sophisticated idea- and fact-filled summaries of the men, their art, and their epoch. Barzun has an ingenious way of moving about his subject freely, abjuring straight chronology and devising, instead, in the true Romantic mode, an "original form...used only for the one unique purpose."

In the community of scholars, program annotations for concerts and jacket commentary for recordings have become metaphors for the lowest form of music criticism—"appreciation" is the shorthand pejorative. One sample of Barzun's contributions to these maligned genres is included here, soundly contradicting the generalization. His informative piece on the *Romeo and Juliet* Dramatic Symphony characteristically presumes a high degree of intelligence and curiosity in his readers, as well as a responsive sense of humor. Describing Berlioz's lifelong love affair with Shakespeare and his total immersion in the text and spirit of this play, Barzun goes on to illuminate the singular musical structure created by the composer as an analogue to Shakespeare's drama.

In line with my plan to collect shorter writings by Jacques Barzun not readily accessible, portions from his own books were ruled out of bounds. But I have found myself compelled to make one exception: "Berlioz and the Bard." Originally adapted by the author from part of the *Beatrice and Benedict* chapter in his Berlioz biography, this article appeared in the *Saturday Review* shortly before publication of the book. Shakespeare and Berlioz make an intriguing pair, their obvious and latent connections demonstrable on many levels; Barzun's imaginative exploration argues the evidence in the loftiest tradition of comparative criticism. The ground rules were waived, perforce, to admit this fine essay.

In respect to Jacques Barzun, the term "cultural historian" implies not only the investigation of social and cultural processes in history but also the clearheaded scrutiny of contemporary developments. For his grasp of the dynamics of society one hundred or several hundred years ago is matched by his keenness as an observer and interpreter of the present. The arts—and the behavior of artists, patrons, and public—have always colored his way of looking at the world; and the material in the last group of this anthology, dealing with a wide compass of philosophical and cultural questions, reflects this disposition.

The early nineteenth-century Romantic movement had fallen into disfavor by the beginning of our own era. During the 1920s and 1930s especially, cultural critics rejected its pervading spirit as out of tune with the times; indeed, according to some, Romanticism was the ideological forebear of fascism. It remained for Jacques Barzun, in a seminal article published in 1940, to reassess the Romantic impulse, turn conventional wisdom on its head, and show that Romanticism, "the offspring of reason by way of the French Revolution," in fact symbolizes "democracy and . . . equality in diversity."[3]

Just as this influential piece compelled a reconsideration of the Romantic phenomenon intellectually, so did the article herein, "Romanticism: Definition of an Age" (1949), trigger a radical shift in taste. Specifically, Barzun's analysis encouraged new modes of apprehending the movement's artistic productions—that heady effusion of arts and letters during the remarkable epoch extending from Goethe's youth through the lifetime of Berlioz. Barzun emerges in this essay as a preeminent Romantic critic, bringing to light the elements that generated and still link together the rough-textured, "unruly" art of Hugo, Delacroix, Berlioz, Balzac, and other leading Romantic artists.

If Jacques Barzun's relentless crusade over the years suc-

---

3. "To the Rescue of Romanticism," *The American Scholar* (Spring 1940).

ceeded in redeeming Romanticism and vindicating Berlioz, his persistent advocacy of nondogmatic and humane criticism has likewise made its mark. The motif comes through repeatedly in his writings on music, as already shown; several items in this final segment of the collection pursue the same theme in other contexts.

"Biography and Criticism: A Misalliance?" (1975), lampooning the excesses of the New Criticism, is a tonic for "comp-lit" veterans of close-reading assignments, experts at forcing out obscure meanings. This solid contribution to critical thought proposes a return to the use of biography and history as reality-based supplementary resources in interpretive criticism. But the *misuse* of such contextual data does not escape his mordant satire either, and the result is choice Barzun: spirited, irreverent, no-nonsense opinions argued with acumen and style. Similarly, "The Case for Cultural History" (1956) examines the nature of the discipline, contrasting it with the conventional Rankean model of "scientific" history. Not obsessional ordering of data but an intuitive grasp of connections and a high tolerance of ambiguity are the desiderata for cultural historians. On the other hand, Barzun exposes and respectfully rejects (in "Leonardo and Freud" [1940]) the illogical reasoning and fanciful conjecture sometimes purveyed under the rubric of psychohistory.

Admirably levelheaded during the turbulence and intellectual disorientation of the 1960s, Jacques Barzun brought his individual stamp not only to the practical affairs of daily campus life but also to the lively discourse—in and out of academia—groping for perspective and understanding. "Liberalism and the Religion of Art" (1967) meets the sovereign issues head-on—a striking example of innovative, risk-taking ideation. Developing the audacious theme that post-Renaissance culture and industrial-society liberalism are both headed for oblivion, Barzun pushes the lugubrious proposition to an unsuspected upbeat ending, igniting the kind of exhilaration usually associated with great theater rather than the written word.

The two most recent pieces in this collection, each originating as spoken remarks in 1980, may serve as a summation of our author's credo in respect to the arts and the cultural life. The sophisticated newspaper interview, requiring a sharp interlocutor and a thinking, articulate respondent, is a disappearing genre—a casualty, perhaps, of the TV talk-show with its curious tendency to sabotage thoughtful exchanges and trivialize the meatiest subject matter. "Let the Artists Decide" is newspaper journalism at its best, the questioner eliciting from Barzun pithy, eloquent reflections on the state-of-the-arts as well as the arts-and-the-state, Modernism and the avant-garde, and the problems of rational and esthetic communication.

The counterpart of "letting the artists decide" is for the rest of us to find ways of grasping just what it is they are up to; and these two notions constitute the dual aspect of the humanist strain informing Barzun's view of man and the arts. For if it is to be laissez-faire for the makers of art, then critical and philosophical verbiage must diminish, not magnify the distance between the perceiver and the artistic product. The final item in this collection, "Philosophy and the Arts," makes a plea for "bringing art back to its first condition as experience" in esthetic discourse. From there, ruminations on the encounter with the work of art, expressed in simple and direct language, are first steps towards "ordered conclusions for others to compare and verify."

A crucial feature of Jacques Barzun's mode of thought is its unswerving honesty—hence his knack of smoking out pretentiousness and cant, however adroitly disguised; the outstanding characteristic of his mode of expression is the invigorating quality of his prose. This bracing effect arises from the concentrated sequence of astute insights—numerous profound and original specimens of wisdom joined together (apparently) by just plain common sense—conveying an impression of continuous discovery, the "aha!" phenomenon of Gestalt theory multiplied many times over. Best of all, these discoveries are felt somehow as *joint* accomplishments, the reader quite as responsible for the revelation as the author. The writings that follow, read casually or purposefully, offer many opportunities for this special brand of intellectual gratification.

Bea Friedland
New York City
January 1982

The Musical Life

1

Music into Words

The world, the mind, is an endless miscellany.
William Hazlitt (1829)

The invitation to deliver one of the Elson lectures under the auspices of the Library of Congress must come to anyone as a great honor, and so it was to me. But I must candidly add that I found myself regarding it as providential besides, an opportunity ideally contrived to suit my own purposes. For the occasion would put at my mercy, for an hour or so, just the kind of audience I had long wished for, an audience interested in music and yet equally interested—or else it would not be here—in discourse about music. I wanted such an audience in order to try out upon it some ideas about the relation of music and words that I had so far been able to test only piecemeal, in private conversation, where the irrelevant, skeptical, and—shall I say—uncalled-for interruptions of my guest or host interfered with full exposition.

Now in the usual kind of audience one is likely to find a mixture of amateurs, who derive their artistic pleasure almost exclusively from listening to music, and of "literary people" to whom music is worse than a closed book; for they can open a book but they cannot penetrate music. This fact defines my problem, which is also indicated by the title "music into words." The problem is, Are there genuine connections between music and words, or only accidental associations, some of them tolerable but most of them forced or farfetched? Is it possible to describe music in ordinary prose,

3

or is technical jargon indispensable? And if description is allowed—perhaps "translation" would be the fitter term—does its possibility imply that music conveys a meaning outside itself, like the arts of literature and painting?

You can see that on the answer to these questions a good many of our activities depend for their justification—the whole status and value of music criticism for instance. You may not care much about music criticism; you may be willing to let it perish unwept. But you are something of a music critic every time you open your mouth about a concert you have just heard. Can it be that your words are meaningless, that you are saying just nothing with great vehemence? Again, the teaching of music is inseparable from comment, appreciation, and interpretation of styles. Are all the words of all the patient souls who push young talents through the mill just so much gibberish? We are inclined to say so even as we go on gibbering. We have been told so often that the adagio of the Moonlight Sonata is not "dreamy" and certainly not moonlight; that there is nothing "stark" about any of Bach's two-part inventions; and that pieces with a title like *Des pas sur la neige* are music in spite of their silly, reprehensible allusions. Snow is snow and music is music; the one is a physical, tangible thing, and hence there is a word for it; the other is immaterial, elusive, absolute, and hence no words can reach it.

If this is so, then only the names of the notes (which are interchangeable parts of no intrinsic significance) can legitimately be used in discussion, and hence discourse about music must remain technical. As such it can only interest professionals, and it finds itself limited to some few salient points within a piece. A bar-by-bar technical analysis of a large work would be unendurable even to professionals—in short, great works of music are unquestionably great but their greatness is as it were unspeakable.

All this, I need hardly say, is the prevailing view. It has an astringent quality which was no doubt needed when the looseness of gushing "appreciation" became general fifty years ago. But on reflection this self-denial about words appears really as a rather crude remedy, which I suspect is now more often used as an instrument of intellectual pride than in any good cause. Indeed it resembles nothing so much as the cant of the old-fashioned scientist and secularist who loved to shock naive believers in Genesis by facing them with some bit of high-school geology or astronomy. At any rate as regards music today, I think we have reached a point where we are in honor bound to avoid the naiveté of both parties: we know of old that a piece of music tells us nothing about snow. So it is childish to keep reminding the world that inarticulate sounds are not articulate. The formidable question remains, why the great musicians, the great critics, *and the great public* keep talking about music as if their words meant something.

The historical truth behind this question was deeply impressed upon me recently when I was engaged in selecting, translating, and editing for the general reader a collection of prose pieces about music.[1] Having to exclude technical discussions, I nevertheless found that I had on hand an abundance of stories, sketches, essays, confessions, letters, and anecdotes, which taken together gave an excellent idea of what music is for, what it is like, how it lives and moves in the lives of those attuned to it.

And when I looked at my cast of characters as a whole, I saw that it included the great composers from Monteverdi to Van Dieren; the great writers from Cellini to Shaw; the great performers (who might also be writers and composers) from Bach to Busoni. It was then I formulated the conclusion that whatever affectation we might be mouthing today about music being undiscussable must be deemed local and temporary. It could not withstand the weight of testimony that had

1. *Pleasures of Music* (New York, 1951; Chicago, 1977). (Ed.)

grown under my hand in support of the proposition that music can be talked about like any other art; and that perhaps it must be talked about if it is to give its devotees full measure in enjoyment and significance.

What was further remarkable as I considered my two hundred thousand words about music was that no author or composer in the total span of four centuries had even tried to make rational the connection between his words and the musical experience that he discussed. All seemed to take the connection as self-evident, which must be because these literary and musical artists lacked on that point the benefit of modern skeptical thought. But given the prevalence of this skepticism we cannot be so lordly, we are compelled by the current opinion to build up a step-by-step defence of the position unconsciously taken in the past by the great composers and critics. At the same time it would be foolish to neglect whatever may be found valid in the negative view, for our whole effort should tend towards something I consider the great desideratum in contemporary American culture, namely a comprehensive grammar of criticism for dealing with art.

To take off from the negative view that music is untranslatable, we must first separate the upholders of it into sheep and goats, that is to say, into musical people, who are usually gentle and much alike but limited in vocabulary—like sheep; and literary people, who feel vaguely put upon by music, and whose intellectual hides are tough—like goats. Both groups maintain that music cannot be talked about properly or usefully, but their grounds for thinking so are exactly opposite. The literary person proclaims that "he knows nothing" about music, and yet he may own a record collection and listen with enjoyment. He infers that he is tongue-tied because of his ignorance of technicalities and he concludes that the only possible criticism of music is technical. His argument amounts to saying: "I am a man of words; if words could be used about music I should be able to produce them; I can't, hence music is an experience absolutely self-contained."

To this reasoning the first rejoinder is that the "literary" listener has perhaps not sufficiently reflected about such musical experience as he has. How can a man "know nothing" about sensations he has undergone willingly, repeatedly, and pleasurably for a whole year, for ten years, for a lifetime? Obviously he is confusing the conventions of a trade with the essentials of human knowledge. He is suffering from the twentieth-century disease which is to suppose that knowledge and professionalism are synonymous; by which principle it is clear that primitive man could never learn to build bridges since there were as yet no schools of engineering.

Turn now to the professional or the accomplished amateur musician. He swims among sonatas like a fish in water, but contents himself with but very few critical terms beyond the strictly technical. Immersed as he is in performance and in judging performance, he has no need to go after more language. Music for him is quite truthfully a self-contained experience. He can share it with his fellows by an almost bodily communication of sympathy. He is moreover so busy practicing or composing or coaching others—not to speak of putting up music stands and dog-earing scores—that he rarely has time to straighten out his impressions. If he ever does so, his temper is bound to be hostile toward anything "literary." The violinist senses that the Razoumowsky Quartets do not pertain to the Napoleonic Wars as does Tolstoy's *War and Peace*. He assumes that he knows all there is to know about music, and concludes that it is an art diametrically opposed to the so-called "representative arts" of literature and painting. If challenged, he clinches his case by pointing out that each word in the language has a distinct meaning known to all, whereas single notes or chords mean nothing. and thus may not mean *any thing*.

It is here that the counter argument must take hold and destroy, once for all, the platitudes offered about words. It is not true that words have intrinsic meanings; it is not true that meanings reside in words. Turn to the dictionary and look up a common noun: the first striking fact about it is that it has eight, ten, a dozen, or a score of meanings. If someone were to break into this room shouting "Chair!" it would be impossible to tell whether he was asking for a seat or calling upon the chairman. He might be a mad professor who had been deprived of his post—for in a University (as you know) a chair is a post—which is why it cannot be sat on. In an eighteenth-century novel a chair is a vehicle, and in a twentieth-century drawing room a chair is almost anything that is not a rug or a lamp. This last fact is very important, for it reminds us how wrong it is to say that a word automatically puts us in mind of an object. On hearing the word "chair" and being told further that it means a seat, anyone will visualize something different; a thousand people will picture thousands of dissimilar objects. "Chair" is really an empty sound which we can fill with meaning only with the help of many other words and of much other knowledge which is not and which never can be put into words.

This is universally true of workaday life, where we can seldom understand the snatches of conversation overheard on the street, the quick undertones exchanged among strangers, or the easy allusions of other men talking shop. In short, there is nothing mechanical about verbal meanings, not even the practical meanings of daily life. All communication in words remains an art, no matter how habitual, and like every art it is made up of more elements than can ever be enumerated. Tone of voice, gesture, and facial expression, choice and placement of words, omission and superfluity of sounds, plus the indefinite sphere of relevancies that we call context, all play their role in the transmission of any one meaning, not excepting the most trivial.

Obvious though all this may be, it can stand being under-scored again and again, because discourse about art and criti-cism usually forgets it. Speech is so common that we seldom analyze its mysteries and as a result comparisons among the arts are strangely distorted. For the sake of simplicity the stuff of each art is assigned some flat, blunt attributes that supposedly exclude one another: words stand for things and ideas; paint reproduces the visible world of nature; music is pure form; architecture is machinery for living—singly or in groups; poetry, dance, and music are time arts, the plastic and graphic arts are concerned with space . . .—none of these aphorisms is without suggestiveness, but not one of them is wholly true. And the terms of each are in some sense trans-ferable to the rest. Thus, on the basis of what has been so far rehearsed about the character of verbal meanings, one can say that the two forms of sound called speech and music are alike in requiring a multitude of qualifiers and modifiers be-fore they can make a significant impression on a human mind. Just as you cannot produce a solitary middle C and expect a listener to be greatly affected one way or another, so you cannot utter the single word "chair" and hope for much of a response.

And even now the comparison still remains a little unfair to words, for the parallel has been drawn between the high art of music and the merely workaday use of speech. If we pass from daily talk to literature proper, the force of all that has been shown is augmented manifold. Augmented and also complicated by the presence of the new element which we recognize as artistry, though it is impossible to define and dif-ficult to isolate. The borderline between the utilitarian and the literary uses of speech is not intrinsic and fixed, as we might casually suppose; it is circumstantial and shifting, and this variability is reproduced in all of the so-called fine arts, in-cluding music. A bugle sounding taps in camp says "go to bed" just as clearly as the vesper bell says "come to church."

This is by context and convention, exactly as in articulate speech. But in an opera those same musical sounds would be quite transfigured and charged with new meanings. Again, certain pieces of music, for instance a jig or a Virginia reel, though they utter no distinct message, are nevertheless little else than invitations to the dance. The appeal to mind or spirit is slight, whereas the pull upon the legs is powerful. Yet a dance movement in a Bach suite or the finale of Beethoven's Seventh Symphony uses the same conventional rhythms and figures with wholly different effect.

It is therefore not the presence or absence of conventional forms and phrases that distinguishes art from messages of utility, or that distinguishes the art of music from any other. All we can say is that art differs from workaday communication in that it transcends the literal—not excludes it or denies it, for it often contains it—but goes beyond. If this is so, then another imaginary barrier between music and the other arts disappears: no art denotes or gives out information.

We can test this generality by considering in its light a passage of literature, say the scene in Shakespeare where Hamlet finds Yorick's skull and says: "I knew him, Horatio; a fellow of infinite jest, of most excellent fancy. He hath borne me on his back a thousand times. And now how abhorrèd in my imagination it is! My gorge rises at it. Here hung those lips that I have kissed I know not how oft . . . ." etc. Clearly these words are not to *inform* us that Hamlet knew Yorick. They do not answer the question that a lawyer might put: did you or did you not know and associate with one Yorick, deceased? Their purpose is quite other, namely to impress us with certain realities of death and thus to heighten the shock with which we shall soon see Ophelia's burial procession. Nor is this all. The words, while disclosing yet another aspect of Hamlet's character, suggest his constant harking back to the old days when his father reigned; moreover, the facts presented fit and sustain the brooding atmosphere of the whole play, so that the effect—as it is the purpose—of those simple words is to reverberate endlessly.

If, contrariwise, Hamlet came on and said: "Death really does dreadful things to the nicest, jolliest people," the gist of his remarks would be exactly what it is in the scene as we have it, but the impression made would be nil. The *meaning* that only art conveys would be blotted out. As a working part of that meaning, altogether unlike "information," notice the small but effective shift from Hamlet's "he" and "him," denoting the Yorick he remembers, to: "how abhorrèd in my imagination *it* is." *It* is at once Hamlet's recollection and Yorick turned to earth. This, if I may say so, is the secret of literature; the adjective "literary" means: doing this sort of thing with words; it does not mean using words to denote physical objects.

For conceivably Shakespeare could have used many other objects, invented other details, to serve his same purpose in the same way. Hence we should never mistake the literal ballast of the sentences for the meaning of the piece. The play—any play—is not about the ideas, people, or cocktail glasses that it juggles with; in a strict sense literature is not *about* anything, it *is*—precisely like music. And precisely like music, like any art, literature offers a presentment having significance. What kind of significance will be suggested in a moment; at this point it is enough to conclude from all we have said that the things signified are not the things named.

If it should be objected that a poetic drama such as *Hamlet* is not a fair test (even though the passage chosen was common prose) I would remind the objector of a scene in *Madame Bovary*, a prose work notoriously designed to exhibit the prosaic in life. Well, in *Madame Bovary* Flaubert makes one of the principal love scenes take place in a cab that keeps driving aimlessly round and round the provincial city; the incident is in keeping with the rest of the story, but it is safe to say that anyone who believes in the literal circuit of that vehicle knows nothing about love, cabs, or literature.

Here, of course, one must beware of falling into the trap of symbolic interpretation: the cab does not "stand for" anything. Such an explanation would only be literalism at the second remove, duller still than the simple-minded sort. Let someone suggest that Flaubert's cab means the wild drive of the passions, or the vicious circle of sensuality, and the very thought makes one groan. Why? Because it is limiting and mechanical; it sets us to solving riddles instead of grasping meanings. Allegories are frigid for this very reason, that they seem to offer significance only to degrade it into information. Similarly, works of literature that communicate by means of broad generalities about love, death, fate or revenge are invariably tedious and, paradoxically, false. We cease to believe in propositions which in other contexts we should readily accept. And this in turn explains why it is fatal for an author to go directly after the eternal verities. He can state them, but the statement won't be art; for let me repeat at the risk of being tedious myself, literature does not reside in propositions; though it may say a great deal, it tells nothing; it thereby resembles music: it is a music of meanings.

If this assertion is true we should expect that great works of literature, in spite of being verbally explicit, would give rise to widely different interpretations. This is exactly what we find. No two critics agree about the meaning of any given masterpiece, and the greater the work the greater the disagreement. This remains true after the most laborious reading of the text and the most honest attention to previous commentaries. From this one can infer what must be the unspoken differences that co-exist in the thousands of minds which have read *Hamlet* or *The Divine Comedy*. We get a glimpse of this chaos of opinion when we discover what an earlier century thought of a work that we think we know well: it seems like a wholly other treatment of the same subject—the movie we gape at after reading the novel.[2]

You have no doubt jumped ahead of me in applying this generality to our continuing parallel between the art of words and the art of music: the well-worn argument that denies clear meaning to a piece of music because no two listeners give the same account of it is an argument that works equally well against clear meaning in literature. Yet, it will be said, no one will ever confuse what happens in *Hamlet* with what happens in *King Lear,* whereas your musical program hunter will hear the waves of the ocean in a piece which another takes for the Rape of the Sabine Women. Quite so, but this contrast is only superficially correct. The plots of Shake-speare's dramas are not likely to be confused because they are the skeleton, not the significance of the piece; whereas what the programmatizer hopes to tell us with his ocean or his Sabines is the significance, the upshot, the net effect. If we want in music the true parallel of plot we must look for the form of the work and its key relationships, a skeleton about which there will be no confusion either, assuming an educated listener.

Returning now to the significance of the given piece of music, we may grant that the inventor of programs is almost certain to fail; he fails, that is, to convince us that the piece is the same thing as, or a true copy of, a storm on the ocean. Being now profound students of literature we know why he fails. He fails because he has tried to equate a work of art with a proposition or with the name of a thing or an idea. And we rebel against this attempt either because we know such an equation to be impossible or, in less conscious moments, because we have a pet name or proposition of our own, which clashes with the other; this conflict itself helping to prove the impossibility.

2. Note that within living memory Mozart has turned from a gay, superficial composer to a profound and tragic one.

Thus when Sir Laurence Olivier produced his motion picture version of *Hamlet* he prefaced it with a short explanation—a few programmatic words—that defined the forthcoming action as "the tragedy of a man who could not make up his mind." My feelings were immediately up in arms against this hoary misinterpretation of a play in which the hero makes up his mind quickly, repeatedly, and brilliantly. But the play would not be more accurately described by maintaining the opposite of Olivier's view, which happens also to be Goethe's view and Coleridge's. Rather we must give up these attempts at summarizing, or at least acknowledge that they are nothing but shorthand reminders, and careless shorthand at that. Is Tolstoy's *War and Peace* a novel about Napoleon—no, certainly not; and yet . . . well, yes and no. Is *Don Giovanni* an opera about a Spanish libertine? Does the Ninth Symphony celebrate the brotherhood of man? Is Velasquez' "Surrender at Breda" a historical painting? Yes and no; yes and no; yes and no. The "yes" answer is correct in the same sense as the statement that the earth is one of the planets. It *is* one of the planets, but to an earth dweller it does not feel like one: there is so much more to say, a myriad qualities to add, which swamp the mere definition.

The analogy is one to which the critic of the arts must keep coming back: a great work resembles an animated world that is perceived and inhabited by the beholder. It is various, extensive, treacherous, perfectly still and yet in constant motion. Like the moon seen from a vehicle, it follows one about while looking down with indifference. The masterpiece mirrors the mind of one man and of all men; it annoys, delights, instructs, and sometimes preaches, though it contradicts itself and other revelations equally true; it shapes the conduct of multitudes who have never so much as heard of it, and it is often powerless to improve the behavior of those who study and believe its messages. It was created out of nothing, but pieces of other worlds lie embedded in it like meteorites; it is the cause of endless unimaginable creations after itself, yet its own existence is so precarious that its survival often suggests miraculous intervention through the agency of fools and thieves. It seems to have neither purpose nor utility, though it commands veneration, it bestows money and prestige, and it arouses a hunger that some find insatiable.

This and much else is the fluid phenomenon named Art, which we try to decant into our little individual flasks of consciousness with the aid of words. The attempt must seem hopeless until we remember that it is quite like another task which we have no option but to perform—the task of organizing the experience of living. We begin this second task as soon as we learn to talk, and the volume of words which comes out thereafter shows how necessary we feel discourse to be, even about familiar acts. But the words by which we capture the flux of life were not given mankind ready-made. Hard as it is to believe, the best words, like the worst clichés, had to be invented; they were once strange and fresh; and the entire charting of our perceptions, from stomachache to religious ecstasy, had to be made bit by bit like a geodetic survey. The coverage is by now so extensive that we forget its historical growth, its slow progress towards sharper and sharper analysis. We come to believe that every experience for which we have a word, be it heartburn, hypocrisy, or ambivalence, was a plain fact from the beginning. Nothing could be further from the truth. Each piece of reality had to be carved out from its neighboring parts, had to be named, and the name elaborately explained until it became a commonplace. I mentioned "ambivalence" to give an example of recent carving and naming: in many places the word and the fact would not be as readily understood as the word and the fact of hypocrisy, while these in turn would in primitive circles be less intelligible than heartburn.

The point of these commonplace truths is that if we agree to see art as a source of meaning, something like the carving and naming of experience has to take place. Something *like* it, rather than something identical with it, for we have not yet considered the way art and life are related, nor the kinds of words that can apply to each. And before we can be critics we must be clear about these relations. Life, art, discourse—an eternal triangle in which it is difficult to avoid mistaking parts, as we discovered in dealing with literature: we mistake words for things and knowledge for information. We can err in the same way about life and suppose that it is made up, simply, of all the things named in the dictionary. The truth is, the experience of life is not by any means exhaustively rendered by words. We have, for example, the word "anger," but each angry man, each bout of anger, is in some respects unlike any other. The common words by which to mark those differences soon run out. We feel about *our* anger, or that of our friends, or about any vivid example of an enemy's anger, an inexpressible immediacy and richness that overflows the poor word. What do we do about that? We turn to art. We refer to Achilles' rage, to the furies, to Othello, or to any other creations that we have "experienced" as if they embodied those fireworks of feeling erupting as it were from the abstract core of human anger. But it is not because Shakespeare copies, it is because he discriminates and distils that we go to him for an extension of awareness. He—or any artist—enlarges the scope of our perceptions without throwing us back into the total stream. For one thing, the use of a single medium, such as words, or paint, brings clarification. Through it the artist gives us not life but equivalent sensations sorted out. There is no anger in the stage-Othello nor in ourselves watching him. I should in fact be willing to define art in relation to life as "equivalent sensation"; it being understood that in a work of art the sensations are purposefully organized.

But contrary to a prevalent notion it is not the organizing that is fundamental, or else we could take no pleasure in fragments of ancient sculpture. The fundamental thing is that the fragment speaks to us. In color and texture it is as unlike flesh as can be, but the equivalence intended by the human fashioner still holds for a human observer.

In other words, the several arts compel the different materials at hand to serve the curious purpose of producing sensations that we recognize as commentaries on our existence. By habit or convention some of these materials seem to be "closer" than others to the original impressions of life, but this is merely habit or convention. "Closer" has no meaning here. Stone is not closer to flesh than word is to thing. Just think of the immense diversity of words used in different languages for the same things, the great diversity of styles used in the graphic arts for the creation of lifelikeness, and the enormously rapid change in musical taste without much change in the effect produced on human beings. The means of artistic communication are infinite, and a tapestry is as lifelike as a ballet. If I were asked to illustrate the situation of the arts in relation to life, I should create a sort of seven-layer cake, with a large ineffable fruit in the exact center. From this a single strong flavor irradiates the whole confection. Each layer is one of the arts; it may taste different by virtue of the different filler within, but all draw a common sweetness and nutritious force from the central fruit. We can eat our slice and have it too, for it grows back magically—art is inexhaustible. But the fruit is to most of us out of reach; much of the time we taste it through art alone, which, in the broad sense that includes language, is the conveyer, distiller, and organizer of life par excellence.

It would be easy but high-handed to argue that since this role is true of all the arts and since music is an art, music must also present an equivalence of life. Many would continue to doubt the validity of the reasoning, or at least would puzzle over the connection. "Does he really mean to say," they would ask

themselves, "that music embodies anger or manifests hypocrisy? Why, I thought he admitted that music doesn't tell us
anything. Of course, he did say that literature doesn't tell us
anything either: it's all very confusing." I am glad you remembered literature, because what was asserted of it was that
it speaks to us *by virtue* of not being literal. So does music, as
I hope an example will make clear. In the introduction to the
first movement of Beethoven's Ninth Symphony, we are
given sensations contrived in such a way that the ear—the
thinking ear, that is—remains uncertain of the tonality, the
direction, the fulfillment of the sounds. This is protracted
until the tutti comes crashing down upon us in D Minor and
all doubts are at an end. This is a favorite effect of Beethoven's, another instance being the transition from the
Scherzo to the Finale of the Fifth.

Now, why is it "an effect"—an affecting thing? Why do we
respond to it, and respond to it, I should imagine, all alike
even though it may cause annoyance to some and pleasure to
others? The impression as a whole has no name, and no good
would be served by calling it Resolution of Uncertainty.
Any such term is limiting, literal, and—you may properly
add—unmusical because abstract. Just so: music is a medium through which certain unnamable experiences of life
are exquisitely conveyed through equivalent sensations for
the ear. As Mr. Roger Sessions has admirably put it: "Emotion is specific, individual, and conscious; music goes deeper
than this, to the energies which animate our psychic life....
It reproduces for us the most intimate essence, the tempo,
and the energy of our spiritual being; our tranquillity and our
restlessness, our animation and our discouragement...—all,
in fact, of the fine shades...of our inner life."[3]

I would qualify this statement in only one way, by pointing

3. "The Message of the Composer," in *The Intent of the Artist*, ed. A. Centeno
(Princeton, 1941), pp. 123–24.

out that although music is not like, or about, namable emotions, being neither literal nor abstract, it has a way of interweaving itself with some of our perceptions that do have names, and so tempts us to tag the music with the experience of which we are reminded. This accounts for the programmatizing, the naming of pieces large and small, and the inevitable amateur comments about passages that are like sunset on the Matterhorn or the kiss of an archangel. Notice that these analogies are usually with the rare and the fanciful, precisely because they are not readily namable in spite of their vividness and intimacy. If you should ask, "what is the kiss of an archangel like?" you would probably be told, "It's just like the close of the Siegfried Idyll."

The fact that music begins to speak to us at the point where words stop accounts also for something rather more important and certainly more aboriginal—the fact that articulate and inarticulate sounds can combine to form one meaning, the fact that songs can be composed and understood. If a good judge can say that one setting of given words is better than another, it is not merely because one tune is better adapted to the conventional accent of those words but also because it wraps itself more snugly around their significance. We appreciate this in reverse when we remark that the Star-Spangled Banner is a tune somewhat wanting in martial fire and ill-adapted to the patriotic feeling of the words. When we know that its traditional form was that of a convivial song "To Anacreon in Heaven," we recognize its fitness to that theme and discover that the awkward wandering of the notes turns from blemish to expressiveness.

Music's same power to present the sensations missing from the verbal signs of an experience explains why as a general rule the text of the best songs and operas is inferior in its kind to the musical setting. A great poem is complete in itself and needs no additions from another art. Great music is complete

in itself, and only a disagreeable overlap of intentions can
result from its being harnessed to great literature. Fortunately, many musicians have shown a certain indifference to
poetic expression and thus have expended their powers on
verse that was literal and required to be made into art. We
then enjoy both the independent beauty of the music and the
pleasure of its adaptation to a rudimentary conception in
words.

This rudimentary conception is still with us, of course, in
instrumental music, to which we must return as the true test
of our entire theory. For music has taken rank among the
high arts by virtue of its relatively recent emergence as a
presentment that can stand by itself: all its claims to absolute-
ness and disconnection from life rest on the fact that intelligent people will sit silent and motionless for twenty min-
utes while upwards of a hundred players blow and scrape
"meaningless" notes. But consider this strange institution. In
order to find one's way in this supposed desert of significance, it appears advisable to distinguish "suspensions"
of sound, "resolutions," cadences (or fallings), appoggiaturas
(or leanings), sequences (something like raised eyebrows),
broken chords and what not other inarticulate suggestions of
bodily experience. Again, the movements are called gay, fast,
walking, dying, joking, or retarded—all in defiance of plain
fact, since nothing moves or dies, is suspended or resolved.
Stranger still, there is often a madman, sandwiched between
the performing and the listening lunatics, who is delegated to
lead and interpret the meaningless sounds by means of a
pantomime which is said to be as necessary as it is expensive.

When the noise and gestures have subsided, the audience
are heard to say whether the new piece has merit or whether
the old one was played right. Obviously they are comparing
the flood of sensations with a preexisting pattern in their
minds or memories, a pattern to which they readily ascribe a
value akin to revelation as well as the power of producing

pleasure. The sensations offered are extraordinarily complex and the receiving mind must be extraordinarily acute, for it sometimes happens that all the notes of a familiar piece are played in the right order at the right speed, and yet good judges declare they could hardly recognize the work. It lacked force or coherence or was subtly bereft of its accustomed virtue. This fairly usual experience surely goes to prove that music communicates something beyond the relation of its audible parts. It conveys a meaning which some people catch and others not; a meaning which is not *in* the notes, since these can be played correctly and yet meaninglessly; a meaning which is not universally intelligible, since listeners vary in their judgment of composers, of works, of performances; a meaning which like verbal meaning depends on a mass of previous knowledge and feeling.

This last truth is not merely one of common observation, it has also been the subject of experiment. The classic statement of the results is that of Dr. Philip Vernon, a British musician and psychologist, who twenty years ago subjected the Cambridge Musical Society to a series of tests proving conclusively that to consider music a purely auditory experience is contrary to fact. His report should be read and pondered by every amateur or professional listener who believes that, whatever vulgar souls may do, his own pleasure in the art is the contemplation of pure form. The facts are so enlightening, and so amusing besides, that I have reprinted Dr. Vernon's article in the anthology to which I referred earlier. The honest reader cannot fail to recognize how much that is commonly deemed non-musical goes into intelligent listening.

The reason for this paradox is that on his side, the artist-composer, even while he attends to the demands of his material or to his formal design, consciously or unconsciously endows the familiar elements with qualities that also correspond to his grasp of life as a whole. The order in which he puts things, the things he repeats and the things he avoids; the suggestions, emphases, and climaxes; the pace of his thought and the intensity of his will; the stops, the false starts, the crashes, and the silences—everything he does or leaves undone—is a signal to the listening mind that recalls to it the qualities of life. The composer has probably no intention of being autobiographical; he may indeed be a dramatist composing the wordless biography of some imaginary being, like Mozart depicting Figaro or the Queen of the Night; but the stream of sound is as surely the equivalent of a lived experience as are the lines of an expressive face or the gestures of an inspired actor.

The conclusion is inescapable that musical meaning relates to the existence of the creature that man is, not solely because music delights man, and not solely because he assigns to it a value beyond mere delight, but because it requires from him a special attention to particulars within and without his own mind. He must, as we say, understand the idiom, that is, he must record and relate the multitude of sensations aroused in him, and so make them into food for his soul.

It follows readily enough that what the artist has put together, the critic can take apart and restate in the foreign tongue of prose discourse. In so doing, he is really doing no more than accounting to himself and to others for what he has undergone. The critic may, for example, ask himself how it is that some works using all the devices of modulation, cadence, anticipation, etc., according to rule are nonetheless unbearably dull; whereas others are not only agreeable but great. One composer, we say, has good or great ideas, another has not. But this is to repeat the fact without explaining it. The ideas we refer to are obviously something else than clever tricks for linking the common elements of the medium, though this cleverness is not to be despised when, as we also say, there is a *point* to it. And the point is always something larger than devices and the linking of devices; for we can recognize the presence of genuine ideas at both extremes of technical knowledge: Bach is not a great composer because he was adept at counterpoint, but because he had a purpose in using it. Gluck is a great composer despite his clumsiness of technique—if art that is successful can ever be called clumsy. Both equally served an intention that we can recover and rejoice in. When we receive a communication we value, it is idle to carp at the means employed, art being the first and truest pragmatism.

But criticism immediately asks how a diversity of means can achieve similar results. This remains a complete mystery unless we admit the proposition to which our long argument has been leading, namely, that the "point" of speech or music or art is to summon up and shape the stuff of human experience. Anything we understand, we understand in the light of human experience, actual or potential. We must bring our little share of wisdom and remembered life with us, and pour it into the given mold, or else remain deaf and dumb to messages the most heavenly; since, as we know, neither words, nor paint, nor music, nor science can take up and unload at our feet the full cargo of even the smallest portion of reality.

For "potential experience" we have the word Imagination, and it is this faculty that the artist possesses in great strength and uses to spur our own. By a combination of instinct and design he so orders the elements of his art that the interplay of resulting sensations produces a decipherable code to new meanings. Our attention is arrested and sustained. The stream of impressions holds us because it refers to our past and future being, to our conscious or submerged memories, to our anxieties and our purposes; it arouses and satisfies our expectations on all planes, from rhythmic sympathy with our heartbeat to flattering our ego by subtlety. When I say that the work of art, the musical masterpiece, does all this, I mean that in any given instance it may do some or all of these things. At first, the very great work may appear to do none of them: it defies our expectations and unpleasantly disturbs our heartbeat. Our ego is flouted and our anxieties increased. We leave the concert hall muttering. But history has taught us that we should expose ourselves repeatedly to such icy showers of seemingly *non*-equivalent sensations until one of two things happens: either we reject the new alien world for good, or we adopt it by adapting to it. In gifted or determined devotees of art, adaptation comes easily, of course, but most of us need help, and even the gifted ones occasionally find themselves face to face with art that looks impossible to assimilate. It is to help digestion by resolving doubts and dispelling mysteries that criticism exists. The traditional belief that criticism is intended to separate the good from the bad seems to be a confusion between means and ends. It may at times be necessary to point out the bad, but only as a corollary to defining the character of a piece by imputing to it an intention that is bad, or an intention that is good but poorly executed. Again, those who maintain that criticism judges and gives grades for the sake of the artist's next performance mistake criticism for teaching. Even the teacher might be said not so much to pass judgment as to show the pupil, like a critic, what the pupil's own work does and fails to do.

The role of critic is, in a word, to act as go-between, as midwife, between the artist's conception and the beholder's recognition of it in the created thing. The critic says: "Where you see chaos, or possibly where you see nothing at all, there exists nevertheless a valuable entity. It has such and such features. Look at this, and again look at that. If you will but subject yourself to its influence once more, noting the truly salient parts, I will try to point out their connection and their meaning. I will, in the fullest sense of the term, identify the object for you, so that you will never again misconceive its place and purport, nor mistake it for another or for a dead thing."

Obviously, an undertaking so ambitious is never perfect or complete, which is why there can hardly be too much criticism, despite one's frequent feeling that there are too many critics. The remedy for this excess is to improve the quality of criticism by making stringent demands on those who criticize. In music particularly we should be very exacting, and also very receptive, because music criticism is still in its infancy. Indeed we may pray that its puniness is not a sign of stunted growth, due to the impediments of prejudice and false belief that it has encountered and that I have been enumerating. Their removal is prerequisite to critical performance, because otherwise the common goal of all critics is hidden from the musician by his own self-righteousness: he denies the possibility expressed in the title of our discussion. And yet, still, notwithstanding, the critic of music must, like the critic of literature, translate one kind of experience into another. To do so he must use words, for they are the most general medium of communication. And he is entitled to translate music into words because all the arts concern themselves with one central subject matter, which is the stream of impressions, named and unnamed, that human beings call their life.

If he is himself at home in life, in music, and in words, the critic may rely on his readers' keeping in mind the difference between life and art and between words and music. His remarks will naturally replace literalism with significance and will automatically show that meaning is always above and beyond the thing said. The stupidest man is brighter than any device of speech because he always finds more in it than a device. Establish that same happy relation between the naive listener and music in general and you have got rid forever of the bugbear of "programmatic" interpretation.

Remains the question of vocabulary. What words are appropriate to lead the listener into the neighborhood of musical understanding and give him the push that will make him land in the very center of direct perception? A full answer would amount to a manual of critical practice. Here I can only sketch out a few general principles, most of them implicit in all that you have heard. First, the criticism of music, like that of the other arts, must be written for the layman; an educated layman if possible, but a layman and not a professor. The educated reader may be expected to pick up some rudiments of terminology; that is all he knows and all he needs to know. Technical terms are used in criticism simply to point to a part of the work. Just as in a painting we draw attention to a "patch of cobalt blue in the middle distance," so we may refer in a piece of music to the cadence, the tutti, the arpeggios, or the second subject. Beyond this the critic must reserve his profundities for the learned journals, exactly as the literary scholar reserves his discussion of acatalectic meters and double syllepsis. All these matters have importance for the trade, not for the public.

Having singled out the parts that he considers noteworthy, the critic then explains what makes them so. Here he uses ordinary words, and the range of possible phraseology is infinite. No one can predict what type of commentary will enlighten a particular mind, though it is safe to say that a critic ought to be aware of current doctrines and superstitions, whether or not he takes one of these as a text for his sermon. He should ideally begin where the unaided listener left off—in bewilderment if the work was new and difficult but well spoken of; in horror if it was new and badly spoken of. The critic begins in some familiar key and modulates to his own prearranged full close.

In the course of this exercise nothing is a priori excluded. Provided they are themselves intelligible at sight, the facts of history, biography, psychology, poetry, architecture, or of any art or science may be equally relevant. Analogies may be drawn from the workship or the boudoir, provided always that anything said really makes a point, that the point is anchored to some precise part of the given musical experience, and that interest attaches to the remark or thesis for people who care about art and life.

This is a tall order and the record shows that it cannot be carried out without recourse to a device I have just mentioned—analogy. The justification for this need not be argued again, for you are (I hope) convinced that in this world things may be alike, though no more than alike. We may say of any group of things: A is to B as C is to D. The statement of a bold critic long ago that the overture to *Figaro* was like champagne, means the sensation in my palate when I drink the celebrated wine resembles the sensation in my ears when I listen to the celebrated overture. The analogy might of course be boiled down to the single adjective "sparkling," but words of this convenient sort tend to lose their sharpness by overuse. They do not discriminate sufficiently deep, and break down under the strain of building up more elaborate analyses. Hence the obligation for critics to keep inventing metaphors and employing their very strangeness to force attention upon what is deemed the critical point.

Analogy is of course not without danger. It can impart an indelible character to the work or the passage it seeks to illuminate. Much nineteenth-century music suffers from having a certain kind of poetical character thus stamped upon it. The Moonlight Sonata, the Pathétique, the Appassionata, have almost become trite through their labels, as if the suggestiveness of the music were imprisoned beneath. Perhaps the most striking example is that of Berlioz's *Fantastic Symphony,* in which five movements differing markedly in atmosphere are heard and spoken of as if all were demonic like the last; the result being that the adagio, one of the loveliest of pastoral movements, hardly penetrates the mind-hardened eardrum. Such misconceptions are perhaps inevitable; they do result from criticism, and better criticism is the only antidote. The mishap only reinforces the need for the best criticism we can produce—informed, sensitive, and above all explicit; criticism fit to reconcile the tone-deaf and raise the spirits of the frightened Philistine, as well as enchant those who do not need it.

The existence of such criticism matters not only to artists and amateurs but to society at large. In a civilization as old and changeful as ours there is a constant movement between art and social thought. Ideas, attitudes, models for the physique and for the mind, come from the hand of the artist and are popularized by critics. New forms arise as the old filter downwards. This is what Shelley meant when he called poets "the unacknowledged legislators of the world." And music's effect is surely as strong as poetry's, acting as it does on the nerves and the very bowels of mankind. But because the art is wonderfully complex in its higher reaches, its action is more uncertain and diffuse. It takes the critic speaking the speech of the literate man to arouse in that man the desire for music new and strange, and to ease the road to pleasure through that desire.

The goal for the critic to keep steadily in view is that of significance. It is meaning that makes sensations cohere, meaning that rewards and justifies the groping eye, ear, mind. In this first half century we have assimilated, among other things, primitive sculpture and non-objective art. In the previous century, a band of geniuses conquered inanimate nature itself as a realm of art—the literal God of thunder had long departed and nature was mute—but the mountain echoes began anew to speak ethics and esthetics and to inspire masterpieces in their own image. There is thus no reason why in the next half century the meaning of music should not become just as well understood as that of the eternal hills. If the critics seek the way, this civilizing effort will not prove a superhuman task, despite the relative backwardness of discourse about music. The language of criticism by which we assimilate and assess literature was not found ready-made. It had to be invented, phrase by phrase and term by term. And so it must be for music. Once made and tested by public use, the critic's grammar and vocabulary are available to all for their several purposes. Music will then no longer be a thing apart, jealously or scornfully cut off from the total sphere of pleasure and significance. At that time the problem that has occupied us will no longer be a stumbling-block. Every literate being will feel as free to translate music into words as he now is to translate love, religion, the joy of living, or the spectacle of nature. It will then be a platitude rather than a heresy to say with Hazlitt: "We listen to the notes of a thrush with delight from the circumstance not only of sound, but of seasons, of solitude, the recollections of a country life, and of our own."

And lastly, under that dispensation, the false division with which we had to start, of sheep and goats using the words "literary" and "musical" as terms of faint abuse or misplaced pride—that division will abolish itself, and all persons with artistic feelers of whatever kind will share equally the blessings of a common tongue.

1951

2

The Indispensable Amateur

To make a point of calling the amateur indispensable should really raise the reader's smile. Who would not smile at the idea of a select group of businessmen foregathering to acknowledge in a big-hearted way The Indispensable Customer? Yet that is the position of most academics and professionals in art when they meet and talk about their place in the world today. They seem to take it for granted that they—teachers, performers, and composers—are fixed species without which the universe is inconceivable. They think of themselves as beginning and maintaining the cycle by which art comes into being. They do recognize that there must at some later point be a public—or as it is usually called today "a society"—which has the duty of keeping the arts alive; but this duty is taken to mean supporting the professionals, out of taxes if need be, and asking no questions. In short, the vocabulary and mental habits of our time foster the illusion that every cultural pursuit is carried on by experts for its own sake—whatever that may mean—or else for the sake of training future professionals.

But this self-sufficiency is not so inveterate that it does not occasionally suspect its own adequacy, and signalize it by calling for the dossier of the amateur and looking into it (as I have been asked to do) for the data on his apparently unavoidable existence.

Once a term of distinction derived from the idea of love, "amateur" now denotes a mongrel type and connotes disdain. The amateur is not a Philistine but he is incompetent, he scatters his energies, and he never sees things from the correct or professional point of view. Like all unclassified people in a world of organized functions, he is a nuisance. For in the last one hundred and fifty years the liberal arts have split and split again, like the original amoeba. The sciences dropped off first, then each separate art or science; and within each, every separate activity, marked by labels and degrees, to a point where mankind is now divided into two cultural classes of haves and have nots. You are licensed or you are not. This demarcation is so strongly reenforced by our institutions, whether trade unions or educational establishments, that it is no wonder the amateur looks anachronistic, primitive in his wholeness, close to the amoeba.

Yet when we examine the "society" to which we assign the role and duty of supporting the professionals, we find that it shows no unanimous, spontaneous desire to maintain the arts and discharge its duty. Certain *persons* have this desire and voluntarily assume the duty; and on inquiring into their status or quality one finds that they are in their diverse ways amateurs. Rightly or wrongly, with or without capacity, they love this or that art, or all the arts, and pay for the privilege. They take lessons, they attend concerts, they read books, they buy discs—some of them strive to become good performers. More, they talk and publicize their tastes. It is clear that they form no homogeneous group of perpetual laymen, but present rather a variety of interests and accomplishments that grow and change with circumstances and the passage of time. As a type "the" amateur does not exist; and as a group he turns out to be "the" public for the several arts—the public we professionals invoke and flatter in the abstract, the indispensable public.

Similarly, "the" professional is a myth, or at best an unlikely hypothesis, presupposing as the term does a near-identity of training, powers, and purposes among a host of people. It is not merely their specialization as teachers and performers, composers and critics, that divide them, but a hundred differences of temperament, ability, and artistic ideology. The professional label spells uniformity only in the great conspiracy against the public. When you go behind the scenes and listen to the heartfelt gossip of the guild, you discover that no one within it really knows his business except the speaker and his revered teacher, now safely gathered.

As a guildsman myself, I can see that this is exactly as it should be: any artistic conviction worth the name implies a stubborn singleness of vision which usually (not always) blots out the merit of others. Add to this the normal dose of envy and jealousy, and you have for every profession no company of mutually respectful equals but a regular gradation of imperfect aspirants to the good. A parallel gradation necessarily obtains among amateurs, and it follows that by applying rigorously any test of pure talent one would find many an amateur high up among the professionals and many a professional down among the duffers.

A test of pure talent is of course quite imaginary, and the distinction between professional and amateur remains real, indeed obvious. Only, it rests on other grounds than those commonly assumed, especially by the professionals themselves. It does not, as we just saw, signify a difference in native gifts, nor in devotion to the particular art, nor in the understanding and judgment of art at large. What it signifies is almost a tautology: the amateur does not earn, or try to earn, his livelihood by exercising the art of his choice; as a consequence he is free from certain compulsions inseparable from being artisan as well as artist.

To put it the other way around, the professionals resemble and recognize one another by virtue of the stigmata that their trade has left upon them. They are like the dog in the fable, whose collar had made an indelible mark around his neck. The amateur is the shaggy wolf whom no dog had better trust too far. Knowing certain things, using certain words, dealing with routine difficulties in a certain way are the characteristics of the professional. Some of this knowledge and prowess is indeed necessary, but much of it is arbitrary and changes with time and place. A professional pianist of 1890 would probably sound "amateurish" today, just as a modern singer would sound amateurish—downright untrained—to an eighteenth-century jury of Italian professionals. There is a sense in which "professional standards" are but conventions for creating solidarity in place of the critical judgment that might destroy the guild. X may not grasp the essence of music but he's heard of tonic sol-fa—and what's more, he's taught it. The counterpart of this is the judgment that defines the amateur: "He doesn't even know . . ."; "he hasn't even heard of . . ." some elementary thing. In the eyes of the diehard professional, no amount of genius will outweigh some glaring deficiency in the supposed rudiments, for the lack strips the man of his blazon and forces his antagonist to test their respective powers in action.

This reminder of the conventionality of professional standards does not mean that other things being equal the amateur is "as good as" the career man. To begin with, in such matters other things are never equal; they are incommensurable. In the second place, the application, the ambition, the obsession of the great professional is bound to make him absolutely superior to the finest amateur in all that is subject to the will. And the time spent on self-perfecting breeds habits that sustain or replace the will when it flags. In this regard, James Agate said the definitive word: "A professional is a man who can do his job when he doesn't feel like it." When the professional does feel like it and deploys the full strength of his native talents and acquired perfections, he is quite simply the great artist of our dreams, the paragon by which all others, professional and amateur, are measured.

But by this very definition, the sublime professional in

whom all is genuine gift and discipline, not tricks of the trade eking out faults of nature, is what the scientists call a limiting case, that is to say, an ideal example constructed from partial observations of life. In actuality the advantages of professionalism are acquired at a price, great or small, and it behooves the critic to assess this impartially, just as it behooves him to spur and chide the amateur. The critic must in fact play one off against the other in the interests of art.

This dialectical opposition of persons is of course the parallel to the tension within the work of art between form and contents. We may properly concede that the distinction lies in the mind rather than in the work, for we perceive contents and form as one thing. Yet it remains a fact that in both creation and performance there come moments when only one demand can be satisfied, that of structure or that of meaning. We accordingly have the right to contrast technique and musicianship, polish and verve, dexterity and intelligence, precision and passion, ritual and spirit; and if we are wise we want all of each that is compatible with its contrary.

The role of the amateur is to keep insisting on the primacy of style, spirit, musicianship, meaning over any technical accomplishment. It is idle to say that he does this because he has the taste of sour grapes upon him. Perhaps he does envy the professional his technique, but he has also good reason to deplore it when offered as a substitute for thought. And it cannot be denied that the congenital disease of professionals is creeping anesthesia. They cease to hear, see, and think. It is for example the professionals who keep in print a large quantity of third-and fourth-rate music because it favors their instrument or is useful in teaching. It is the professionals who misguide the public by vain displays of virtuosity, competitions of speed or trivial accuracy, appeals by specious means to irrelevant emotions.

When I say that the professionals do this, I do not mean to

imply that they are not tempted and abetted by the public. The corruption moves along an endless chain in which both public and performer prefer mechanics to art as being more showy, easier to command, less of a strain on the judgment—and hence sure-fire as regards applause and box-office returns. The by-product is to make still more difficult and uncertain the success of true art.

On this score the testimony of history is overwhelming. The best critics of every generation have groaned at the dearth of genuine artists amid a plenty of professionals. They have railed and stormed at the vulgarity of accepted tricks or traditions that denatured the meaning or quality of master-pieces. This purging of professional error can only be carried on with the aid of amateur taste and amateur performance: the critic is seldom himself a singer or actor, and he derives his notions of the possible from what he observes outside the professional arenas: "Miss Z. has no voice but how she can sing! If only our professionals, etc . . . ."

Again, the history of creation is but a succession of battles between amateurs of genius—inspired heretics—and or-thodox professionals. Every art has escaped sterile imitation and Alexandrianism only because men of genius broke up the old routines. We should remember more often than we do how many great artists were never "properly" trained and so remained, in the eyes of the rest, rank amateurs: Schumann, Wagner, Tchaikovsky, Delius, Moussorgsky are a few that occur from recent history. Their genius, we say, overcame their lack of instruction—just as in opposite instances, it had to overcome an excess of same. No one but a mediocrity has ever been heard to approve his own education, and the reason is plain. It seems part of the nature of things that all advance, all success in the unattempted, should be the work of the "irregulars." This is true even in the simpler world of machinery. We must take it as indicative that Edison and

Ford both had a strong aversion to experts. As Ford put it in a brilliant phrase, the amateurs seem "less familiar with the impossible," and so conquer it more often.

The price the amateur pays for his singular power is of course very palpable: he wastes time, rediscovers what is known, and makes colossal blunders. But to dwell on any of these faults after they occur argues a weak, not a healthy, critical judgment. We should expect failings and should dismiss them from our minds without outcry, reserving our strength to praise the successful new achievement. If this suggestion seems unfair after the advocacy of strict dealing with professionals, we must remind ourselves of their respective moral positions. The professional has pretensions; he has made a contract, registered a vow, to serve a particular art, and we hold him to it when he commits a breach of faith or palms off a counterfeit product. The amateur as such has no pretensions, whatever may be his personal egotism or self-delusion. In fact and theory he is deemed superfluous and marginal and he usually acts apologetic. Yet it is from him that historically we receive our best gifts. It follows that to treat him justly his hits should be counted and his misses forgotten. Unlike the professional's faults, the amateur's are harmless because they are atypical and no one will take them as models or precedents.

But there is a further reason why leniency is called for, and that is the neglected truth that all professionals are themselves amateurs in some part of their own domain and therefore must sooner or later claim our indulgence. This reversal of roles is due to the same cause that produces the professional's chief virtue, and that is: Concentration. The pianist, for example, has trained his hearing in a particular way; when it comes to playing with a string quartet he is probably insensitive to the refinements of their medium, cannot hear or gauge—much less direct—their efforts at perfection: he is an amateur in strings.

Doubtless a good pianist would soon conquer so elementary and physiological a handicap, provided he had the desire and the time. But an acquaintance with musicians or any other artists in the mass shows that the higher reaches of knowledge present the same unsuspected inequalities. Very few professional musicians respond with their whole mind and soul to the several kinds of music. Some actively dislike choral or orchestral works, others are devoted exclusively to the piano. Some will not listen to the organ, or to any music composed after 1700. The assumption that the term musician denotes a complete artist who can compose, play, hear, and lead any music is as obsolete as the notion that a doctor is a man who can treat a patient from head to toe. The professional of today is inevitably a specialist whom competition has made very searching in depth and detail, and very ignorant—if not scornful—of things outside his purview.

Nowhere is this more evident than in educational institutions, where the student is required to develop an interest in the liberal arts under the tuition of men who put their pride in ignoring all but one. This paradox of bad pedagogy seems invulnerable to reason, and in truth it is due not so much to intellectual rigor, or to the sense of one's limitations, as it is to laziness and misplaced fear. From this *mauvaise honte* the amateur is largely free, and being free he can recognize and cherish the unity of culture. In the art or arts of his predilection he moves easily among the various forms, styles, periods, persons. Usually he has an intuitive grasp of the identical relation of all the arts to human experience, and in his stumbling uninhibited way he helps to promote a common language of discussion and criticism. To that extent he works for true culture and for the ideal solidarity which the professions cannot help breaking up into exclusive camps. We should remember that the meaning of *esprit de corps* originally was (and in France still is) derogatory: it means clannishness at all costs, particularism; and it accordingly needs the corrective of otherness and cosmopolitan freedom.

To say all this is to say that in effect the relation of the amateur to the professional is that of the individual to society. The profession *is* a society. It conserves what the outsider creates, he being an outsider by the mere fact of his difference from the compact body. To be sure, he draws from them most of his knowledge and possibly even his desire to innovate. But what he brings is more than what he takes, and all in all his services to the community are irreplaceable. A world of professionals is an image to shudder at; it would not be a world peopled, and hence capable of novelty; it would be *staffed* and rolling in accredited grooves. We may complain and cavil at the anarchy which is the amateur's natural element, but in soberness we must agree that if the amateur did not exist it would be necessary to invent him.

1949

The Passing of a Free Spirit: Erich Kleiber

In the death of Erich Kleiber last January[1] the world has lost a very great artist, though the United States, for understandable reasons, is not sufficiently aware of it. It is one of the paradoxes of modern communications, so-called, that public notice is intense and concentrated on a few figures that revolve within a given orbit. Luminaries outside that orbit might as well belong to other universes. A living example is that of Dietrich Fischer-Dieskau, the baritone about whom musical Europe has been raving since the Edinburgh Festival of 1952: he could vanish from the scene tomorrow, the American public would hardly notice it; he has been here just once, last fall; he is still a stranger.

Kleiber's odyssey was something quite different. He did come to this country, and it was here that I came to know him, twenty-five years ago, in the midst of the Depression, when he was being tried out as conductor of the Philharmonic. I was then near the beginning of my labors on the biography of Berlioz, and I wanted to hear as much of the music as I could. Since the repertory at the time consisted of the *Roman Carnival*, the three excerpts from the *Damnation,* and an occasional tossing off of the *Fantastique*, I used the simple device of a word and a two-cent stamp to arouse a little venturesomeness in conductors, especially newcomers.

During the 1930 season Kleiber had given a superb performance of the *Fantastique*. The first and last movements—the touchstones of conducting intelligence in that work—had been done with a control, animation, and sense of

1. This essay was published in 1956. (Ed.)

line that I have never heard equaled. Kleiber's rhythm, prime requisite for Berlioz, was faultless, and he had the art of balancing his dynamics so that one actually heard everything going on at once, instead of merely knowing it from the score while being given a thick paste of sound.

Moved though I was, I find from my letters that diffidence prevailed and I waited till Kleiber's return in October 1931 before asking for more. I then compiled in German—and had vetted by a colleague—a message in which I respectfully requested a couple of things off the beaten track. I suggested *Harold in Italy* and the *Roméo* excerpts, including the Love Scene.

To my delight he played these, with the adagio, which had not been heard in New York since the days of Theodore Thomas. I expressed my gratitude. Kleiber replied suggesting that I come round after his next concert. Such was the beginning of a friendship sustained by correspondence and brief meetings here or abroad for a quarter of a century. Kleiber's lovable, devoted, omnicompetent wife, who was an American from Iowa, served as our indispensable go-between on paper, for his English was strictly utilitarian and my written German is of an angularity which might pass for archaic if it were not ludicrous and worthless for the exchange of ideas.

Fortunately, the year after our first acquaintance I went to Europe for eighteen months as a research fellow of the American Council of Learned Societies and spent a large part of that time in Germany. It was 1933–34, the dismal period of intellectual *Gleichschaltung* under Hitler's minions, to which the best antidote was recourse to the unverbalized—music and painting. In Berlin, I followed Kleiber's season at the Staatsoper and really came to know him and his work.

As in every great mind, the most striking thing about him was indefinable, but if a single word can suggest the character of the unique, I should for Kleiber choose Vivacity. What I mean by it is something equidistant from the impetuous and the repressed. It is the quality of men in whom strong impulses are steadily harmonized by *quick* intelligence.

Men of slow judgment can have powerful minds, but they are at an obvious disadvantage in dealing with violent emotions. The strong and quick have vivacity. One is not surprised to find it in, say, Toscanini; we expect it from the culture to which he belongs. But there is always the possibility that the forms are there without the substance: there are many Italian conductors but only one Toscanini. And even he is a stranger to some of the artistic impulses which move a temperament such as Kleiber's. This is evident in the way the two men conducted Beethoven. Toscanini was always admirable, but without the right kind of strength. Kleiber (as one can verify from his recordings of the Fifth and Sixth) had both strength and lightness. The clinching example of Kleiber's amazing sinew struck me during his performance of *Parsifal* in Berlin twenty-two years ago: without tampering with tempos or using any specious tricks, he made me forget the clock. The tireless repetitions were saved by a truly angelic grace and I lost my fear that the Good Friday spell would end only on Monday morning.

It was only some years later, in Paris, that I saw Kleiber rehearse and I then understood more thoroughly why he had not greatly pleased the inelastic minds which still set musical fashions in New York: he did not seem to conduct, that is, to earn his fee on the podium. All his histrionic ability went into rehearsal: there he gestured, danced, chattered, pantomimed his way into the subconscious of his players until the right musical utterance came out of their fingers and lungs. But it was not all comedy; he could be severe and—God help us all—impatient. This is but to say that he was an artist, a man who wants results and is appeased by nothing else. Once he had finished his work behind the scenes, all he had to do was call it forth again by quiet cues and reminders—nothing to see from in back.

It is not true to say that the test of musicianship in conducting is furnished by opera. But it is true that opera discloses the dramatic conductor, the one who in any work that allows it will stress the elements of vivacity as against those of decoration. That vibrancy, that compulsion to believe and be moved, takes precedence over the contemplation of design, which is for calmer moments. Now the printed score does not adequately record the dramatic elements. While design is evident, drama has to be imparted. And of all types of scores that need the vivifying injection, opera needs it most.

Kleiber felt all this and studied his means of vivification as deeply as he did the purely practical difficulties of performance. And that is no doubt how he managed to make *Wozzeck* a vivid reality for our generation. I remember his telling me, however, that for perfect bliss he would choose what he called the three F's—*Figaro, Fidelio, Freischütz*. I concurred in his choice from my selfish consumer's point of view, but wondered a little at the "bliss" of making *Fidelio* come right. "Ah," he said with a toss of the hand, "there are ways, there are ways!" Though I never had the luck to hear his *Fidelio*, I do not doubt that he had "ways." Those who know his great recording of *Figaro* can confirm the surmise.

For his live work one had to go abroad. At last in 1944, Kleiber came once more to the United States. I heard him at Juilliard, where he put on *The Abduction from the Seraglio*: a memorable performance due not only to his seemingly effortless skill, but also to a good English translation by Robert Lawrence and Albert Stoessel, and an uncommonly able young cast. Not long after, the papers announced that Kleiber had been engaged by the Metropolitan for the following season. Good news, but not borne out by fact. Kleiber's orbit, as far as it was transatlantic, kept him in southern latitudes. Buenos Aires claimed him for her own and so did other Latin American cities as far north as Mexico but not beyond. In Europe, it was the magic square Vienna-Berlin-Paris-London.

Latterly London had really discovered him; that is, audiences did not merely listen and applaud, they knew what they were doing. This recognition was both expressed in and caused by the spreading renown of his recordings and the enthusiasm they aroused in connoisseurs. The Beethoven symphonies were a revelation to the jaded eardrum, even after the Weingartner re-pressings. London (the firm this time, not the place) would not let him go, though Westminster, whose adviser, Kurt List, knows a good man when he hears him, tried hard to entice him into their fold. It would be gratifying to add at this point that a solid backlog of Kleiber recordings existed on tape in London's vaults. But, I am told that there is only one, an *Eroica*, which we may have the opportunity of hearing this winter.

The upshot of the demand for his records was that at the time of his death Kleiber was scheduled to tour this country with the Vienna Philharmonic in the autumn, sharing the task with André Cluytens.

In our present state of wide-awake receptivity to sound, there is no doubt that Kleiber would have at last crystallized in our minds the image of himself and his art, the deprivation of which has been one of our incalculable losses. We barely escaped a similar one when Toscanini emerged from the pit of the Metropolitan into the light of concert halls, but we muffed our chances with Kleiber by reason, I suspect, of his qualities. During the two critical decades of his mastery we paid our respects to the severity of high art through Toscanini, but actually indulged ourselves in semimusical trances, presided over by a succession of well-intentioned mediocrities, ranging from the orgasmic to the sentimental. All the while time was running on, and whatever may have been

Kleiber's ambitions or desires regarding this country, he ended by showing us, as if in a final act of self-respecting indifference, that he did not mean to wait forever.

In one connection, it is true, Kleiber did receive a good deal of notice in the United States. This was apropos of politics and in a way not likely to make him congenial to music lovers less clear-minded than he. His background as an Austrian belonging to a family of unregenerate Imperialists reinforced in him an artistic point of view on modern statecraft which it is difficult for the mass mind to appreciate. His was really a nineteenth-century outlook, but as so often happens with nineteenth-century ideas, it resolved for him the confused choices that have faced contemporary artists, from Richard Strauss to Prokofiev and from Cortot to Gieseking.

Kleiber conducted in Berlin under the Nazi regime, in Milan under Mussolini, in Buenos Aires under Perón, and once again in Berlin under the Communists. Yes, but he broke with every one of them, openly, loudly, and explicitly as soon as each began to interfere on political grounds in artistic affairs.

As an Aryan (so-called), Kleiber was *persona grata* to Hitler, whereas Mendelssohn, a pious Lutheran of Jewish descent, was not. Word came to Kleiber to remove Mendelssohn from his programs. Kleiber removed himself. In 1936 in Milan, learning that Jews could not be opera subscribers at La Scala, Kleiber laid down his baton and departed. When the Peronistas were in power and interfering with the direction of the Colón in Buenos Aires, Kleiber refused to conduct. He toured the country under private management. The same lamentable tale was repeated eighteen months ago when the East Berlin government started defacing their own opera house to remove the inscription about "Frederick the Great, Friend of the Muses." Once more Kleiber dissociated himself, penning a letter of resignation which in an age of true friendship to the Muses would have covered with ridicule those to whom it was addressed.

The philosophy behind these acts of Kleiber's rests on the premise that an artist is not a political man, not militant except on behalf of the republic of art. This last is a full-time job which unfits him to be a useful ally in civil strife. The artist's partisanship and critical strength are given to art, just as the physician's knowledge and skill are given to the sick. When the state begins to treat art politically, then the artist expresses his solidarity with other artists and amateurs of art in the defense of their name and privilege.

This position is by no means perfectly logical or satisfactory, but it avoids some of the worst pitfalls of the other tenable ones. It begins at least with self-knowledge: very few artists, even supposing they have the time and interest, possess the ability to survive in politics. They perish there pointlessly—a massacre of innocents. In the second place, Kleiber's principle certainly does not prevent any other musician, such as Casals, from engaging in political war if he is so minded.

To the objection that every artist is also a citizen and therefore has a duty to fight fascism or communism (in Russia it would be capitalism) it may be answered that no such duty exists in law or tradition. An ambassador is also a citizen, yet he has no duty to seek the overthrow of the government to which he is accredited; and he too receives from it smiles and civilities. In short, though coexistence is a difficult game, it is one which the artist has a special duty to master. If he moralizes his role too far he becomes a conceited fool: he cannot entertain dictators because of their crimes nor capitalists because of their profits; he refuses to countenance listeners who do not share his musical enthusiasms or religious doctrines; and if he is truly upright, he will not sing for people who drink and smoke, some of whom, he suspects, also commit adultery.

At the other end of the scale, of course, an artist who knowingly lives off crime or depravity is bound to be contaminated by it. Art and life mix unevenly, but they do mix.

And for that very reason, the public's judgment of artists' moral and political careers should be tempered by the sobering thought, "What could *I* do in such perplexities?" A mind like Kleiber's, tracing out consequences in imagination, is strong in the belief that by reasserting the independence of art, its independence both from political dictation and from public clamor, he contributes most to the ultimate virtues of civilization.

It was in London, before his return to his well-loved Berlin and his break with the rulers of the Eastern zone, that I last saw Kleiber. The date was 1951, the season Christmas, and the mood still that of privation. The previous year had seen the first signs of national resurgence in the great exhibition on the South Side, which included the new crystalline concert hall where Kleiber was conducting. He pronounced it acoustically admirable when filled, but difficult to rehearse in—and brutally, Britishly cold.

We three—for Ruth Kleiber was there—were away from home and spent Christmas Day together in the gaunt, old Waldorf Hotel, drinking its superannuated champagne and speaking of those absent, particularly of Kleiber's son Carl, who seemed disposed to follow his father's career and has since taken the first steps, in Germany, with encouraging success. I kept urging Erich ("Pepito" to his family) to give the United States another try. I told him of the increasing, the alarming passion for music which he could help at once to satisfy and to moderate with the strokes of his wand. To which, having seen and talked about America with E. M. Forster the day before, I felt I ought to add a word of assurance that one could lead in this country a reasonably comfortable existence. Ruth Kleiber's heroic endurance of innumerable hotels deserved surcease, even if only in anticipation, and I expressed my conviction that life over here need not be noisy, hectic, frazzling unless one preferred it so. The United States, I could guarantee, had vastly changed since their earlier long stay in 1930–32.

Ruth was readily persuaded, and I turned to Erich for his doubt or assent. But the question did not really interest him: it was the country's conversion to music that absorbed his thoughts—Was this musical renaissance genuine? What was the meaning of the chamber-music craze? Did the leading orchestras still recruit the choicest players? What kind of audiences did the dozens of new city symphonies attract? What did it all mean? Being no prophet, either at home or abroad, I could not answer this all-inclusive question. But I could report on the changing repertory—and deplore his absence from the Metropolitan, where he would infallibly have given us "the three F's." And with the inconsequence of free association, I added: "Do you know that the only satisfying performance of *Freischütz* I've ever heard was yours, in April '34?"

"Was it now?" For a brief moment his face was pensive.

"Yes—wonderful in every detail!"

"No wonder, really: Weber put them there."

1956

4

The Playwright as Critic—of Music

If by reading Shaw's *How to Become a Musical Critic* you expect to learn how to become a musical critic, give up the idea at once: you are out for an impossible self-improvement when you should be out for pleasure. Likewise, if you think you have to "know music" (that mysterious state of beatitude), or even be interested in music, in order to read a volume of Shaw's previously uncollected pieces on the art, you are mistaken. The reason—aside from pleasure—for reading Shaw on music or any other artistic subject is to feel anew what criticism is. Nine-tenths of what goes by that name, even in an age like ours, which is alternately proud of being critical and despondent because it is nothing more, is not criticism at all, but an accepted kind of flatulence.

Shaw's six-page essay, which gives its title to the volume assiduously collected and edited by Dan H. Laurence, begins to specify what true criticism is, and the list of requirements shows why the real thing is as rare as rubies. The critic must have a cultivated taste in the art he criticizes, he must know how to write, and he must know how to criticize—three distinct powers, not guaranteed by any law of genetics to occur in one individual. The critic moreover must understand the economics and politics governing the production of his chosen art, he must understand the minds of his public and invent infinite ways to keep them interested, and he must understand the several arts with sufficient intelligence and zest to frame for himself and his readers generalities, critical and esthetic, that may in time teach and reform the mixed public of consumers, managers, and other critics. Shaw adds that this paragon should also have an independent income, for the wages offered to even the leading critics will not attract an able man who knows he must subject himself and his talents to a punishing round of recitals, concerts, or other exhibitions.

Shaw himself fulfilled the requirements and endured the drudgery for more than six years (1888–94), after an early apprenticeship at the age of twenty, when he ghosted the musical reviews which form the opening pages of this well-organized volume. Between that first sally and the years of solid weekly performance, Shaw wrote two-and-a-half-dozen pieces which show the ripening of his powers, native and acquired. Finally, we find here a last series of articles, written between 1904 and 1950, and dealing with such themes as Richard Strauss, radio music, *Messiah,* the quality of modern singing and, in questionnaire form, the inevitable "Music Today."

The dim recognition that criticism is at any time extremely scarce, and that it differs *toto caelo* from the well-meant, ill-wrought utterances that justly inspire the scorn of artists, leads a good many people to suppose that criticism is art. This not true. Criticism relies, of course, on the art of writing and it may be put under the head of art as prose. But this is not what people mean when they want to dignify criticism with the name of art. They mean that it is "creative" and they imply that we should cherish its products as we cherish a poem or a piece of sculpture. This seems to me all wrong. Criticism is not an art: it is an intelligence. It does not create, because it starts from a created thing and owns an obligation to it. And its products cannot be cherished like a work of art, because the pleasure they afford is that of analysis, not synthesis.

Shaw's critical writings form a continuous demonstration of these truths. Anyone next to him in the audience could theoretically take in what he took in, feel as he felt, move his lips or his pen as he did to utter English words. But only he could disentangle his feelings and perceptions, choose the diagnostic ones, relate them to others of a like kind, extract general propositions from this exercise, and convey the results of these complex operations without effort, in the form of a coherent essay measured to the line.

Even though the end of criticism is, as it were, analysis in aspic, the special quality of the critical intelligence is comprehensiveness. That is why a correct technical description of a symphony is not a criticism of it, and why Shaw is seldom technical. He could have shown off, like the others, by pouncing on harmonic oddities and peppering the page with the jargon of the trade, but he knew that this was only evading the real, recurrent difficulty of criticism, the difficulty that is never permanently solved: how shall I render my understanding of this piece or this performance, through words, to an unknown reader who was not there? Which points matter and which do not? What prejudices must I counter, what ignorance dispel without seeming to? And above all, how keep criticism ethical, that is, refrain from taking advantage of the critic's power to misrepresent, wound, and cause public harm, not out of malice (though malice is not unknown), but out of heedlessness, high spirits, and the desire to shine?

Shaw's greatness as an intellect and a moral being is that he shines and indulges high spirits—the highest, perhaps, in all literature—without ever being heedless. In every critical piece, long or short, his control is absolute. He is gay, not irresponsible; he hits hard but is never cruel; his energy animates the scene and the reader, it does not destroy the occasion or the performer. No one can rise from reading a page of his criticism without feeling elated at the existence of art itself, at the thought that in the muddle and misery of civilization such an activity as a concert can take place, and such thoughts and feelings be generated by it in an organized mind and body.

Nothing could be further from the self-protective scurrying and snarling with which many among us take to the arts, read and write criticism, and pursue a chimera of perfection. We are all very fine fellows but we cannot criticize like Shaw. And we cannot, not merely because we lack his enormous sensitivity and strength and intelligence and memory, but because we are no longer capable of being interested exclusively in the subject before us. We have an ax to grind and we chop off our fingers and our pleasure in clumsy attempts to satisfy the ulterior motive.

Open your Shaw anywhere and see what I mean. But, if you will, pay particular attention to what he says about Mozart and Berlioz, those kindred artists of whom Shaw, almost alone in his generation, had the right intelligence. Here is "the problem of Mozart" anatomized in 1891:

> It is not possible to give here any adequate account of Mozart's claims to greatness as a composer. At present his music is hardly known in England, except to those who study it in private. . . . Mozart, if left untutored, would probably have arrived at the conclusion that a composition without a poetic or dramatic basis was a mere luxury, and not a serious work of art at all. As it was, he was trained to consider the production of "absolute music" as the normal end of composition, and when his genius drove him to make his instrumental music mean something, he wasted the most extraordinary ingenuity in giving it expression through the forms and without violating the usages of absolute music . . . .
>
> This combination of formalism with poetic significance has been much applauded, not only for its

ingenuity, as is natural, but as a merit in the music, which is perverse and absurd.

Now on the practical side, but no less an act of imagination, a good part of "the problem of Berlioz," apropos of the Funeral Symphony:

The effect was unsatisfactory and the composer's reputation unfairly damaged by it: a result which those who were present at the production, on a similarly reduced scale, of the gigantic Te Deum at the Crystal Palace in April were quite prepared for. To play either of these works without at the very least doubling the ordinary numbers of a concert orchestra is as unjust to the composer as a performance of a Haydn quartet on the jew's harp would be.

And after this, the whole of the essay "Mozart with Mozart Left Out." Then you may speak of criticism.

1961

5

Men, Women, and Pianos

Our century's self-conscious interest in culture and society has produced valuable attempts to retell the Western past with the aid of such organizing principles as technological change, art collecting, and—in a humorous but informative vein—the modes and means of sanitary plumbing. It was left to Mr. Arthur Loesser, a pianist and musician as well as a musical journalist, to hit upon an idea which seems obvious now that he has given it body and form, but which had not occurred to anyone before, despite its patently rich possibilities.

Taking the piano as a "center" for writing the social history of the last three hundred years was an inspired idea. It combines all the virtues and advantages: the piano being a creation and plaything of men, its story leads us into innumerable biographies; being a boxful of gadgets, the piano has changed through time and improved at ascertainable moments and places; and every Western land has both contributed and succumbed to it. Indeed, for the last century and a half the piano has been an institution more characteristic than the bathtub—there were pianos in the log cabins of the frontier, but no tubs. As a result of this ubiquity, the identification of piano with music took such deep root as to constitute a superstition. We are only now emancipating ourselves from it, and it is thus doubly fitting that we should review its origin and spread.

All this Mr. Loesser must have seen at a glance when his great idea struck him, and his work proves that he also perceived how in itself the piano is a perfect symbol of Western civilization in modern times. I suggested with undue scorn a moment ago that the piano is a gadget; it is in fact a machine. More than any other music-making contrivance until the advent of radio, its growth has paralleled that of technology. There is something of the power loom in the ultimate "grand" of the nineteenth century, and a fair likeness between note-spinning virtuosos and cotton-spinning magnates.

Again, the piano is the social instrument par excellence. It is drawing-room furniture, a sign of bourgeois prosperity, the most massive of the devices by which the young are tortured in the name of education and the grown-up in the name of entertainment. It is a rallying point for the convivial when letting off spirituous fumes through song and for the amorous conducting a romance with the aid of romances. At the same time, too, the piano is the individualist's instrument for nursing the illusion that he is a host in himself. With bare hands and intermittent foot he can unleash quasi-symphonic storms and discharge the tensions induced by a world increasingly populated and oppressive, a world in which standardization and noise-making power jointly increase, the inevitable concomitants of machinery—including the piano.

But this summary is not the tale itself, and we cannot really be said to know what the conclusion stands for until we have read Mr. Loesser's admirably balanced and leisurely account. In the hands of a less versatile writer, the story might have left deplorable gaps or pitched into impassable technicalities. A breathless narrator would have choked on his own learning and given us vertigo instead of pleasurable instruction. Just think: in his progress from country to country and from age to age, the historian must tell us how the piano grew out of its various keyboard ancestors; he must explain the mechanism, the manufacture, and the playing of all these hybrids; he must describe the music and its patrons, the cost and arrangement of their diversions, and the economics of their lives. Equally his concern are the printing and publishing of music and the tastes and fads, reputations and charlatanisms of an industry which culminates in vulgar idolatry as well as high art. These in turn, as Mr. Loesser shows, reflect the image of the great intellectual and political movements, from the Reformation, which lies just behind his starting point in 1648, to twentieth-century democracy and totalitarianism. Almost his last words connect the rise of Hitler and the failures of American banks with the nadir of piano manufacture and the victory of airborne music.

Nothing that is or was relevant is too slight for his notice; nothing that can entice the imagination of the curious and the thoughtful is too impalpable for him to convey. He evokes (without solving) the mystery of how four-hand duets were played at one keyboard when hoop-skirts were wider than the instrument, and he knows how to sum up what is not at all mysterious: "The lyrichord, the musical glasses, and the guitar earned but short rides on the wheel of time; the pianoforte was the object that fulfilled the needs of a longer day. It had expression; playing it required only a slight adaptation of an existing skill; and it was expensive enough to be socially desirable."

We do not of course expect Mr. Loesser to rewrite the history of the French Revolution or tell us "all about Chopin." But wherever we test him he gives us the grateful feeling that he has seen and thought for himself. He may err in judgment—as I think he does whenever he deals with Rousseau—but the mistake, if it is one, does not matter, because it is part of a considered whole which in turn rests upon firsthand impressions. Mr. Loesser has undoubtedly fingered and examined all the types of instruments he speaks of; he has studied illustrations and exploited foreign sources; played or read the music, good and bad, which has adorned or compromised the costly apparatus which is his theme. In a word, Mr. Loesser is a good craftsman in research.

But he could never have made a book, in seven years or in

seventeen, if he had not started with a large fund of general culture and miscellaneous reading. No amount of research into the lives of baroque organists would suggest an analogy of their trios with Leibniz's "windowless monads." No degree of conscientious reading about the eighteenth century would lead a man to characterize Richardson's novels as "viscous." Mr. Loesser, it is clear, is a man of strong and vivid opinions, and they color his work. No one but a pedant would want it colorless.

His prevailing wind of doctrine, one may say, is the astringent. He prefers the aristocratic ideal to the bourgeois, polyphonic music to homophonic, art to trade, the individual to the mass, the definite and elegant to the atmospheric and passionate. These are temperamental choices which also help account for the sustained lucidity of his prose—no mean advantage when so much that is intricate in mechanics and sound, in costume and chronology, has to be imparted without tables, diagrams, or notation. Indeed, the author's power to convey the quality or purport of a piece is most unusual in an age when music is generally supposed to make us speechless. See how Mr. Loesser manages: "Variations now were made to open with a magniloquent introductory section containing a number of attention-raping chords and flourishes ranging over a good portion of the keyboard. A clever composer might also incorporate into these a sly anticipatory allusion to a measure or two of the tune to come. The bustle would subside, and a hold would be arranged upon a leading tone or chord, whereupon the simply attired melody would come forth, effectively set forth against the suspense just accumulated. In other words, the tune was made to 'make an entrance' in the best theatrical or operatic manner." A writer who always knows what he means will assume other writers carry meaning too. And so when Mr. Loesser quotes from foreign authors, his translation has point and character and sounds as if written in English. Thus his entire work is of a piece, free alike from witless gush and from hollow gravity.

But who am I to praise a performer in whose pages a colleague can learn innumerable lessons? It is much more modest and becoming to point out that Mr. Loesser's chapter titles do not come up to his own standards of expression and might even mislead the unwary. Let the intending reader sample the text rather than the Table of Contents. His eye is bound to fall upon such happy phrases as:"light music is a good lubricant"; "Vienna was built dense"; "musicians were invited to many salons on terms of putative equality"; and even before he encounters such a problem as "the need of the thumb in strained digital situations," he will have been convinced that in order to discover all and enjoy the exploration he must begin at the beginning. This is the spot where, having held a candle before the sun—or perhaps the herald's trumpet before the grand piano—we now leave the reader, confident that he is setting out on a memorable journey.

1954

6

Toward New Musics

Harry Partch and the Moderns

Neither Mrs. Peyser nor her book needs an introduction from me.[1] Her intelligent scholarship, by which I mean her desire and ability to tell the reader clearly and comprehensively what happened in music between Wagner and Varèse, is more than sufficient warrant for her to address the public without screen or sponsorship.

But perhaps the world in which the events she describes took place can stand a little explanation and apology, if only because it is the world in which we all have lived from day to day, too busy or too bewildered to reckon up sums and work out answers. The only trouble with attempting such cultural arithmetic in a preface is that a couple of sheets of paper are not enough. Still, one can at least try to set out the problems in common form: If A has a tank full of water and B's machinery pumps out 100 gallons an hour, where are we?

From Mrs. Peyser's excellent account of Schoenberg's driving obsession, it is evident that by 1911 (the date of his *Harmonielehre*), the European system of major-minor harmony and tonal enharmony had yielded all it could possibly give. It had been exhausted in a few centuries by an extraordinary number of composers and their patrons. After Richard Strauss any further exploiting of it could only fall into meaningless repetition, clever allusiveness, or deliberate pastiche. From every derived hint the accustomed mind could call up the great original from which it sprang. The

1. Introduction to *The New Music: The Sense Behind the Sound*, by Joan Peyser (1971). (Ed.)

truth is that in any art at any time, meaning is conveyed only when the practitioners are struggling with a new style or medium, not when they are torturing an old and juiceless one. Such was the predicament of Western music by 1920.

And what had happened to music was also happening to the other arts. Five hundred years of creation and logical evolution were everywhere coming to an end; an era of civilization was reaching its close—political, social, and cultural. New paths must be cut in the unknown or else— stagnation. Desperate chromaticism, the 5-tone scale, polytonality, atonality, the 12-tone row and its variants were at once symptoms of decadence and groping efforts to find a new organizing principle for sound, just as the technical innovations of Cubism, Futurism, Surrealism, Simultaneity in poetry (the choric poem), and Joycean discombobulations of language were the groping efforts of other artists to leave behind them the barren ground to which a half millennium of high art since the Renaissance had brought them. The surrounding fads, marked by self-conscious humor and bright charlatanism, were the normal devices by which a culture destroys itself and ensures its leveling down to nothingness.

I happen to think that only in music have truly new directions been found, and that these are two and only two: electronic music and the 43-tone works and instruments of Harry Partch. This conclusion may, as I reflect on it, be at variance with Mrs. Peyser's estimate of the composers she discusses before reaching Varèse. (Partch she does not mention, but he is implicit in her Epilogue, where pop art and the Beatles figure as important, for knowingly or not, the Beatles partake of Partch, who antedates them by twenty years.) Any such difference of opinion in no way invalidates her survey, or my stage-setting. It merely shifts the point at which the observer chooses to mark off end and beginning, always a matter of considerable discretion.

It may help the reader to make that choice if I add a few

words in support of my own. It seems to me that the wanderings of Stravinsky, the brevities of Webern, the unassimilabilities of pure Schoenberg, and the solemn pedantries of his disciples all suggest a terminus, not a fresh start. They prepare the way, as Mrs. Peyser so lucidly shows. They exercise the ear and disabuse the educated mind of its refined prejudices. But they bequeath little we can treasure without these very arguments of "functional importance."

On this question Mrs. Peyser's title is a splendid touchstone: What *is* the sense behind the sound? Or even more forcibly, what is the sense *in* the sound? Allow as much time as is reasonable for the cultural lag, and it remains a fact that our very best ears, our most antiphilistine minds are not yet enamored of the music which fills the time since Debussy. I speak of enjoyers, not producers. Alban Berg, yes; early Stravinsky, bravo; transitional Schoenberg, to be sure. Sample pieces by Webern, Wellesz, Messiaen, Boulez, granted. But as to the rest of the output—an output more eagerly nurtured and welcomed and studied than its nineteenth-century counterpart—who can say that it has ever shed its laboratory smell, its taint of the *voulu* and the demonstrative?

To say this is not to damn the workmen; it is merely to assign them their due and heroic place in history. We must be enormously grateful to them. It was genius and courage that said good-bye to harmony and sought a new principle of musical unity in melody and rhythm. Perhaps, if critics and musicologists had been more alert, that lesson would have been read long ago in Berlioz, where it was first embodied— Debussy at Bayreuth had a glimpse of it when contrasting him with Wagner as regards modal writing. But never mind: Wagnerism obscured the facts, and while all the professors kept reanalyzing the *Tristan* chord, the creative minds discovered that the age of dissection was also the age of despair.

At that juncture there are no positive principles, only negative: "Let us do just the opposite; let us forget what we know; let us not even suppose that we possess the simple means of our art." Thanks to the genius of Varèse, exploration along these lines, coupled with technologically new sources of sound, led to a genuinely new *possibility of music*; and here we are, listening to *Ionisation, Déserts,* and *Poème électronique.*

Before we can listen properly, though, a certain cleansing of the intellect is required. Exactly like Varèse, we have to reach the point where we naturally and abruptly remember what music is for. It is not to provide chapters in books about music and win a place for profundity in said chapters. Making music is for delight; it is intended and designed for sentient beings that have hopes and purposes and emotions. Music does not *tell about* these movements of the human spirit, but it somehow transfixes them, elaborates them, and gives them enduring form and self-renewing vigor. This raison d'être of music is what our electronic composers must exhibit, and what we listeners must learn to find in their works.

That double need (as I said a minute ago) requires that we clear our minds of the verbal pedantry and affectation of the past half century. Mrs. Peyser quotes, much to the point, a large emetic dose of this nonsense. We should bear in mind that it, too, has only functional importance. Nearly every remark by these contemporary masters was a shot fired in the battle; we may hope it killed some dreadful enemy of music. But it is only spent and twisted metal now, and as bad for us to harbor as any foreign body under the skin. Forget and disbelieve! For did any artist ever utter such false and absurd notions as Stravinsky? Was any genius so narrow and vicious in his abstractions as Debussy? Was any profound musician so megalomaniac and irrelevant in speech as Schoenberg? They and their peers have filled the books with angry words, demonstrable untruths, and selfish animus that can only pollute the environment for music as a whole. Alas, their own music undoubtedly suffered from this rankness of the soil out of which it sprang. Let us by all means understand why they spoke as they did, unable to help themselves; but let us also, and permanently from now on, open our minds to the broader and purer thoughts that belong by nature to the fit concourse of sounds.

1971

A Request for the Loan of Your Ears

Your presence here, at a concert of electronic music, is a compliment to the composers, as well as to the two universities that sponsor their work; and while I extend to you a welcome on behalf of those universities, I also wish to convey the composers' hope that you will be as gratified by hearing their works as they are by your willingness to listen.

No doubt your expectations are mixed. You are ready to be surprised, to have your curiosity satisfied, and possibly even to experience snatches of enjoyment as you would at an ordinary concert. If that is your state of mind I am fairly sure you will not be disappointed. But it may be that you are here in a mood of combined trepidation and resistance: this, after all, is the Age of Anxiety. Or you may be bent on proving that electronic music is not music—doing this by the most painful test of endurance; or else you may be feeling caught because you have been brought by a friend and friendship is dearer to you than prudence.

If for these or any other reasons you are ill at ease, allow me to suggest a few considerations which should make you more serene, while leaving you your full freedom of opinion, your entire right to dislike and reject. I suggest, to begin with, that we are not here to like or approve but to understand. And the first step to understanding a new art is to try to imagine why the maker wants it the way it is. That attempt is interesting in itself, even if we ultimately disown the product. To understand in this fashion does not mean to accept passively because someone says that the stuff is new and therefore good, that many believe in it, that it's going to succeed anyway, so it's best to resign oneself to the inevitable. This kind of reasoning has gone on about modern art for some thirty years, and nothing has been more harmful to culture itself. It is an inverted philistinism, which eliminates judgment and passion just as surely as did the older philistinism of blind opposition to whatever was new.

What then is the decent, reasonable attitude to adopt? Very simple: make the assumption, first that the old style—whatever it is—has exhausted its possibilities and can only offer repetition or trivial variations of the familiar masterpieces. I am not saying you should believe that the style of your favorite music is obsolete. I invite you to *assume* that it may be: for by trying to think that it is, as the new composer obviously has done, you will begin to discover what he is up to. By way of encouragement let me remind you that you make this very assumption automatically four or five times in every classical concert, in order to adjust your ear to the changes in style between Bach and Mozart, Mozart and Richard Strauss, and (if you can) between Strauss and Alban Berg. If styles and genres did not suffer exhaustion, there would be only one style, one genre in each art from its beginnings to yesterday.

But, you may say, electronic music is something else again; it is out of bounds; the jump is too great. There is no semblance of scale, the sounds are new, most of them are in fact just noise. Ah, noise. Noise is the most constant complaint in the history of music. In the heyday of music it was not only Berlioz and Wagner who were damned as noisy; it was Mozart before them, and Haydn, and even earlier Lully and Handel. I suspect that the reason Orpheus was torn to pieces by women, as the myth tells us, is that he made horrendous new noises on his lyre which they thought not at all modish.

The argument of noise is always irrelevant. The true question is: does this noise, when familiar, fall into intelligible forms and convey notable contents? To supply the answer takes time. One hearing, two, three hearings are not enough. Something must change in one's sensibility as a whole, in just the way that permits a foreign language suddenly to break into meaning and melody after months or years of its being mere noise. As a veteran of the premiere of Stravinsky's *Sacre du Printemps* in Paris, I can testify to the reality of the transformation. At the end of the work, in 1913, the conductor Pierre Monteux turned around amid the furious howls of the audience and said that since they had liked the piece so much he would play it again. The response was no better, and the police had to come in to quell the tumult. But now, fifty years after, the young accept those hammering rhythms and dissonant chords as if they were lullabies. They relish them while dallying in canoes, at the movies in consort with Disney's abstractions, and at the circus, where the music is used for the elephants to dance to.

Associations, in short, and assumptions and expectations rule our judgments. They govern our feelings, which we think are altogether spontaneous and truthful. But our sensibility is always more complex and more resourceful than we suppose, and that is why why I have ventured to bring to your conscious notice what you knew all the while, but might not sufficiently allow for in listening to electronic music for the first time.

The word "electronic" suggests a final objection with which it is well to come to grips. Most people of artistic tastes share the widespread distrust and dislike of machinery and argue that anything pretending to be art cannot come out of a machine: art is the human product par excellence, and electronic music, born of intricate circuits and the oscillations of particles generated by Con Edison, is a contradiction in terms. Here again the answer is simple: the moment man ceased to make music with his voice alone the art became machine-ridden. Orpheus's lyre was a machine, a symphony orchestra is a regular factory for making artificial sounds, and a piano is the most appalling contrivance of levers and wires this side of the steam engine.

The application of this truth is obvious: the new electronic devices are but a means for producing new sounds to play with. What matters is not how they are produced but how they are used. And as to that we are entitled to ask the old questions—do we find the substance rich, evocative, capable of subtlety and strength? Do we, after a while, recognize patterns to which we can respond with our sense of balance, our sense of suspense and fulfillment, our sense of emotional and intellectual congruity? Those are the problems, beyond the technical, which our composers have tried to solve. We shall now attend to their handiwork with pleasure and gratitude (I hope), and certainly with a generous fraction of the patience they have themselves invested in their efforts to please us.

1961/1972

To Praise Varèse

It is, I think, a reproach to our civilization that in commemorating a great artist we must rely on the feelings and thoughts of the moment and the halting words that they provoke. Why are there not some ritual words to mark the passing of the artist as there are in the various churches to mourn the man? For the intention of ritual in rededicating the listeners through the words is to remind them of certain permanent truths, and surely the conditions of art and more especially the tribulations of the greatest, most innovative, artists have not changed in 500 years.

This generality is proved again in the figure of Varèse. Everybody now celebrates him. The newspapers run editorials, the auditoriums resound with his music. Where was this collective interest and effusive good will when he was alive and still able to produce? His was the standard case and it must not be misunderstood. He was never *un*recognized. He had warm friends and admirers and helpers from the start and all along the road. His genius was manifest and his efforts enlisted their due following. But what a creator needs is public facilitation—and for his particular work, not for something else—facilitation to perform, to exhibit, and as we say, to *establish* his idea; not medals or prizes or fame in themselves, but the kind of acceptance that enables the man's energies to concentrate on creation, instead of the necessity to waste these energies on mere contrivance and management.

And that facilitation Varèse was denied. It is the old story and nothing will change it. It is so familiar that one is even led to suppose that an artist who does not undergo this odyssey cannot be great. That is not true. One of the deplorable aspects of our blindness is that it confuses judgment in this way, making us value real things irrationally, by the volume of public talk or by the absence of talk outside the small group of the faithful. Now that these two groups converge at last in support of Varèse, what we must be on the watch for is the next man who is ignored and who should be recognized, not for his own sake but for that of his work.

Meanwhile, it is evident that Varèse is the man who solved in music the generic problem of the twentieth-century arts, the problem of creating a new idiom by creating new materials. The half millennium of high art since the Renaissance has exploited its characteristic means to the utmost, and there is nothing more to do along those lines in any art. What we need now is not new technical tricks or new variations on old themes and feelings, but a new substance and its appropriate new feelings. In contemporary music, Varèse provided the first usable answer to this historic demand.

Let me now present testimony in support of what I said at the outset, that it is possible for a great man to be recognized by the best judges and to be a great unknown until his death. By chance, a few days before Varèse died on November 6, I was reading here and there in the correspondence between Richard Strauss and Romain Rolland, and my eye fell on the following: Rolland in Paris writes to Strauss on February 21, 1909—"I talked a great deal this morning with one of the heads of the Orfeo of Barcelona and with a young French composer who has been living in Berlin for a couple of years and who admires you so much that he is afraid to call on you. His name is Edgard Varèse. He has great talent and seems to me particularly gifted as an orchestrator. I think you will find him interesting. He possesses what I believe you love as much as I do and what is so rare today—I mean *life*."

Varèse, it is clear, belongs to that extraordinary generation that came to maturity between 1905 and 1910, that so-called Cubist generation which is only now coming to be viewed as the founding fathers of modern art. Curiously, an important group of these men came together again in this country during the First World War. I was reminded of this in a note I received not long ago from Marcel Duchamp. "With a deep feeling of nostalgia," writes Duchamp, "I remember when Varèse and I arrived in New York and the groups of friends we made or met there again at the time: Walter and Louise Arensberg; Picabia; Albert Gleizes, the Cubist painter just recently exhibited at the Guggenheim Museum; Ozenfant; Henri Barzun; and Louise Varèse who has been our friend's devoted companion ever since." And he concludes, "A bientôt, cher Varèse."

My father, whom Duchamp put in his list, not long ago published these words about Varèse: "He is the architect of the new simultaneity in pure sound, the master of our only living music, of which we who are leaving the scene will not hear nearly enough before we go. Hail and farewell."

Igor Stravinsky wanted to write a special note, but illness prevented him. I therefore quote from his tribute of a while ago in *The New York Times*. "I became acquainted with Varèse myself," he said, "only at the end of his life, and then only slightly. But that was enough to know his genuineness and his unauctionable integrity. I am deeply saddened by his death."

Others, too, who could not attend this commemoration wrote letters in his honor. William Schuman, who took part in the first performance of *Ionisation*, writes: "Edgard Varèse is surely among the giant creative artists of our time. It seems at least a hundred years ago that I was snared by Nicolas Slonimsky into taking part in a performance of *Ionisation*. It was not merely that I had never played the instrument that was assigned to me—I had never even heard of "the lion's roar.' As in in everything else, Varèse was ahead of his time.

Buckets as musical instruments are no longer a rarity. But Varèse was no trickster. His scoring called for the same nuance and delicacy afforded any conventional instrument. How astonishing, little by little, to glean the remarkable combinations, gradually to understand the relationships, and finally to know that the banquet set before us was indeed grand, the appointments of the table properly germane to the exquisite cuisine and that even my humble role as tamer of the 'lion's roar' had its place."

Norman Lloyd also writes, "Varèse was an elemental force. He brought new concepts of sound to a world which, whether it knows it or not, needs to understand itself in tone. As original as he was courageous, Varèse was a pioneer of the space age in the arts. If there were a true sense of values in the world, Varèse would have been honored as one of our few originals in a time of conformity."

Elliott Carter, a lifelong friend, tells us the following: "Having been an enthusiastic admirer of Edgard Varèse for forty years and a friend for thirty, I am still impressed by the fascination which his music never ceases to awaken by its originality of conception and execution. It was a special concern with sound, with music as a thing in itself, and its compelling assertion which gives his work so much meaning to these confused and distressed contemporaries under the conflicting, unfocused pressures of American musical life. The commanding imagination that demanded these musical formations challenges by its provocative, revolutionary position so characteristic of the man himself, no doubt the only position possible for a composer today confronted by a musical life of complacently accepted routines, administered by the docile to the somnolent."

And to conclude, Leonard Bernstein, whose interest in Varèse's *Amériques* will, I hope, lead to a new performance, adds these remarks: "It grieves me to be unable to attend this memorial concert. Varèse meant much to me both as musician and as music lover. Many words have gone forth in praise of Varèse as a composer and innovator, but it is as a music lover that I must spontaneously think of him. Involved as he was in electronic devices and sounds of the future, he never for a moment lost his love for the great sounds of the past. I recall him in my dressing room after a concert of Beethoven as enthusiastic and filled with joy as a student just discovering the magic of this music. And it was certainly this intense love for music, which he never used for his own ends but in whose service he used his own person, that enabled him to make all his experiments into deeply musical and human experiences. His influence and vitality and contribution to music are forever immeasurable."

From boyhood I have also been a student and enthusiast of Varèse's music. *Amériques* transported me in the mid-twenties. *Ionisation* convinced me that here was the music of today. I believed this so strongly in my own twenties that thirty-two years ago when I was asked to contribute a chapter to the required readings for Columbia freshmen taking Contemporary Civilization I devoted a page to Varèse and concluded it with the superb encomium which the late Paul Rosenfeld devoted to *Ionisation*. Those freshmen of long ago didn't know what they were getting in for, but I still believe they were getting the right thing.

These witnesses-in-chief have been heard, and what they prove is that genius does not simply need or want recognition and praise; or rather, he has no need or want of them unless their absence causes the big world to roll on heedless until the task is done and the man is gone.

1965/1966

7

The Life of Stendhal-Rossini

The twentieth-century adoption of Stendhal as one of the great masters of the novel is in part a proper recognition of his genius and in part a warm fellow-feeling due to the large doses of irony, skepticism, and witty debunking of human pretensions that we find in his novels. If we do not exactly make him into our image of sophistication, into a malicious modern ego of Stracheyite birth, we account him nevertheless a dazzling precursor of the true revelation about man and society, and we marvel at his elegant autonomy of thought and act in the times of *Schwärmerei* (as we think) in which he was forced to live.

But this assimilation of his character to that which has prevailed in literature since the 1920s runs into contradiction as soon as we leave the two great novels and one or two of the autobiographic sketches. If we read *On Love* or *Racine et Shakespeare* or, still better, the *Life of Rossini,* we come upon a different man—different from our image of the sophisticate, and seemingly different from the thin-lipped unmasker of "bourgeois society."

This other man is not in fact incompatible with the first and he has the great virtue of making us see that we misunderstood Stendhal in limiting our love of him to what suits our book. The second man is a creature full of headlong enthusiasms, ready—almost eager—to risk being ridiculous; he is a man whose emotional life unwinds itself to an accompaniment of intimate recollections verging on the sentimental. He cherishes what catches at his throat and makes him weep. And in keeping with this cultivation of soft feelings and tender memories as the redeeming moments of life, his view of art is diametrically opposed to ours.

The *Life of Rossini*, as full-fledged *beylistes* know, forms together with the *History of Painting in Italy* a sort of journal of Stendhal's artistic experiences in the country he loved so much. The first of these books is not a life of its subject; it is not mainly about Rossini; it is not even altogether Stendhal's work—not that he again plagiarized a predecessor as he had done in an earlier essay on Haydn and Mozart, but that he stuffed into the delightful hodgepodge he named after Rossini the best anecdotes and reports on music and musicians that he could find in contemporary magazines or could extract from his friends in Italy and Paris.

The result is a unique piece of work. It keeps the reader going because its author was passionate about the *sensation* of art. He was not musically trained, but he was, by his own admission, transported when listening to music. "By dint of being happy at La Scala, I became a connoisseur." He conceived of art as a stimulus to *rêverie*. Imagine! Our severe esthetic moralists would have sneered behind his broad-gauge back and laughed in his dreaming face, even though what Stendhal called *rêverie* was a controlled dream—intense but controlled by what is given in the artistic presentment. From the comments and analyses in the *Rossini* it is clear that Stendhal did not mean *day*dreaming, but some sort of communication between the deepest motions of his spirit and those he discovered in, and attributed to, the artist. That is why he could say that he preferred such *rêverie* to everything else, including being thought a man of wit.

Logically, too, music reminded him of love—opera is always steeped in it—and being almost always an unfortunate lover, Stendahl recouped his lost opportunities through the imagination of love in sound. This addiction does not mean that Stendhal was insensitive to form; but with him form is known by an instinctive response, not by study and reflection. What matters much more, he thinks, is fitness and accent, plausibility, drama: unmistakable passion must be provided, no substitutes accepted. Music—all art—exists to be expressive. On this notion he is eloquent; he recurs to it, sensing the difficulty of distinguishing "expression" from programmatic illustration. It is still *the* problem.

The reader who opens this new edition of the *Rossini* will be grateful to Mr. Coe for the skill with which he has translated and annotated the text. To be sure, Henry Prunières did the heavy digging for the centenary edition of 1923. But in preparing an English version there was still a large field left for knowledge, tact, and judgment. Without the help provided, the modern reader might be more bewildered than he will in any case be by the sudden asides on politics and persons, the strange or superb comments on Mozart and Beethoven, the rapid comparisons at the expense of the French, the shifting scale of merit (for Rossini did not begin by being a favorite with Stendhal), and all the other oddities and profundities in this astonishing stream of consciousness about art.

1972

8

The Meaning of Meaning in Music

After the Music Critics' Association had met in New York last May[1] and discussed sundry professional matters, some of the members adjourned to Washington, where the French Festival was opening at the Kennedy Center. There, in four lively sessions that followed performances of the *Symphonie fantastique*, the *Requiem, Romeo and Juliet*, and *The Damnation of Faust*, the subject of discussion was Berlioz and—inescapably—the main issue debated was the relation of his music to something outside, to literature, to a program. One critic, a close and admiring student of Berlioz's oeuvre, introduced his remarks by saying that Berlioz only composed music that was *about* something.

Despite this as-it-were traditional caveat, a noticeable change from the past marked those sessions: not only were the participants extremely well informed about Berlioz; they were now referring to his kind of music with entire approval. I was reminded of a passage in a novel I once read, where a naïve character boldly spoke up: "The program notes said the music was antiphonal, but I liked it." One gathers that the second stage in the study of Berlioz's music has been reached: it's always "about something" but they like it—even if is not like other music, not as the best music ought to be, purely musical.

This attitude is confirmed by two important articles that have appeared in *The Musical Quarterly* recently: "The Sym-phonie fantastique and Its Program" by Nicholas Temperley, the admirable editor of the *Fantastique* in the New Berlioz

1. 1979.

Edition, and "A Return to Berlioz's *Retour à la Vie*" by Peter Bloom, whose thorough scholarship entitles his views to the best attention. Both writers maintain that the music of Berlioz presupposes in the listener a knowledge of some story or series of events which it follows or illustrates. Therefore the contention I have always made that the master's music was no more and no less tied than any other composer's to something outside itself is an error—and a serious one. I ought to be satisfied now that Berlioz's musical powers are recognized as great, side by side with his attachment to various "programs" that it behooves us to study and remember.

But I am not satisfied and I persist, not in Berlioz's behalf: this conclusion of mine was never a piece of special pleading for his sake. I see it as broader and more far-reaching than the standing of any composer and his works, or even than the nature of music. It is a proposition in esthetics. The question of program has to do with art as such: what is art in relation to objective reality and to the perceiving mind? Or conversely, what meaning applicable to art do the terms "pure" and "absolute" stand for? Whether musicians know it or not, there is a sizable literature about pure poetry and pure painting in which the same assertions are made as in discourse about pure music. To answer these questions of purity and autonomy is a prerequisite of any intelligent critical practice. And the failure to raise them accounts, I think, for the continuing debate about "program" in music; for the use of such terms as "extramusical," "literary," and the like; for the clichés about "all the arts striving to become pure form, like music"; for the classification of artists (with or without implications of better and worse) as more or less musical, painterly, and so on; and—most important—for the unresolved mystery that in certain works the material is worthy, the technique is unexceptionable, the form is clear, but the result is "uninspired."

The ramifications of the simple query, What is program?

are obviously many and of great moment. They go far beyond the limits of an essay. Accordingly, I propose to deal only with three main points that I believe should concern those who write or speak about music, including concertgoers walking out of the hall after a performance. These points are: (1) that all music is programmatic, explicitly or implicitly, and in more than one way; (2) that keeping out so-called extraneous ideas or perceptions while composing, hearing, or analyzing music is impossible and unnecessary; and (3) that musical people who call literary the elements or the influence they deprecate in music do not fully understand what literature is.

The first proposition has to be considered from a number of points of view, for critical practice shows no agreement as to what a program is. Berlioz's *Fantastique* visibly has one, since it takes up a couple of pages of print. But does *Harold in Italy* have one, with its two dozen words in four phrases of place setting? Further, is the text of a song or the libretto of an opera a program? And what of pieces of instrumental music with titles? Does *Des pas sur las neige* constitute a program—in the melting mood, perhaps? This reference to mood is not altogether frivolous; it leads to the next question: when a work bears the name of a musical form qualified by a nonmusical adjective, have we a "literary," programmatic work? What is a *Tragic* Overture? What makes a bourrée *fantasque*? Finally, in what sense of program dare I maintain that musical works usually described as pure forms (or called absolute music or pattern music) also follow a program?

To cover all cases, it seems necessary to define as programmatic any scheme or idea, general or particular, that helps to determine the course of composition. It would be hard to deny that the words of a poem constitute for the composer of songs a program in this sense. The words exert a constraint; they face him with a set form not of his own making and quite different from the set forms of music. I say *the words* affect the course of composition, for it is possible to sing without any such constraint, on "ah" or some other vowel. But words in poems follow the rules of accent, grammar, and syntax, which are not musical rules but linguistic. And so composers of songs fitted to words and, by extension, composers of cantatas, Masses, operas, and oratorios are composers of music determined in part by a program. They bend their musical impulse and their technique to something preexisting and—as the critical phrase has it—extramusical. It is true that in the interests of music the words are more or less distorted; they are not uttered as they would be if they were unaccompanied. But it is equally true that at the same time the music is continuously shaped in the service of words. We acknowledge this in saying that the music is *adapted* to the text.

Nor is it only in such things as the placing of accents and the length of phrases that the words dictate "from outside." Those words carry a meaning and the composer, in his naïve, unmusicological way, tries to follow it, to make his inarticulate sounds "appropriate" to the articulate ones. He may not know how he does this; he may never have thought whether it is possible to do it; but he does it. And the critic who comes along later can somehow tell whether the setting is successful in both respects—fitting the words in their structure and in their meaning at the same time. That this judgment is not an illusion based merely on the association of certain words with a tune is shown when two technically adequate settings of one poem exist: one will probably be found better, "closer to the meaning of the text."

That verdict is clear enough, though not explained by critical theory. Even so, the conclusion is forced upon us that music, which in its barest definition is ordered sound, is capable of following at least two types of order—one which we may call formal and the other significant. What is to be said of the significant order I shall discuss shortly.

The formal order, as we have just seen, is given shape at times by the order of something "outside" the music, such as verse, and this may well have been, historically speaking, the first program governing sounds, before set forms were devised. But every kind of physical matter that the arts employ has properties of its own, and it is to be expected that each should give rise to ways of handling peculiar to itself. Inarticulate sounds invite repetition, steady pace, clear rhythm, small alterations, and return to origins. Such ways inspire plans and procedures which by tradition become accepted "forms" of the art, and when developed and made habitual these seem "inherent," inevitable, every detail preordained from the beginning. The history of music tells us how resistant to change these conventions have been and also how, when they do change, their variants or opposites seem equally inherent and unchangeable.

The truth is that they are all choices "from outside," that is, made by individuals from motives more mixed than pure. Nothing "inherent" in rates of vibration causes the major third to be felt or not felt as a consonance, parallel fifths as diabolical, dissonances as grating or attractive. They are made so by human fiat, not necessity. It is the same with the set forms. That the movements of a suite should be fast-slow-fast answers the human desire for variety, which is not a specifically musical desire. A-B-A form corresponds to a widespread liking for departure and homecoming; it applies to much else than sounds. Exposition, Development, and Recapitulation—an extension of A-B-A—is the fundamental form of public oratory; it is persuasive and satisfying. A fugue—"pure" music par excellence to the purists—is a construction of the most deliberate kind, which moreover requires tampering with the scale in the most arbitrary way. And equally artificial—"artifactual"—are sonata form, rondo, trio, da capo aria, and the rest: none would have germinated on their own if selected notes had been shaken in a test tube with a sonic reagent.

The fact that these forms serve admirably to bring out and organize the musical impulse of gifted minds does not conflict with the truth that forms are schemes imposed upon sound for various reasons, and that these reasons are preferences of the human mind: balance, coherence, unity, variety, surprise, suspense, conclusiveness, and the like. Nor can these preferences claim a special affinity with the realm of sound. This being so, it follows that the set forms of music each supply a program that the traditionally trained composer may elect by itself or at the same time as he elects the program furnished by a poem—or by a purpose such as hunting, dancing, or church ritual. For neither of the two programs is so rigid that it cannot be accommodated to the other; or to put it more concretely, the skillful composer can order sound so as to fit both together by modifying the articulate or the inarticulate sounds within the limits of intelligibility.

The musician is then following a double program, constrained and also helped to create order by two preexisting patterns that intersect only at certain points. Part of his merit consists in the deftness with which he reconciles the independent demands of the two schemes. The tension between them is a spur to his artistry and technical skill, just as it is a source of the listener's admiration and pleasure.

If we scan the history of Western civilization, it is clear that musicians have devoted by far the greater part of their talents—whether as composers or performers—to music fashioned according to this double program. The amount of music for religious uses, for dancing and hunting, for singing words, for accompanying stories in opera, cantata, or oratorio vastly outweighs the remainder. Most Western music has been composed "about something." It has more often than not used the human voice, and that voice or those voices have been discoursing explicitly about something. It is only within the last two centuries that solely instrumental music has assumed preeminence and so has come to represent the art as a whole and to serve as the theoretical model for all music. Within instrumental music itself, the critical enthusiasm for the pure and absolute is the product of a very recent estheticism. It belongs mainly to the second half of the nineteenth century; and judging from the theorizing about the other arts, it appears as part of the hostile reaction to the modern world, as an expression of distaste for objective reality and common emotion. "Pure form" in all the arts is meant to reinstate spirituality in the teeth of vulgar materialism and practical life.

It is therefore unhistorical and absurd to single out Berlioz as the composer whose works, unlike others, are always "about something," that is, follow a double program. On the contrary, he is in this respect with the overwhelming majority. Only his early works—three symphonies and part of a fourth—are without a text to be sung, whose presence everywhere else shows his adherence to tradition.

But the critical situation, both about these works and about music in general, is complicated by the fact that Berlioz's century was the time when instrumental music developed new powers, thanks to the perfected orchestra and the genius of composers such as Mozart, Beethoven, Weber, and Berlioz himself. They enlarged musical expressiveness and also added to the confusion of terms and ideas by speaking of *Tondichter*, by expanding familiar musical forms, by devising the symphonic poem, by writing about *le genre instrumental expressif*. Since most of their music lacked the interpretative aid of a vocal text, explanations of "meaning" were given "outside"—in programs or program notes written with or without

the composer's authority. The ground was thus prepared for
the later conflict between the musical purists and the de-
bauchees.

To sort out this critical tangle, one must recall the practice
as well as the theory of musical expressiveness before the
nineteenth century. What did composers do with sounds in
order to express, imitate, heighten, underline, reproduce,
adumbrate the meaning of a text? I use these various verbs,
because none really says what happens when the formal program which a text amounts to is adopted by a composer
concerned to follow significance as well as form. The kinds of
things he does that lie on the surface and are more or less
apparent could readily be classified if it were necessary. Actually, musicians find most of these devices established in the
tradition. Thus by association bells, hunting horns, fifes and
drums evoke the scenes of their utilitarian use. Certain other
sounds, such as thunder, cannon, the crash of an earthquake,
or the tearing of cloth (cf. Bach's *Passions*), can be "imitated"
sufficiently well. But it is mainly by rhythm, pitch, and
dynamics that most representative effects are achieved. For
reasons organic to the human body and the human mind, a
slow pace and deep tones seem to go with what is sad, serious, solemn, majestic, menacing; whereas high notes in rapid
time are felt as appropriate to gaiety, joy, triumph, the mood
of celebration and the carefree life. What is more, certain
keys and the minor scale generally show an affinity with the
darker or more pensive moods; other keys and the major
scales suit their opposites. And modulations, sudden or
gradual, smooth or harsh, produce impressions adaptable to
feelings and thoughts.

All this is, I repeat, obvious and on the surface. Nor is
there (fortunately) anything fixed or absolute about these
linkings. Much depends on context—the double context of
the surrounding music and of the known "situation." This is
what permits the critic to write of Haydn's setting of "Es

werde Licht" in *The Creation* that it is "a flood of C major brilliance and one of the most vividly pictorial strokes in all of music."[2] I question the term "pictorial" for reasons that will appear, but it can hardly be denied that the words "Let there be light" did not leave the composer of so dramatic an event as the Creation indifferent as to what he could do with sounds to match the program. The enormous flexibility—one might even say the permanent willingness—of sounds to be ordered for such purposes is shown by the fact that the experience of light after darkness (and its parallels) occurs in innumerable texts, secular and religious, and each finds a musical expression different from Haydn's.

Yet so fitting did these marriages of sound and thought seem to earlier composers that in modern times down to the end of the eighteenth century theorists have tried to establish formulas for the musical rendering of ideas and feelings. There has long been argument, for instance, whether Bach was a strict adherent of the Baroque doctrine of the Affections, according to which certain ideas called for certain musical figures. It should have been clear from the best empirical evidence—the scores—that whereas some "affection" (emotion) named in the text brought on certain tempos and note values in Bach's music, those same features also occurred in linkage with other affections, thus raising an important question and giving a clue to a more exact understanding of meaning in music.

But the Age of Reason was bent on rationalizing all practice and discovering in the arts the uniform workings of "nature"; hence the many efforts directed at codifying the scientifically correct "poetics of music." Although it gradually fell into disrepute, such theorizing did not end with the eighteenth century. It lingered on into the time when Berlioz began composing. Students of his work and his times should

2. Donal Henahan, *The New York Times*, February 21, 1979.

pursue the subject in the admirably comprehensive dissertation by Professor Katherine Reeve.[3] For in supplying the ample background of critical thought that Berlioz inherited she shows what preconceptions the composers of the early nineteenth century might expect in their critics and in the educated portion of their audience. The bane of literalism—not literature—hung over dramatic music, and when music happened to forgo the stage and use the orchestra by itself, public and critic alike wanted a rationale for the proceedings. In the absence of text or plot they wanted a program.

I have been taken to task for calling Berlioz's program for the *Symphonie fantastique* a promotional piece. His recent interpreters are apparently solicitous for his fair fame. I withdraw "promotional" and substitute "educational." The program certainly was meant to guide, instruct, appease the curiosity of listeners unprepared for an orchestral work in five movements of which the sequence and character could not be known in advance. And it had its intended effect, just like the rigmarole of *Le Retour à la vie*, to which Professor Bloom attaches so much importance. However called, these two pieces of prose must have been timely, for they brought Berlioz the only two enthusiastic responses he ever got from the Paris public. And why did they succeed? Because the public wanted something as explicit to latch on to in the concert room as it was accustomed to in the opera house. It is inconceivable that without the farrago of *Le Retour à la vie*, with its quasi-autobiographical manifesto about art and Shakespeare, Berlioz could have got his random collection of fragments—some of them exam papers for the Rome Prize—listened to as something meriting attention.

It will not do to say that the need to have music situated and explained was a stupid French habit, the Germans having always known as far back as their forest wanderings that sym-

3. "The Poetics of the Orchestra in the Writings of Hector Berlioz" (Ph. D. diss., Yale University, 1978).

phonic music was pure and absolute. The argument about Bach is enough to show that this is not true. But still more telling—for Bach, after all, was setting music to words—is the fact that the first German commentators of Beethoven's symphonies all agreed that these works embody a sustained thought which, for some, distorted the recognized forms into so many puzzles. So to help their own understanding and the public's, the critics would supply programs of their own devising. Musicians as sophisticated as Schumann and Liszt wished that Beethoven had given a clue to the intended meaning of each symphony. Preceding them all, E. T. A. Hoffman had put the common assumption in words that we must not ignore if we wish to know the history of criticism "wie es eigentlich gewesen": The symphony, he said, "has become . . . nothing less than the opera of the instruments."

In short, the early nineteenth-century musical dogma was the antithesis of ours, and though mistaken it was at least an attempt to grapple with the evident fact that somehow music has meaning. Contrariwise, our dogma that music is important because it affords the contemplation of pure form leaves criticism full of verbalisms and contradictions. On the one hand, critics of works and of performance cannot carry on their trade without imputing qualities and defects worded in terms of human experience; on the other hand, no one can say what a pure form is or why the spectacle should make us rejoice. If form means "outline," arrangement, balance of parts, then it would seem as if one specimen of each musical form should suffice for all time; it could be contemplated with bliss over and over again. If the material that exhibits the form makes a difference as being more or less agreeable, then we are back at the heart of the eighteenth-century debate, when some connoisseurs maintained against the literalists that music was solely for the pleasure of the senses. That is a tenable position, but it puts music below the other arts, next to interior decoration and fine cuisine. Pure-form ecstasy and simple ear-tickling come together from opposite extremes to deny significance. For both schools of theorists sounds are incapable of carrying, embodying, conveying, expressing anything. Listeners who think otherwise labor under an illusion; they import a meaning "from outside."

The issue, then, boils down to: sounds with or without connotation, those voting aye to "Without!" being divided into pure sensualists and pure Platonists; those voting aye to "With!" being still at a loss to account for music's connotative powers beyond the few effects based on association—church bells or military trumpets.

The difficulty is due to a customary error about the implication of such words as *carry, convey, express*. They need to be entirely reconceived when applied to art. We commonly say: "In speaking to a crowd he always knew how to express their feelings"; or: "You express my thought exactly—and better than I could." Such remarks imply an action in two parts—first, a conscious or nearly conscious feeling or thought; then a form of words to make it manifest. Likewise, we may suppose a subject complete in itself and an object that stands for it which enables us to name and recognize the subject—in brief, an imitation. So familiar is this hookup that we forget there can be any other. As soon as we hear "expression," we ask what it is an expression *of*. That is the great stumbling block in the way of rightly conceiving musical expression—nobody can say what it is an expression *of*. Verbal accounts seem inadequate if not silly—and also unauthorized, unprovable. Worse still, it is on reflection absurd that when music goes with a text it should express what the text is about: why do the job a second time?

What we forget is that there is such a thing as meaning and understanding in one step, immediate and without imitation. Take a sudden cry. It bursts from someone near you, whom you know. The cry is an expression, and from the looks of the person and your sense of the situation you usually know whether it is a cry of joy, or of pain. But that is a mere tag. What the cry expresses is not the general subject pain or joy, nor a localized pain or cause of joy. It contains infinitely more than either emotion, general or particular. It expresses the whole being, that person at that moment. Strictly speaking, the cry is unanalyzable and undescribable. You may surmise that along with pain there was fear and self-pity and guilt; along with joy triumph, pride, relief, or anything you like; you cannot exhaust the expression by using names, but you understand what you heard. In telling of it you find yourself saying, with renewed horror or delight: "You should have heard that cry."

Music—and every other art—is expressive in the same sense as a cry or a gesture. We say to the same effect a "facial *expression*"—it has no name, but it *means*. Music is of course far more complex than cries, faces, or gestures, but like a brilliant pantomime its consecutive intention is immediately perceived and understood. No need of mentally guessing, translating, converting its passing forms into another realm of abstract or concrete perceptions. The better word for this power is not expression but expressiveness, which—to me at least—gets rid of the imagined second term that cannot be named but would be tacked on to "of" if one could name it.

Expressiveness constitutes the composer's third and fundamental program. He may begin with a set form, or a text, or both, but unless he is writing an exercise, composing a work that listeners will call academic, this inexplicit, part-conscious, part-unconscious program will shape the music. The program does not preexist in any clear sense; it is simply the maker's intention at any given moment of composition. When music is not making use of ready-made formulas, and sometimes even then, it is expressing. Through that expressiveness we come to learn the composer's style, to read his mind, and thus to share his meaning.

For example, the Bach Chaconne for unaccompanied violin has, so far as I know, never been associated with any subject, but when well played it affords a tremendous dramatic experience. The drama is *in* the music and only Bach can have put it there. Almost certainly he was not thinking of any drama or situation whatever: he felt dramatic—and we follow suit. The "program" is forever hidden in the mind that can thus communicate, but it exists. For sounds do not generate their own order, much as they may seem to in the happy act of creation and the enchanted act of listening. Nor is there any way, usually, of knowing the degree of deliberation that went into each instant of the design, what prompted not so much the doing of this or that as the *wanting to do just that*, the aim which that particular move satisfies.

Now that aim is not an idea in the ordinary sense. It has no name, though it can be linked more or less aptly with ideas and feelings that are namable. And that is how critics come to write: "He then introduces a jaunty little tune in D major." Who told him it was jaunty? But the audience agrees, even though nobody could explain the adjective "little" applied to a tune that contains more notes and uses more instruments than "the big majestic theme of the introduction in G minor." All these quite unreasonable words are attempts to get into the neighborhood of the hidden program and help the thick-eared or inattentive to follow it *in* the music. Those who know the work or are quick-eared do not need words and are made impatient by them—until they want to point out to someone else a merit or defect in the performance. For then, apart from wrong notes, the only appeal is to the hidden program, which has been misconceived or violated. Thus the critic quoted earlier on Haydn's "pictorial" effect had led up to that observation by saying that "the genteel thumping and flutterings that came with the words *Es werde Licht* can in some performances be a flood of C major brilliance . . . ."

Performance good or bad brings out the truth that an

underlying significance inhabits music, for it can disappear from the notes played if these are not filled with the right intention.[4] That is why an RCA synthesizer cannot play a waltz, no matter how expertly the notes, rhythm, tempo, and accents are fed into the machine. The life-inspired "program" is absent from its programming. And living performers will sometimes act like synthesizers. In his letters Mozart writes of a virtuoso much admired by audiences: "Hearing, thinking, feeling, they experience no more than he does"; and elsewhere, when he had given his beloved Aloysia Weber "Ah! lo previdi," he sent her instructions for singing it: "Put yourself into the person and situation of Adromeda... reflect on the force and meaning of the words." The hidden program is visceral, for, as every performer knows, the composer's markings for tempo, phrasing, and dynamics furnish only a rough approximation of what is called for by way of intention. A phrase marked *p* or *mf* is not played so throughout; it goes through a curve of dynamics between beginning and end, and this according to a meaning which is not in the *notes* but in the *music*, that is, added by an intuitive knowledge of what the hidden program calls for at that point, if the phrase, the passage, and the movement are to have the right meaning. True, that addition will vary with each interpreter, for in art nothing can be rigid and still give the sense of life, but that very fact proves the connection with life and the error of calling a work of art "autonomous" or a pure form.

This visceral program, then, this expressiveness, which the good listener follows undeviatingly without being aware that he does so, is the vivifying principle. Its shape and character make the difference between a routine piece and a great

4. That excellent musician, Dorothy L. Sayers, recalled that once, when singing in an Oxford choir under the direction of Hugh Percy Allen, he said of a single-note entry by the sopranos: "It should have sounded like a single star on a clear night. You make it sound like a damp firework." Conductors have no recourse but to "programmatize" in order to obtain the effect they want.

work, and some of its elements are consciously struggled for
by the composer, as we can tell from surviving sketches, from
Beethoven's notebooks, from verbal accounts of difficulties
while composing or dissatisfaction with the result. A letter of
Mendelssohn's is especially enlightening on this point. Of all
his overtures, *The Hebrides* is surely the finest; indeed, it is a
masterpiece. He was moved to compose it by a visit to Fingal's Cave in 1829, and he soon wrote part of his score, of
which he quoted the main theme to his family shortly afterwards. He kept working at it during the next two years while
traveling to Italy and France, but was not satisfied. In January,
1832, he writes home again: "The working out smacks more
of counterpoint than of train oil, sea gulls, and salt fish and
must be altered." These are casual but suggestive words. In
the first place, the work is not programmatic in the imitative
sense. The main theme does not sound like waves or caves,
nor can one imagine train (=whale) oil, sea gulls, or salt fish
begetting musical renderings. Those words stand in the writer's ironic mood for what he does want to render, which is
the force and meaning of his experience. That is his program,
and he knows he has not fulfilled it when, looking over the
working out, he finds it only counterpoint. With Mendelssohn that counterpoint was doubtless irreproachable and
it would have made a nice little section, but it was pro-
grammatically null. What he did by his alterations was to
infuse meaning—the meaning stored up in his memory of a
passage in his life.

That this meaning had nothing to do with representing
objects—animals, rocks, liquids—is shown by the variety of
titles the composer used to name the piece. To his family he
called it "The Lonely Island." At the première it was called
"The Isles of Fingal," the next year "The Hebrides," and a
little later "Ossian at Fingal's Cave." The orchestral score of
1835 is entitled simply "Fingal's Cave." One is reminded of

the variation in title of Berlioz's "Corsair" overture, which went from "The Tower of Nice" to "The Red Rover" before acquiring its final label. With both composers their ostensible subject actually recorded a biographical, travel-stained occurrence.

Their real subject was something deep inside their minds and obviously something universal, within the reach of all minds, since we can by listening to the music rediscover the quality and shape of Mendelssohn's experience in Scotland and Berlioz's in Nice. Now what makes possible this transmutation of life-as-it-is-felt into ordered sounds and back again into an experience not similar but corresponding? It is simply the nature and activity of human consciousness, which experiences the world and its own memories in clusters of percepts and concepts charged with feeling. These clusters know no limits as to what they may include; the more powerful and wide-ranging the mind is, the richer each pulse of consciousness will be in associations, parallels, and meanings.

All such pulses, moreover, have an affective tone. This phrase must remain vague in order to be correct, for, although this tone will often be clear enough to be called by the name that language gives to the common emotions, it may also possess a definite quality for which there is no word, or a distinct shade of familiar feeling not covered by any name, or a mixture that defies analysis. The most abstract idea, the most fleeting sensation as it comes and fades is suffused with such an affective tone, whether or not it is noted as it passes. By deliberate attention it will of course stand out as a component of the thought. And as everyone can verify for himself, the evocative and affective power of shapes, odors, and sounds goes far beyond the actual objects that trigger the idea or the memory. That is the explanation of the surprising fact that architecture can move us so. In a sense, everybody is synesthetic, that is, feels with all the senses at once, feels the self and the world simultaneously through his whole being. It is on that plane that the experience common to artist and beholder takes place; it is there that the hidden, visceral program takes shape for embodiment in one medium or another.

In the light of these fundamental traits of consciousness, it seems idle to go on classifying music and its listeners as "emotional" and "intellectual," formalists and affectists. It would be more in keeping with the facts to say that some listeners' attention is more comprehensive, taking in more fully the stream of sound, so as to grasp—in Schumann's words—"the finer shades of passion" and thus to understand "masters like Schubert and Beethoven, who could translate every circumstance of life into the language of tone."[5]

Whoever wants a detailed account of the interplay of the mind and its objects in experience will find it in William James's *Principles of Psychology*, Chapter 9, the famous chapter on the stream of consciousness. And whoever needs to be persuaded that the perception of music as pure form, as an absolute sonic experience, is a myth should read the report of P. E. Vernon's empirical studies in his essay, "Non-Musical Factors in the Appreciation of Music."[6] Preconceptions, pre-perceptions, prejudices; associations random and relevant; errors of thought and of hearing; knowledge or its absence about theory or history or biography—these and dozens of other influences stream through our consciousness along with the stream of sound, just as a similar mixture presided over the composer's work of putting order into his material. This is not to say that in the concert hall a symphony is heard

5. *Neue Zeitschrift für Musik*, 1 (1834):10. Ernest Newman showed the same concern, pointing out that one source of the prejudice against "subjects" in instrumental music was the implied summons to *follow* instead of letting the stream wash over one's head with an occasional response of nervous thrills. (*Musical Studies* [London, 1905], pp. 105–6.)

6. Reprinted in Mr. Barzun's anthology, *Pleasures of Music* (Chicago, 1977). (Ed.)

in the midst of perfect chaos distributed among 500 heads. Habits of attention give some discipline. But it is still fair to say that the so-called esthetic experience detached from life's miscellany is an abstraction from what happens and is never vouchsafed in its purity, even to the most spiritualized and emaciated of devotees.

It would be strange indeed if the arts, were they divorced from the actualities of human life, could take the hold they do on both naïve and sophisticated sensibilities. The mystery of music's power; the attribution of profundity, moral value, psychological penetration to its masterpieces; the incorrigible habit of saying what they "really" mean; the criticism of performance in the very terms we use to describe action, scenery, or mood—all these common realities compel us to acknowledge that music is in its own inarticulate way an extension of human experience. And since we cannot help pondering and discussing our experiences, we reflect and discourse on music as best we can, in words that simultaneously capture and belie the experience, the hidden program.

That effort to pin down what is felt inside is of course what mankind has been doing since the invention of language. Words do pretty well when rightly used, but in the great moments we know they do not reach the heart of things, the fullness of being. We end up saying "I can't tell you how moved I was by . . . ." This is where other means come in, including music. *It* is able to tell you, or rather show you, not everything but more than words can; which is why it can go with a text without duplicating it, giving us, for instance, the feeling *other than visual* that comes with light breaking upon darkness.

That was my reason for querying the word "pictorial" for that "revelation." As a shorthand term it may do, but I think it obscures the actual inwardness of the sensation. The fallacy in the doctrine of the Affections was the fact that a specified musical figure, let us say for joy, could be used again for haste or any other form of trepidation. Haydn's "C" major brilliance" would go as well with "relief after anxiety" or "vindication of innocence after being under a cloud." This last phrase is chosen on purpose to show how words themselves play upon likenesses that defy analysis. Why should suspicion of guilt resemble being under a cloud? Never mind. There is, as in the metaphor, an indefinable kinship between light in *The Creation* and light after a beclouding suspicion, and it is this likeness that a contrast of certain sounds—Haydn's or someone else's—will evoke in us at the inarticulate level.

By an interesting paradox, as soon as one is persuaded that this essence of experience cannot be brought out in literal language, one is freed to talk about music in similes and comparisons, for one knows that these do not refer to the experience but merely orient the reader or listener toward a quarter of human life where one thinks that essence may be found. I say "a" quarter and not "the," for as we just saw, light after darkness = relief after anxiety = feeling whole after grave illness = etc., ad infinitum. The proof of this is the practice of self-borrowing among the great composers. At first, one is shocked to learn how much of the superb *Boris Godunov* is taken from disparate earlier projects of Mussorgsky's. We are less upset when we know that the barcarole in Offenbach's *Tales of Hoffmann* was originally the Goblin's song in *Die Rheinnixen* or that material in the original music for Verdi's *Don Carlo*, Act IV, was used in his Manzoni *Requiem*. But shock returns, at least for the pure-minded, when they are told that Bach was willing to have nine sections of the *St. Matthew Passion* adapted to words by Picander in a memorial service for Prince Leopold of Anhalt-Cöthen.

The truth is that the feeling of shock implies our belief in the very literalism of music that we rightly deny in the abstract. We think: how can Walter Scott's *Rob Roy* reappear as Byron's *Harold* in Berlioz's second symphony? And this literalism is applied to the "program" also: can the hero march to the scaffold in the *Fantastique* to the same music that guards of the Vehmrichter would have used, had his *Francs-Juges* ever been staged?

Bach, Mussorgsky, Berlioz, and their peers knew what they were doing. They understood that in just the proportion that music is not literal, denotative, it can connote the essence of diverse experiences. So we might as well cease to be troubled by verbal programs, explanations, or the loose poeticizing of amateurs and reviewers. They are all wrong and all right at one and the same time, the wrongness being really in those who take the words literally. And what should keep us from denouncing their practice is that we understand quite well what they mean. When a distinguished conductor says that after Debussy he cannot drink beer, we get his drift without effort. Likewise, when a critic says of Busoni's *Fantasia contrappuntistica* that "it holds you spellbound by its overpowering spiritual qualities" or when a composer explains how he worked with electronic means to achieve a gong sound that was "somewhat pale but tremulous."[7]

There is further legitimate use of words in connection with instrumental music: to indicate occasions. The title of Strauss's *Till Eulenspiegel and His Merry Pranks* gives us an inkling of what the musical jollification sprang from. The mind likes to know why things happen, what comes next, and how the object came to be. These are externals, not "about" the music but around it. And this is what Berlioz did in his first (and only) program and in the monologue portions of *Le Retour à la vie*. They encircle the pieces and control nothing inside them. That he had no darker purpose is shown by his later statement that for the *Fantastique* the titles of the movements suffice. In so saying, he was in effect putting behind him 150 years of literalist dogma, as well as teaching

7. Respectively: Alan Rich in *New York*, July 23, 1979, p. 69; and Vladimir Ussachevsky in *Problems of Modern Music* (New York, 1962), p. 68.

future composers what they could do. They have gone in not
only for *Tragic Overture, Dante* symphony, *Ein Heldenleben*
but also for *Enigma Variations* "portraying" friends,[8] *Dover
Beach*, from a poem about the history of ideas, *Epigraphes
antiques* (with subtitles), technologisms like *Ionisation,* and
mysteries such as *Le Marteau sans maître*. It seems as hard to
approach the public without a placard as to compose without
a starting point in life or in books.

But if this is so, why is it still assumed that alone among the
symphonic composers of the nineteenth century Berlioz's
music needs close reference to its tag or title? One reason
may be the awareness that he was a great writer with a passion
for literature, as well as a musician. Double talents invite
distrust—the case of Delacroix and the critics is identical with
that of Berlioz. But more important is the lack of attention
given to Berlioz's methods of composition. Until very recently and except for his instrumentation, his ways of ordering sound, though called original, highly individual, were but
casually treated, in asides. The programs were supposed to
explain what went on in the music. It was a vicious circle
from which we are only now breaking out. The splendid
studies by Professor Edward T. Cone, "Inside the Saint's
Head" and "Berlioz's Divine Comedy," are pioneer efforts[9]
one hopes to see supplemented by other research into special problems.

As for the role of literature, not only in Berlioz but in the
music of his contemporaries and successors, it should cause
no surprise. Musicians have become more broadly educated
than they once were; they read poetry, novels, and plays—
the main channel of ideas and feelings in a secular age. Formerly the musician's library was the Bible, with some of the
ancient classics providing additional stories. But nothing has

8. Compare Mr. Virgil Thomson's charming piece entitled *Henry McBride.*
9. Respectively: *The Musical Newsletter* (July 1971) and *Nineteenth Century Music*
(Summer 1980).

changed in the relation of music to words. What *is* new is the suspicion that when literature inspires instrumental music, as evidenced in the use of titles, something alien has got into the hitherto pure stream of sound. The preceding pages have tried to show how mistaken that belief is. From the beginning of concerted music, composers have used rhythm and timbre to "imitate" nature and the activities of man—as far back as Janequin's "Battle." They have shaped melody and harmony to provide what they felt to be audible equivalents of situations, moods, atmospheres, and even abstractions—witness Mahler. We know that those devices do not really copy or denote. Beethoven's brook sounds nothing like a brook, Wagner's motives are anything but informative. But this conversion of life's impressions into "pure" sound is legitimized by the simple fact that composers have done it and nobody can stop them. Criticism has therefore a duty to account for the frequent and unmistakable fitness of the means to this end.

It only remains to point out that a title, a few words denoting a source, a setting, an atmosphere are not literature. They are just words like "Exit Only" or "Post Office Around the Corner." Literature is the art which makes out of commonplace words a new subtance that is expressive in the same manner as music: it does not tell, it shows. The words of a play or poem are chosen for what they connote, they are figurative, not declaratory. When Hamlet says "Oh what a rogue and peasant slave am I!" he is not giving information to the census-taker; he is exhibiting his whole being's consciousness at that moment. Likewise, the events in a play or a novel are so organized as to reveal the essence of some experience: they are not a factual report. Nor is a poem an affidavit, which is why its meaning vanishes in a prose paraphrase. Such being the nature of literature, it cannot possibly infect music, and the epithet "literary" is as inapplicable to music as "pictorial." The meaning of literature resides in the same motions of the spirit as those aroused by music; only the means differ. And both are programmatic in the same sense of following inner experience while adapting material to set forms and sometimes giving, by association, reminders of the objective world.

1980

Berlioz

9

Berlioz after a Hundred Years

Musical anniversaries are generally little more than reminders that somebody died or was born later than we think—or possibly earlier, depending on our historical sense. Our remembrance of Berlioz's death, on March 8, 1869, carries far more meaning. A hundred years ago, he died honored, fêted, bid for by America (the *summum bonum* for many artists), and in many quarters deeply loved. But something was wanting to the consecration of an arduous, indeed a heroic career: his native land scarcely paid attention to his coming—or going.

Such a deprivation, in the nationalistic Europe of the nineteenth century, had an effect on fame out of all proportion to its intrinsic worth. "Our Wagner," "our Verdi," "our Shakespeare"—these wholly false proprietary claims meant that the casual or formal propaganda machine was at work, keeping the market acquainted and supplied with the national product: almost from the beginning, Bayreuth and tourism were a combo.

Well, it is only now, a hundred years after Berlioz's death, that the asbestos curtain which France kept lowered against one of her greatest creators has finally caught fire. A national association has been formed to study and promote his works, and his birthplace has been restored as a museum. And in contrast with the sesquicentennial year 1953, when two French orchestras managed to celebrate the composer through concerts containing not one note of his music, the year 1969 has seen genuine devotion to the music and the beginning of a comprehensive scholarly publication of the

prose works, including Berlioz's voluminous and musico-
logically important correspondence. In this undertaking the
influence of André Malraux, sustained by the urgings of
his friend Edgard Varèse, must be noted with gratitude.

The reason that the French are studying and reissuing the
prose is that in the parallel work to be done on the music they
were forestalled by the English. It was in 1965 that a United
Kingdom Berlioz Committee was formed under high social
and musical auspices (and soon sought and received a grant
from the Gulbenkian Foundation) for the editing and publishing of the complete scores. This first true edition will
appear in twenty-five volumes at Bärenreiter's in Kassel. It is
symbolic that 1969 saw under this plan the issuing of the two
volumes of *Les Troyens*, for the first time edited and *published*.[1]

These curious historical facts are of course external to
Berlioz's music and even to the general feeling about it. Why
have the French awakened? Why have the English adopted
the French master like a second Handel or a double Mendelssohn? Why are they convinced that, as several recent
writers have maintained, it was a cabal that long kept Berlioz
from the public and that the cabal has been destroyed?

Setting aside cranks and other exclusivists (who, by the
way, are a great force in the determination of all artistic
fame), I think one can discern the operation of two inter-
twining causes. One is certainly that Berlioz's music has been
heard more frequently, in more places, and at shorter intervals, during the last twenty years, than was possible before.
And this indispensable frequency is due to one cause and one
only: the long-playing disc. In other words, Berlioz's reputation has benefited from the same influence that has replaced

1. Until now the work was in print but not on sale, the Choudens firm as original
purchasers of the score from Berlioz having chosen to recover their investment by
renting score and parts to all eternity. The rented scores were in a frightful state
under the tampering of successive users. Conductors who, like Beecham, wanted to
know Berlioz's intentions could not find out except by independent research.

the old local and time-bound repertory by the quasi-universal and timeless repertory. In that regard he stands with many others, notably Vivaldi and the Handel of the operas.

The second cause was the violent re-education of the modern ear and mind as result of phenomena and experiments to be mentioned in a moment. Here I think it important for musical history to attempt a closer description of this interesting shift itself. And perhaps its contents will have something for the critics as well, since the long commemorative article of March 9, 1969, in the *New York Times* found Berlioz still puzzling in his modernity.[2]

Let us replace outselves at Berlioz's deathbed a hundred years ago. After a career of undeviating effort at imparting his conception of music by his writings and his scores, as well as by directing orchestras all over Europe, from London to Moscow and Paris to Prague, the man who stands next to Beethoven as the fountainhead of modern music died in stoic resignation, convinced that his message had fallen on deaf ears. His message was that music is an independent art, whose resources were still not fully explored.

Berlioz had taught hundreds of European musicians new rhythms, new melodies, new tone colors, and a new precision in vocal and instrumental performance. He had admirers and followers among the young; he had a particularly strong body of supporters in England; he had captured the imagination of the Russian Five, with Mussorgsky in the lead. He had cut Europe loose from the old ways and taught it the new.[3]

But in France or Central Europe, independent orchestral music on dramatic themes could not compete with fireworks on the piano or the solid comfort of familiar opera. And when the public finally tired of fireworks and developed in-

2. At a public meeting in London on October 23, 1969, French and English scholars and musicians discussed various aspects of "Berlioz, Our Contemporary."
3. Referring to Berlioz's account of his own activities in Central Europe, Hanslick says: "That is how it was. Berlioz did not exaggerate in the least." (*Deutsche Rundschau*, 1882, pp. 369ff.)

somnia at the old opera, the clean sweep was made by the
steamroller of Wagnerism—not merely Wagner's great
music, but Wagner*ism*, a fanatical tide that rose like Moham-
med's horde to conquer thousands.

Berlioz continued to be played, in small doses. He continued to be the subject of books and critiques, in large doses.
He always had his devotees, from his very first concert at the
age of twenty-two. But after his death the general public saw
him as a gifted forerunner of Wagner; a genius undoubtedly,
but wild, a successful creator of new effects, yes—but of what
besides it was difficult to say. On the programs he would
recur as the composer of a curious work called *Three Excerpts
from the Damnation of Faust.*

That was the position until recent times, when the advent
of the LP enabled the public to hear whole works instead of
fragments. For many listeners Berlioz suddenly turned into
the composer of *The Damnation of Faust*—the whole
thing—plus many other whole works, including nine overtures, the song cycle *Nuits d'Eté*, and *L'Enfance du Christ*—
familiar music now, but unknown to all but specialists twenty
years ago.

The switch from rare and often bad performances to the
repeated hearing and comparison of complete scores effected
a small revolution. To begin with, critics could begin to demand correct renderings. Thus a recent reviewer in one short
paragraph lists half a dozen grave faults in a new recording of
the *Requiem.* He concedes that the conductor "makes some
effective big lines, but the colors of this performance are Old
Master with lots of warm brown varnish on top. The original,
in all its glorious and terrifying brilliance, is more impres-
sive." Two decades ago the unimpressive mush would have
been taken for the original.

By hearing Berlioz in his own guise instead of his interpreters', the public began to notice that he was not an inventor of effects, but a composer, a whole composer. And

meanwhile some of us were overhauling the entire perspective on Romanticism and the nineteenth century. This allowed Berlioz to be seen otherwise than through anti-romantic clichés and post-Wagnerian slogans. Program notes about the *Symphonie Fantastique* began to discuss the music instead of the love affair that it was supposed merely to reflect. And readers began to be told about the interesting progression in the third movement which curiously crops up as the Thought motif in *Siegfried* thirty years later. A different sort of attention given to the fugue in the last movement began to suggest an artist whose fiery soul was disciplined to a highly conscious technique—at its most conscious and disciplined when it departed most from the textbook rules. Seeing Berlioz more nearly as he was had the effect of opening a passage to the ear, just as hearing the works as wholes divested his figure of imaginary characteristics. Each experience helped the other, for no perceptions are pure. We see in large measure what we expect to see—or are taught to look for.

An autobiographical example of this last truth is instructive. I remember bringing light unexpectedly to the groping mind of a distinguished writer on music by pointing out a neglected piece of chronology: though Wagner was only ten years younger than Berlioz, their works belong to different halves of the century. When Wagner is about to reach the summit, with *Tristan* in 1859, Berlioz's output is virtually complete. So these two men, who were natural and chronological antitheses, but whom their contemporaries damned as one, can now be regarded each for himself. The Siamese twins have been split and every man can choose his favorite, forgetting the muddle of history.

Yet there is one more contrast to be drawn in the historical mode. Wagner has been absorbed. Berlioz is still before us, in many ways a tantalizing novelty. More and more people think they know him and know him well. But there is an element of illusion in this confident feeling. In the Berlioz repertory alone there are important discoveries to be made. To take a small example, in the concerts at Aspen commemorating Berlioz this past summer, no one in the orchestra (or in the audience as far as I could tell) had heard the *Funeral March for Hamlet*, a small but characteristic work. Generally speaking none of Berlioz's songs, cantatas, and other small-scale works (except the *Nuits d'Eté*) are at all known. Nor is this because they are all negligible: it remains to be seen which are and which are not; for at one time the *Nuits d'Eté* themselves were neglected—which is something quite other than negligible.

Among the large works, too, there are still unknowns, *Benvenuto Cellini* being the principal item. Its production has been attempted several times without due preparation, and also without a precise understanding of the difficulties presented by a score whose checkered history made it the victim of too many rearrangements. The impression left on several good critics is that it is "a flawed masterpiece—like *Boris*." This is doubtless just, but there are not so many scores "like *Boris*" that we can afford to overlook a single one.

In still other large works, it is right performance that we still lack. The finale of *Romeo and Juliet* has not been heard as it should sound, not even under Toscanini in the late 1940s. When we have singer, chorus, and orchestra in balance and in tune, we shall at last perceive that the conclusion of the work, instead of being the spiritual letdown that some have termed it, is as noble as the music of love and death that comes before. And to this list of "novelties" one could add the *Te Deum*, a work as dramatic as the *Requiem* when it is not played with an in-churchy attitude and when it is given complete with Prelude (No. 3) and March (No. 8).

The quality, apart from plain musicianship, which is most often lacking in the music we are invited to accept as being Berlioz is his peculiar fusion of energy and control—or as one modern critic put it: fire and ice. Conductors who fling themselves at his score in what I can only believe is a kind of primitive courtship by violence get only broken rhythms and impotent melodies as the price of their oestrus. At the other extreme, the unimaginative time-beaters get only the award for endurance, which in fairness they should share with the listeners.

This last result is not a consequence peculiar to Berlioz's music. In my youth, when Mozart was dismissed as a trifler, I have heard a valiant Mozartian on the podium turn the G-minor Symphony into inexpressible boredom. And we are all familiar with Shakespeare crucified on the wooden limbs of his unfit interpreters.

The comparison between Berlioz and Shakespeare is not limited to this plain truth about performance. It goes deep, both because Berlioz found in Shakespeare principles of dramatic art that confirmed his own youthful intuitions, and because the works of these two creators have passed through strikingly similar phases of acceptance, neglect, and re-discovery. At first, for both, enthusiasm and worldly success, coupled with objections of incompleteness and lack of polish. Ben Jonson's words about wishing William had "blotted a thousand lines" could be matched by suggestions offered to Berlioz in the same friendly spirit.

Then, after death, the phase of semi-eclipse: who *is* this man? How shall we take these strange, asymmetrical compositions and willful or ignorant eccentricities? Shakespeare was "improved" by a dozen hands in the two centuries after his death. When, in the 1750s, *King Lear* did not seem likely to pay for itself, even cut down, performing bears would come on to enliven the mood between the acts. Shortening Berlioz's *March to the Scaffold*, denying him his full instrumentation, removing harps and adding cymbals, putting the brass choirs of the *Requiem* in the corners of the hall instead of at the corners of the performing group, mingling the music of the *Damnation of Faust* with that of *L'Enfance du Christ* in order to put the former on the stage, or whittling down the epic *Trojans* to two sides of a disc—all these are the performing bears and tasteful refinements that were reserved for Berlioz's music until recent times.

For Shakespeare it was only at the beginning of the nineteenth century that critics grew sober and thoughtful enough to study his technique through his purpose—or vice versa. As late as 1764 a stout admirer like Dr. Johnson could declare without a blush that "one cannot find six lines without a fault." It was Coleridge's lectures of 1811 and 1818 that put forth what the lecturer himself termed a paradox: "that Shakespeare's judgment was, if possible, still more wonderful than his genius." In short, the wild, irregular, faulty, or ignorant poet and dramatist who (as was said) grew immortal in his own despite, turned out to be a figment of inadequate criticism.

With Berlioz we are on the verge of the same conclusion.[4] The revelation of his judgment as equal to his genius has been made—not all at once by a towering mind such as Coleridge, but in bits and pieces by lesser men. They have shown that the many faults imputed to Berlioz are in fact the indices of an art not as yet fully grasped, much less analyzed. Its logic is but dimly seen so far, because the apparatus for recapturing it is as yet incomplete, only partly invented. Older systems will not work, and there is no use continuing to apply them to Berlioz in the manner of Procrustes. This conclusion was brilliantly illustrated by a conversation which a noted contemporary composer once had with a distinguished musicologist, for whom incidentally I felt admiration, despite his strong distaste for Berlioz. Looking at the second movement of the *Harold* Symphony, the historian pointed out false relations. "All right," said the composer, "but then you must explain to me why the passage is sublime."

4. See note 5, p. 110. (Ed.)

Nor is it Berlioz's counterpoint alone that evokes tsk-tsks under the tongue. "Faults" have been found in his harmony. His modulations used to call forth anathemas. His rhythms petrified performers. His melodies remained unnoticed by the most elongated ears. And his form!—his form could not be found, even with a dowser's wand. Toscanini himself, who loved to play Berlioz, was sometimes uneasy, as he confessed to me, about *la mano sinistra*. He reveled in "those beautiful chords" at the opening of the *Romeo* love scene, but elsewhere . . . .

The remark about the left hand is symptomatic. Toscanini responded like the musician who thinks and composes at the piano. He was worried by often finding the bass a third higher "than it should be" and (I imagine) by the blocks of harmonies that seem autonomous from each other. Or again, in vocal accompaniments especially, he missed the familiar cadential organization, which makes a song both coherent and lulling. The continuous molding of the harmony on a long and dramatic vocal line readily gives the impression of "going nowhere" and thereby irritating equally sensibilities trained in the German and in the Italian tradition.

For standard practice, which has conditioned feeling to the point where it seems aboriginal nature, is to put reliance on the bass, which is identified, by an unconscious pun, with the b-a-s-e of the musical edifice. Well, Berlioz did not *hear it* that way. What emerges from recent studies is that he conceived a new kind of music, which holds together by different means than a succession of normally related "fundamental " sounds. There is no reason to suppose that Berlioz was being deliberately archaic, though his practice bears a likeness to that of the sixteenth-century polyphonists, who preferred to let the true bass be "understood," because, precisely like Berlioz, they were keen to have their melodies stand out. They found hinting more subtle than pounding. There is indeed something dull and repetitious about the grind of an unimaginative continuo.

Berlioz went further and thereby looks forward to innovations of our own day: as early as 1838, in one section of
Juliet's funeral march for the *Romeo* Symphony, he takes the
bass pedal away from the instruments and throws it into the
voices above, quite as if he knew from Einstein that there is
no up or down.

Moreover, Berlioz knew long before Duke Ellington (to
whom the "discovery" is ascribed) that so-called tone color
affects harmony to such an extent that a sensitive ear revolts
at the purely abstract idea of a chord being absolute by virtue
of its constituents and regardless of the timbre (upper har-
monics) in which it is sounded. Certain repetitions in Berlioz
are thus repetitions only on paper or in words; in sound they
are alterations or progressions. And in other cases, by the
same token, the wrong chord is the right chord—provided
the ear is attuned to hear it before the analytic mind reduces
auditory experience to academic nomenclature. The reader
will find further instructive details in articles by Jacques
Chailley and Philip Friedheim, both written within the last
fifteen years.[5]

It is worth noting that Berlioz belonged to an age when art
was still defined as the concealment of art, and when accordingly artists did not make metaphysics out of their genius or
their ingenuity. He never condescended to defend or explain
his own practice. He hated pedantry—and this deep feeling
was one cause of his revulsion against Wagner's cortege of
theories (if the tautology may be allowed). "Music alone," as
Berlioz kept repeating, "like Medea sufficient unto herself."

The one time Berlioz permitted himself a piece of self-
regarding theorizing, he did it very briefly, and only because
the subject seemed to him an entirely new domain of specu-
lation. The subject is rhythm, and the essay in which he deals
with it is one of his *feuilletons* in the *Journal des Débats* apro-

5. Respectively, "Berlioz Harmoniste," *La Revue Musicale*, Berlioz Issue (1956) and
"Radical Harmonic Procedures in Berlioz," *The Music Review* (November 1960).

pos of Johann Strauss's visit to Paris in 1837.[6] He calls it "The Future of Rhythm," and in it he tells us what we should have long since discovered in his works, namely, that rhythm is a facet of music capable of great development like any other, though hitherto largely neglected. There are, says Berlioz, "such things as rhythmic dissonances; there are rhythmic consonances; there are rhythmic modulations." And he adds that no formula exists for rhythmic inventiveness, any more than for melodic.

Add to this a concern with space—what we now call the stereophonic effect—space as an element of structure, and one begins to see that, entirely apart from its dramatic interest, Berlioz was fashioning out of sounds a kind of six-sided music, a cubist structure, which did not have to sit on any of its sides or on the ground, but could fly through space and neither lose motion nor fall apart. When, therefore, we pounce on this or that measure in one of his scores and discover false relations or false basses or anything we deem false, it is because we fail to understand the place and function of that part in the manifold composition. It is obvious that in giving shape to substance, its properties set up conflicts that can only be resolved by adjustment, subordination, sacrifice. Making these regardless of "local error" is the real meaning of technique, not what the textbooks think it is—a mere recipe.

How is it, though, that only we in this blessed age have first come to perceive what Berlioz was up to? One cause is that we have wanted to, for the reasons already given, and have been more systematic than the critics of his own day who, like Schumann, noted only what bore upon the issues then regarded as important. But the great cause of our newfound wisdom is the complete (though unconscious) re-education of the ear which we have all undergone. Just think: the piano,

6. See Supplement 5 in *Berlioz and the Romantic Century*, 3d ed. (New York: Columbia University Press, 1969). (Ed.)

to begin with, is no longer the sole ruler and maker of music.
We can hear true intonation whenever we like. We have
rediscovered the classic guitar—Berlioz's own instrument,
which certainly influenced his harmonic preferences. We are
captivated by the divided scale and the instruments of Harry
Partch. We have become inured to polytonality, atonality,
and the complex rhythms of Shankar. The sounds of electronic music, of *musique concrète*, of Theremin's machine, and
of the machine that bears the name of one R.C.A. Victor; and
yet one thing more: jazz. There are the experiences that have
opened our ears to Berlioz's conceptions and realizations.

Looking back over the century since his death, we can
understand why the well-disposed clung desperately and for
so long to the idea that Berlioz made "program music": they
felt the dramatic force of his melodies, rhythms, and harmonies, but they could not hear their unity. Others, deaf to
the sustained melodies, contented themselves with praising
the orchestration—as if color could redeem an ill-shapen
thing, instead of showing it up. For the rest, Berlioz's supposedly gigantic conceptions evoked either sympathy or de-
rision, depending on the settled convictions of the observer.
In short, it was the blind men confronted with the elephant,
an elephant, moreover, that wouldn't stand still.

I said at the outset that Berlioz is still puzzling. Yet it is
clear that better and more frequent rehearings, together with
the march of mind in music-making have removed part of the
mystery, while special studies have begun to supply needed
theoretical perspectives. What, after all this, can be still
puzzling? The wording of that last clause gives an answer:
studies have *begun*. The elephant has been identified and
drawn to scale, with palms waving in the background, but the
internal anatomy of the beast is not fully charted. We need
many more special studies, all strictly technical: counterpoint
has hardly been touched, harmony not fully explored; modulation and rhythm deserve treatment; after which, a scholar
competent not only in orchestration but in acoustics should

attempt to bring the whole together as a study in the first reconceiving of music as auditory experience. Once these investigations are done, it will only remain to classify and analyze Berlioz's numerous melodic forms, and with the results so obtained to demonstrate how his formal structures, which are almost always melodically determined, justify or fail to justify themselves. In other words, the bones and muscles having previously been enumerated, the secret of how they function organically will have been shown.

To be sure, even when scholarship has caught up with the "puzzling" subject, the sensibility of any given listener may remain unmoved and his mind therefore unconvinced. That is perfectly right and proper. It is the common lot of artists, and criticism on the basis of sensibility is always legitimate and respectable. It is reported of the young Boulez that he admired Berlioz and felt repelled at the same time "because Berlioz lacks the voluptuous texture of the great masters." That is an entirely sound judgment, even though one might question the generality about great masters. The important point is to recognize the given object for what it is, and not take it for a defective form of some other object. One characteristic of Berlioz's art will always repel people like Boulez in his nonage: Berlioz "appeals to the intellectual emotions." The phrase is Froude's about Shakespeare, and it does not mean "ideas" or "literature"; it means the imagination as against the senses.

One sense, of course, the sense of hearing, must be strong and fine, but when hearing Berlioz it is a channel to a multiple awareness of reality, rather than to pure feeling, voluptuous well-being. Those who want transports are bound to be dissatisfied, for the ecstasy Berlioz affords requires the mind to come into play, not the analytic mind, still less the discursive or descriptive mind; but the mind that has stored experience and possesses the swift imagination of the real. These awkward phrases are but another way of saying that Berlioz is a dramatist in music. Just as a few common words in a great drama will derive enormous power from their placing, so in music certain sounds, chords, rhythms, timbres, and even silences achieve the highest art because of their choice and their place in a structure which is dramatic in itself, with or without any reference to a story or poem. And the whole exists because sound can be shaped, like paint or articulate meanings, to produce in human beings the thrill of recognizing, transfixed in those substances, the mysterious gestures of the spirit.

1970

10

Benvenuto Cellini in Wembley

Everybody knows how an opera is recorded. It is played in bits and pieces, all out of order, each fragment done over and over up to eight, ten, or more times in succession. But it is one thing to know this in the abstract and another to undergo the experience. In July 1972, I lived through the three weeks that it took to record Berlioz's *Benvenuto Cellini*, and I can testify that to hear the work ten times, day and night, without even hearing it once, is a strange, exhausting, and instructive way to spend the time.

David Cairns, then Director of Classical Music for Philips International and famous as a Berlioz scholar, had asked me to attend the sessions at Wembley Town Hall outside London, and join the little knot of discontented men who listen to each "take" as it comes hot off the spool and who then bombard the conductor—Colin Davis—with opinion and advice.

In the stuffy backstage cupboard housing the machinery were: Erik Smith, an imperturbable technician, German-born and gifted with an extraordinary ear; Mauritz Sillem, seconded from Covent Garden, where he assisted in the production of the work some years ago; and Janine Reiss, of the Paris Opera, who, with the quiet and meticulous David Shaw, helped rehearse and supervise the vocal side.

From time to time one or two of the singers would troop back with the rest of us to hear and criticize their own performance—Nicolai Gedda, always debonair and ready to talk in any language including the Scandinavian; Christiane

Eda-Pierre and Jane Berbie, both enchanting women as un-like the stereotype of the tempestuous prima donna as possi-ble; and in the midst of this junta—arbiter but not autocrat—Colin Davis, whose good temper never deserts him, who listens to everybody and even seems to believe everybody, but who knows what he wants.

This functional Utopia was a lucky accident, for the work in hand bristles with difficulties, and it would have been easy to develop militant passions over one's pet points. The problems range from text and interpretation to performance. As to the text, the vicissitudes of the work in Berlioz's lifetime altered it from two to three acts, with various con-tents in various sequences, and from a comic opera to some-thing else, hybrid and false to the composer's original idea.

For it was Berlioz who conceived the theme (essentially that of Wagner's subsequent *Meistersinger*) and who supplied the principal scenes. The Davis recording—the first and only one—goes back to his conception and gives us a drama in the mood and genre of *Don Giovanni*, which also started life as an *opera giocoso*. True, in both works the "joke" often verges on tragedy, but that is the very nature of high comedy.

From all this it is easy to imagine how often in the Berlioz score a true rendering means a delicate balance on the knife-edge between fooling and genuine emotion. Some scenes, such as that with the innkeeper, the strolling players in the carnival, and the fake duel with Cellini's rival, are clearly buffoonery. But what of Cellini's meditative arias about art or nature? True feeling inspires them, but it must not become too gripping and throw the rest out of kilter. Yet the murder scene in the middle of the carnival is the real thing and very moving. As for the pomp that ushers in Pope Clement VII, it must be both majestic and satirical—difficult!

Throughout, Colin Davis got what he wanted. Tireless and articulate, he kept his head despite all confusion. While the gentle concert-master left the hall to hush the cups and sauc-

ers in the canteen next door, the conductor made jokes—
very mild ones—that would tide the orchestra (the cellos in
particular) over the ninth repetition of Ascanio's solemn aria
in the first act. Then again, he confers with Jules Bastin, the
heavy father, to find the needed accent just short of burles-
que, and presently all sounds right.

The day had begun at ten-thirty and might end at seven or
as late as midnight, but there was no slackening of attention,
or intention. The numerous guests who came and went—
musicians from abroad, critics from the London papers, students from the R.C.M.,[1] conductors on furlough—thought
themselves rewarded by a couple of hours' sojourn on the
hard creaky chairs (by the end there was a whole barricade of
ostracized chairs), but the company serenely went on, day
after day, Sundays included.

The routine included morning and afternoon mid-session
breaks in which card games would erupt. At 4:30, tea of
course. On the long days, hot or cold lunch or dinner, on
trestle tables, for the members of the cast and the musical
politburo; and at almost every interval, the careful shifting of
the overhead microphones, looking like Picasso giraffes,
from here to there, two inches away.

As the haphazard scenes unfolded, it became plain that the
backbone of the work is rhythm. In an article that Berlioz
wrote in the very year of composing *Cellini* he advocated
"counterpoints of rhythm, harmonies and modulations of
rhythm." Here they are. The score is in a sense the textbook
of the course on rhythm he wanted to offer at the Conservatoire. In the playing of no other work is a disciplined
nervous system more necessary. In fact, when one thinks of
his contemporaries' notions on this subject, one is amazed
that this opera could be performed at all in 1838. And one is
reminded of Hofmannsthal's writing to Richard Strauss that

1. The Royal College of Music. (Ed.)

"the secret of comedy is in the rhythm and not in the occasional titillating of the sense of the ridiculous."

Keeping rhythmic inventions from being flattened out into
more familiar shapes, making sure that the steady use of
simultaneous melodies and timbres gives dramatic contrasts,
not blurred outlines; and—most arduous—making out of all
the bits, mechanically chopped-up for recording, one high arc
of sustained energy—these were the things that taxed the
sum of musicianship gathered in Wembley Town Hall.

The burden fell primarily on the conductor and his performers, but vicariously also on the listeners and sideline
critics. Fatigue matched exhilaration. But those large demands did not blot out each man's concern for his favorite
details. David Cairns, who has the knack of looking at once
alert and preoccupied, gave the impression that for him there
was no such thing as a detail. Everything mattered on life-
and-death terms, which was true enough, since he was ultimately responsible for everything. His assistant, Liza Hobbs,
had done the translation of the libretto (an excellent one),
and when she was not busy dispensing tea and cakes she
would scan it and follow the French text, just as Mme Reiss
monitored the pronunciation of the English chorus. When it
came to the repetitions of *pendu* as Cellini is being con-
demned to hang, she put a stop to the audible *pondu* which
would have turned the hero into a fresh-laid egg.

Meanwhile Mauritz Sillem was hypnotizing his photocopy
of the autograph score to conjure up a trombone part that
somebody had blotted out—who? when? why? If we could
only recover those few bars, what a precious addition to the
treasure of sound rippling past our ears! In another corner a
discussion was going on about the right object to hit for the
short passage of metallic noise in the forge scene. Nothing
had been provided and in the end nothing proved satisfactory. Like the cannon of Fort Sant' Angelo that ends the
carnival, it was scamped—two tiny and exceptional flaws.

But why cavil at the absence of two spots of noise when again and again the collective devotion to Berlioz's thought enables us to hear new and delicious things, such as the somber chorus of workmen preparing to cast Cellini's great statue—the quantity and quality of choral writing in the score is amazing—or again, in the final tutti, when everything is banging away fortissimo, the sudden little figure for tuba, which must be even more comic when played on the original ophicleide.

Apropos of this cavernous wind, John Canarina, the American conductor who is an old friend of Davis's, wondered why the BBC Orchestra did not keep an ophicleidist in reserve. He would have come in handy for the Petrushka-like interlude during the Roman Carnival—except that the tuba player did a virtuoso job with that solo, and why risk an antiquarian note? The opera is modern fore and aft: the foundrymen go on strike and Cellini sings some pre-industrial blues.

As for myself, what justified my presence, beyond the duty of conscientious carping described above? Well, I chatted with Mme Eda-Pierre's husband and little boy, neither of whom spoke English. I enjoyed myself by day and then stayed awake nights to let the cascade of sound pour out again. And as I left the last session on July 20, I pondered Colin Davis's wonderful remark to one of the men about Berlioz's musical mind: "You never know where the thoroughbred horse will jump."

1977

11

The Postman Rang Thrice

An Exchange

Columbia University
in the City of New York
February 25, 1958

Dear Dr. Starkie:

I have just read your new *Baudelaire*, having long valued the earlier, and my admiration for your scholarship and biographical art is refreshed and renewed. Indeed, this, with your *Rimbaud* and your superb *Petrus Borel*, forms a contribution to the understanding of both recent history and the modern temper which seems to me unsurpassed for breadth of knowledge and sureness of judgment.

It is this conviction which makes me venture to point out in the latest *Baudelaire* the survival of an old error, small in compass but important in implications, for it affects the character and critical ethics of a great artist.

I refer to your description on p. 417 of Berlioz at the Wagner Concerts of 1860. I know this is a traditional tale, repeated in many "trustworthy" books. But it does not withstand examination. One has only to read the review Berlioz wrote of these concerts to see that he was not moved by jealousy. Wagner had as yet no success to be jealous of, and even had Berlioz felt any such emotion—which nothing in his entire life gives ground for supposing—he would have had too much pride to show it in public by a "disdainful expression." Knowing the Paris world of letters as you do, you can imagine that there was at all times a strong anti-Berlioz party, and the slander you reproduce is but one of the assaults in a lifelong war.

Yours sincerely,
Jacques Barzun

120

41 St. Giles
Oxford England
18 March 1958

Dear Professor Barzun:

It was very nice of you to write and I was very glad to get your letter. I am always glad when mistakes and misstatements are pointed out to me. I am ashamed to say that I haven't yet read your book on Berlioz, though I have often intended to do so as I am told that it is the best book written about him—certainly the most authoritative. I have read, and possess, your book on Romanticism, and I have found it very stimulating.

I got the material for the reception of Wagner by Berlioz from Combarieu, I believe, and I thought he would be reliable, and would have gone through all the documents. I can't remember, at the moment, whether he, Combarieu, has an anti-Berlioz bias. I am glad to know that this is a false opinion because I admire Berlioz very much. When I do another edition of my *Baudelaire*, I shall correct that mistake—as well as many others. I don't think any point is too small, and there is no point in saying something if one is not accurate, and I had used it to show that Baudelaire was amongst a small number of people who saw anything in Wagner's music.

I may be coming to the United States in 1959, and I hope then that we may meet, as I have wanted this long time to meet you.

Again many thanks for your letter, which I very much appreciate.

Yours sincerely,
Enid Starkie

1958

The Three B's

To the Editor
of the *New York Times*

Sir:

Your recent review of Harold Schonberg's *Lives of the Great Composers* states in its headline that the author has added Berlioz as a fourth to "the three B's." It would be more exact to say that he has restored him as the original third. The fighting slogan "Bach-Beethoven-Berlioz!" was first launched by Peter Cornelius, in an article published in Berlin in 1854.

Much later, Hans von Bülow made over the three B's by putting in Brahms—whom Berlioz had admired and encouraged as a youth.

Jacques Barzun
New York City

1972

12

Berlioz and the Bard

"To be past forty and not know *Hamlet* is like having spent one's life in a coal-mine!" Thus wrote Berlioz in the 1860s about some friends at whose house he was going to read the play aloud—they knew none of it but the name. When we think of the nineteenth century as one of Shakespeare idolatry we forget what limits of place, provincialism, and educated ignorance confine even a world reputation. It was not merely the French of that day who neglected the poet; Berlioz tells us also that his Irish friend Balfe, the composer of *The Bohemian Girl*, had just "discovered" Shakespeare in the Fifties. And the performances, comments, and inter- pretations then current often seemed to Berlioz in the last degree discouraging about the fate of art.

His own discovery dated back to 1827, when the first En- glish actors to win success in Paris had brought to the young Romantics *Hamlet* and *Romeo and Juliet,* together with *Jane Shore* and *The Rivals*. From that moment, Berlioz was not only an admirer and an evangelist, but in a very real sense a disciple. Shakespearean form and something that may be called the Shakespearean temperament were to be integral elements of Berlioz's art.

When the revelation came, it was of course combined with the living charm of the beautiful Ophelia, Harriet Smithson, who in time would become Madame Berlioz; but even at the earliest date it was the spell of Shakespeare that kept Berlioz infatuated with a woman he had never met, and not the woman who endowed Shakespeare with power over Berlioz's mind. After seeing a few performances the young composer begins at once to learn English and to qualify as one of the most thorough readers and users of Shakespeare that the world has ever seen. For his work then in progress—"Eight Scenes from Goethe's 'Faust'"—he chooses a number of Shakespearean mottoes, and thenceforth we can trace the poet's words in all that Berlioz wrote and composed, down to *Beatrice and Benedict,* adapted by himself from *Much Ado,* and the last page of the *Memoirs,* which ends with "Life's but a walking shadow."

This lifelong study of the poet-dramatist by the music-dramatist had a quasi-religious quality as well as an artistic significance. Shakespeare's work served Berlioz through life as a secular scripture—a book of devotions, for Berlioz felt as central to his being and creativeness the debt he owed the playwright for his liberation. It was Shakespeare who woke him from the dogmatic slumbers induced by eighteenth-century French criticism and who taught him the "versatility of form" that he needed for his musical purposes. The lesson was not merely that one could disregard unity of place and continuity of action in dramatic works, but that every established genre in a given art could find room within a drama provided there was sound reason for the choice. The uneven texture that resulted was a merit, not a flaw: just as in Shakespeare's *Romeo and Juliet* there are two prologues, two sonnets, prose and poetry, eloquence and catchwords, couplet and blank verse, so in the *Romeo* Symphony of Berlioz, which neither illustrates nor resembles the original, we find a transposition answering to the same esthetic principle. This principle Berlioz never abandoned, in spite of his century's return to older models and his nation's prevailingly opposite tradition. When he inaugurated the "serial idea" in *Les Troyens,* whose subject matter is drawn from Virgil's *Aeneid,* his remark was that the double drama with characters from the first recurring in the second was nothing new: it followed the scheme of Shakespeare's histories. And Berlioz's increasing mastery in fashioning librettos and making lyrical ideas develop into drama grew with his knowledge of the poet.

At the same time Berlioz's admiring discipleship was no piece of secret self-identification which hides personal conceit under an attachment to a great name. Shakespeare was a god in the antique sense, like Virgil and Beethoven, and Berlioz continued to think of himself as a mortal. Still, the choice of our idols, if it is conscious and free, defines something in us—a kinship or an opposition; we may seek something we lack or something close to what we possess. In Berlioz's relation to Shakespeare it is safe to say that the link through similarity is the suggestive one, and English critics such as W. J. Turner and Francis Toye have not hesitated to dwell on the likeness. This cannot be taken as sacrilege once it is agreed that the Shakespeare who is under discussion is the great but fallible writer of plays, not the fish-eyed figure of the schoolbook whose name is merely a synonym for: "Supreme! And don't let's hear another word about it!"

The question of great power allied to great imperfections is of course the significant one for critics. From Shakespeare's time to ours—that is, from Ben Jonson to John Crowe Ransom—competent judges of literature have not ceased to point out Shakespeare's singular combination of mastery and ineptitude. He is said to be transcendent and also crude, careless, vulgar, incoherent, rhetorical, exaggerated, naive, cheap, obscure, unphilosophical, and addicted to bad puns and revolting horrors. Dryden, who admired Shakespeare just as Wagner admired Berlioz, found his master's phrases "scarcely intelligible; and of those which we understand some are ungrammatical, others coarse; and his whole style is so pestered with figurative expressions that it is as affected as it is obscure."

The remarkable fact, of course, is that these faults, any one of which would be enough to sink an ordinary writer into oblivion, did not keep Shakespeare from exacting and receiving the highest praise—often at the hands of the very same critics—and from rising ultimately to a position where we simultaneously see his faults and see that they do not matter. Nor is this double vision to be called idolatry; it comes rather from the knowledge that each critic and each age finds Shakespeare's flaws in different places, and that the blemishes seen from one point of view turn into marks of genius when seen from another. This, if anything, is the meaning of the conclusion so often repeated that Shakespeare transcends criticism, baffles our judgment, and outtops knowledge.

Perhaps because Shakespeare was a writer—hence more amenable to diverse uses, including that of supreme academic hobbyhorse—criticism has not inquired whether his art is unique in the respects cited above or whether by those tokens it belongs to a class. The architecture of the cathedral occurs at once as presenting similar contrasts of crudity and finish, so that in one sense Gothic and Shakespearean are interchangeable terms and do define a class. We easily understand why Henry Adams juxtaposed twelfth-century stained glass and Delacroix; it is for the same reason that the parallel between Shakespeare and Berlioz is hard to resist.

Had the objections to Berlioz's taste, judgment, and knowledge, no less than to his sense of form, harmony, and counterpoint, been artistically founded they, too, would long ago have made an end of him. But from his own day, as Schumann bears witness, the "inevitability" of these presumed errors and the power of the music with all its flaws have had to be acknowledged. For Berlioz as for Shakespeare there has been a reversal of opinion on details formerly thought settled beyond appeal; his crudities have turned into subtleties, his noise into melody, his harmonic ignorance into bold forecasting of methods now current. Since at the beginning critics faced the necessity of accounting for Berlioz's baffling power, there grew up the hypothesis (still in the textbooks) of a volcanic genius, imperfectly educated, in whose work fine inspirations abound, though always in a context of sulphur and brimstone. But thus did the eighteenth century talk about Shakespeare's wild untutored genius, regret that he "wanted art," and deplore his taste for the macabre.

The parallel, let it be said again, does not mean that Shakespeare and Berlioz are identical but that their respective works may be usefully compared as cultural phenomena. We may liken them as "makers of great imperfect dramas," of "flawed masterpieces"—the term does not matter so long as we use it to trace indicative consequences. Can it be simple coincidence, for example, that it was through reiterated performance, instigated by great actors or great conductors, that both Shakespeare and Berlioz finally found fit critics? And by an involvement which only strengthens the bond between the pair, it was the men of Berlioz's own time who forced the last step in Shakespeare's canonization. Scott, Lamb, Hazlitt, Coleridge, Goethe, Herder, and Berlioz himself had to combat their fathers' diffidence, and (to use Goethe's expression) "labor long to show him in a good light." It was they who destroyed the "clumsy genius" hypothesis and made good in its place Coleridge's assertion that in Shakespeare "the form [is] equally admirable with the matter, and the judgment of the great poet not less deserving of our wonder than his genius."

The reader of Shakespeare and hearer of Berlioz will find for himself a good many other facts connecting the two and confirming the suggestion of a Shakespearean temperament producing art of the "Gothic" sort. The notion at any rate explains what is "mysteriously unsatisfying" about some of the greatest artists and why it is that their afterfame is so uneven.

One thinks of Rabelais, Bach, and Rembrandt, as well as of Shakespeare, Delacroix, and Berlioz.

As regards the last-named, it is not enough to murmur "Shakespearean" and hope to suspend criticism. One must also recognize the peculiar property of dramatic form. For it can be shown that the combination of a rough, diversified artistry with objective drama accounts historically for much of the resistance to Berlioz. It accounts for the paradox that he is known at once for his wire-drawn refinements and for being "absolutely devoid of taste." No one can repeat for him the cliché which has served for Shakespeare that he deliberately composed his works in layers of increasing fineness corresponding to social gradations—puns for the pit and philosophy for the earls. The cliché is almost certainly false for Shakespeare too. What we have in both instances is the state of mind of the dramatist working at an "open" form, which demands fine tooling close by relaxed effort, a willingness to let a flat motive do duty side by side with concise or delicate workmanship. And by inversion it would seem plausible to reconsider that other stereotype of Shakespeare as a careless writer, for we know full well how Berlioz polished and revised scores that have been judged careless. Why suppose that Shakespeare alone among writers could reach the sublime as the pen runs? Does not Jonson-of-the-blotter himself speak in his "Memorial Verses" of Shakespeare's "sweat" and "true-filed lines"? Whatever be the fact, it is evident that in both artists there was a purposeful abdication of sophisticated taste in order to make the finished work approximate the reality sought for.

It is this ultimate naturalism which is both Berlioz's strength and his weakness. Since it is his fundamental outlook on the world which makes him a naturalist of this type, we are not wrong to feel that he is unsatisfying, his naturalism being but the outward expression of his pessimism. "Unsatisfying," however, need not mean unsatisfactory. The beholder seeking for Berlioz's reasons and for Berlioz's order is not in the end disappointed. When close scrutiny has done with these rugged, resistant, and intermittently glowing works it must confess that the idea of correcting or improving or de-blemishing them is untenable. Somehow, as Schumann said, the whole thing "has an air," a necessity of its own. And when the noble, moving, or delicate passages have led us to assimilate the rest we find everywhere the same passionate desire to achieve exhaustive expression, the same disinclination to linger or repeat, and the same richness of invention and suggestion pressing as it were behind the externally dull or flat design. The four adjectives by which Scott Fitzgerald summed up his judgment of Shakespeare will therefore serve anyone who knows his Berlioz well: "whetting, frustrating, surprising, and gratifying."

The different degrees in which these qualities attract or repel determine the feeling one experiences on hearing Berlioz's several scores. It is a fact that musicians of similar rank have expressed widely different preferences among them. Brahms thought *The Infant Christ* Berlioz's masterpiece, Wagner chose the *Funeral Symphony*, Liszt adored *Benvenuto*, and Mendelssohn could truly admire only the songs. What is more, the opinions given by capable scholars show that every one of Berlioz's dozen great works appears to some as his greatest, while the rest are unhesitatingly dismissed as inferior. It is clear that if each man's negative vote were accepted this would make a clean sweep of Berlioz's music and, conversely, that if we add together the same men's positive votes they validate the bulk of the composer's output.

This may be another way of saying that Berlioz's range extends on every side beyond the sensibility of his judges. One perfection at least must be granted the creator of such works—that of being inexhaustible by any single mind. And this in turn explains the situation which has been erroneously thought peculiar to Berlioz, but which is merely characteristic of his kind, that of not being finally placed. Meantime, it must be set down as a statistical fact that nine-tenths of all the

music Berlioz wrote has evoked the highest possible praise of
those who know. Their consensus is distributive, as for
Shakespeare—a consensus rather than a unanimity, but it is
emphatic and unmistakable.

Shakespeare remains Shakespeare and Berlioz, Berlioz
—in spite of all similarities—for the common points define a
common type of art and not a reincarnation of souls. But if
art has links with both the culture and the self, it is to be
expected that kindred species of art and of character will
intertwine. In history as in music everything repeats, though
in altered form, and the critical question always is: what have
we here—the same (essence)?—or difference (accident)? The
nineteenth century bears a likeness to the sixteenth, Berlioz's
work to Shakespeare's; why not also the man to the man?
Any answer involves a risk, but when we consider how
Shakespeare seemed to find himself in Montaigne and how it
took a second Romantic period to turn both into great world
figures we are tempted to attach diagnostic importance to
Berlioz's feeling of kinship with Shakespeare. "I have to keep
consoling myself . . ." he says, "for not having known Virgil,
whom I should have so much loved, and Gluck and Beethoven and Shakespeare—who might have loved me. (But
in truth I am not in the least consoled.)" Berlioz found an
uncommon number of his sensations and impulses put into
words by Shakespeare. He found the same intensity of feeling, the same "rush of metaphor" and "lucid confusion" answering to his own. He shared also the fierce pleasure in
seeing nature dwarf the individual, mixed with great tender-
ness, humor, and compassion for men. Unwittingly, too—if
The Tempest is in truth Shakespeare's last word—both men
ended on the same note of half-melancholy fantasy. *Beatrice
and Benedict* skims lightly over the conflict between sweet
purity and Calibanism and uses grotesque humor, airy
figures, and festive pageantry to half-conceal the purblind-
ness of evil. From the composer's artistic serenity we can

infer little as to his day-to-day disposition, but we know that after his Shakespearean comedy Berlioz had said farewell to his art. Like his revered prototype, he meant to live on his patrimony and his accumulated earnings from the stage. Only the unimaginative would complain: "How unromantic!"

1950

13

Sketch of the Artist as Musician

The son of the country doctor had dutifully gone to Paris to study medicine, but although he liked the lectures on science, he hated dissection—and besides, his heart was already pledged to music. He spent his nights at the Opéra and much of his days reading scores in the library of the Conservatoire, then the leading music school in Europe.

He soon found teachers ready to help him, for he had scores of his own to show. Lesueur, who had been Napoleon's court composer, found the young Berlioz an apt pupil and soon got him accepted by his colleagues at the Conservatoire, Reicha and Cherubini. Following the tradition of that school, Berlioz competed for the Rome prize, to which he became eligible in 1827. But his musical ways were too unconventional, and he did not succeed until 1830, after four tries. Some of the music he composed for these competitions—notably *Cléopâtre*—now amazes our concert audiences: it is as if Keats's odes had been rejected as exam papers.

But by 1830 much else had happened to mold the mind and spirit of young Berlioz. First, he had discovered Beethoven, then a foreign bogeyman, and come to know not only the symphonies but the late quartets. Next, he had seen Shakespeare—another crude foreigner—and fallen in love at a distance with the leading lady who acted him in Paris, Harriet Smithson. Third, he had read Nerval's translation of Goethe's *Faust* and out of his enthusiasm, with incredible rapidity, composed eight scenes from the First Part of the poem. Finally and most important for the history of music, Berlioz had completed his first great work, the *Symphonie fantastique*, performed on December 5, 1830. Franz Liszt was in the audience.

In counterpoint with these decisive events, Berlioz's quarrels with his family and with Cherubini, his temporary starvation and hackwork, his mad and unsuccessful courting of the distant "Ophelia," and his engagement—on the rebound—with Camille Moke (the rising and seductive pianist) appear less important and ultimately less interesting, though writers of program notes seize upon them as spice they badly need. The development of Berlioz's mind is thus obscured by the vicissitudes of his early life.

In Rome, where the prize required that he spend two years, Berlioz was at loose ends, his friendships with Mendelssohn and Glinka being ostensibly the chief gains of the sixteen months that he actually lived in Italy. But he wandered much over the countryside, took endless notes of melodies and projects—and dashed home on hearing that Camille Moke had broken her engagement and pledged herself to a prosperous piano manufacturer. A by-product of the latter release was the pair of superb overtures to *King Lear* and *The Corsair*.

Back in Paris, Berlioz gave as a concert of re-entry the hodgepodge he called *Lélio, or The Return to Life*, a supposed sequel to the *Symphonie fantastique*. It contained lovely music, but none of it new, and the work does not form a whole, especially when one knows Berlioz's exacting sense of unity and coherence. Amid the usual troubles of Parisian artistic life, Berlioz married his Ophelia in 1833. What the young composer then faced, until nearly the end of his life, was the question: how to live and compose music? Nineteenth-century Paris expected everyone to write operas, and thousands did who were not even musicians. Awaiting his chance, Berlioz became a music critic. Out of his Italian memories he composed his *Harold in Italy*; then, after political entanglements, the stupendous *Requiem*. At last in 1838 came the opera: *Benvenuto Cellini*, based on the memoirs of the Florentine artist. The music was, once again, too advanced, and a cabal opposed to Berlioz's backers helped to scuttle the work.

Though Berlioz could not suspect it, the pattern of his life was set by this, his thirty-fourth year: he was to create one musical model after another, meeting both fervid response and set hostility. To promote his music and his esthetics, he would crisscross Europe from London to Moscow again and again, until the orchestras of Europe had learned under his baton what the modern style and technique were. Wagner acknowledged that they were revealed to him in that way hearing Berlioz's *Romeo and Juliet* in Paris in 1839. The later scores—*Grande Symphonie funèbre*, *Nuits d'Été*, *La Damnation de Faust*, *L'Enfance du Christ*, *Te Deum*, *Les Troyens* and *Béatrice et Bénédict*—were nearly all imposed upon Europe in that fashion, while in articles and books the assumptions of these *dramme per musica* were expounded by the composer.

Understanding such riches of sound was undoubtedly difficult, especially since performances were infrequent and—under other conductors than Berlioz—often inadequate. The fact that he was probably the greatest melodist since Mozart did not help, for the nineteenth-century ear expected tunes to be *like* Mozart's—or Rossini's. A different melodic line, in turn, required a different harmony, and so did the new element of structure that Berlioz introduced: timbre. It is only now, with the aid of recordings that permit us to rehear, and after the education we have received at the hands of Wagner, Strauss, Debussy, and Stravinsky, that we have begun to hear Berlioz properly, that is, as a creator who—to quote his own words—"took up music where Beethoven left it" and fashioned a medium for his own dramatic and psychological conceptions.

Fame and influence came to him at last—official honors, adulation from young hopefuls, and (ultimate test) invitations to tour the United States. Berlioz preferred Russia, where "The Five" were his ardent disciples. Toward the end the story of his achievement was complicated, as in a Shakespearean tragedy, by the philosophical and musical pachyderm that Wagner called "the music of the future." As a result, Liszt's head was turned and the critics crystallized confusion by taking Wagnerism, program music, Liszt's symphonic poems, and the works of Berlioz as interchangeable parts. Only now is the tangle being teased out, with the consequent emergence of Berlioz for what he was—a lyric and dramatic composer of the first rank, who needed no programs to buttress his work, and who influenced all those who came after, without being imitated by any.

1971

14

The Berlioz Style

To anyone familiar with the Berlioz literature, even that of the last twenty years of general reconciliation to Berlioz's existence, it must come as a shock—agreeable or outrageous—to read on the jacket of Mr. Primmer's book[1] these few words meant to entice the reader: "Because of the richness of its melodic, harmonic, and tonal resources, the musical language of the nineteenth century needed to be controlled by a very firm hand indeed. Berlioz possessed just such a hand." This quiet assertion is the theme developed in four chapters of admirable prose and pertinent musical examples.

Mr. Primmer necessarily began by hearing accurate performances of Berlioz's works, such as are to be had, so far, only in England; and he obviously went to them with his ears open to the sounds and shut to 150 years of conventional criticism. Finding in the music order, precision, control, and self-supporting musical intentions, he bethought himself of the French tradition, musical in the first place and artistic generally, and he reached his first important conclusion: "Berlioz is a solitary figure not because he stands outside of his tradition but because he stands at its head."

This seeming paradox the author demonstrates by brief but telling references to Lesueur, Reicha, Grétry, Méhul, Cherubini, and even Rameau. But by itself the point leaves unsolved the historical mystery of why Berlioz as heir and embodiment of the French tradition struck his French con-

1. Brian Primmer, *The Berlioz Style* (London, 1973). (Ed.)

temporaries as alien and won his most enthusiastic supporters in the Germanies, England, and Russia. Virtually until today in France he is a tolerated eccentric and not a national possession. The solution of the mystery is given in Mr. Primmer's three chapters on musical substance and technique, that is, on Berlioz's melody, tonality, and harmony. By showing how Berlioz used, regrouped, and expanded the elements and principles of the Baroque and transitional periods, by pointing out how the hints found in talent were transmuted by genius, the analyst explains how Berlioz "achieved a revolution without a rebellion."

At every turn Mr. Primmer's perceptiveness, judgment, and fertility in comparison and analogy serve his undeviating purpose. He is much too modest when in his eight-line preface he defines that purpose as "no more than to provoke discussion." One can think of but few works of criticism so compact and yet so well designed to overturn and remake the existing conception of a great artist. It is the sequel and fulfillment of Tom S. Wotton's pioneering work of 1935, executed on a plane of cultural knowledge and esthetic sensibility transcending all previous efforts. And, being addressed to students of music, it is as thickly, solidly, and clearly technical as all the professors of all the conservatoires could collectively wish.

Some of Mr. Primmer's choices of technical illustration will surprise the connoisseur of Berlioz's music; for example, the use of the first two themes of the Funeral and Triumphal Symphony to show subtlety of melodic structure. Our critic thinks the work as a whole underrated. Certainly it is underplayed, with the result (invariable for Berlioz) of its being seldom played right. The upshot is that when Mr. Primmer makes his point it is seen to be at once cogent and plain, and one wonders how it can ever have been overlooked. That is genius in criticism as it is in art: all miracles are simple. It may be a natural confidence in this sort of power that also led Mr.

Primmer to take the first themes of the *Corsair* Overture and of the Prelude to the *Trojans at Carthage,* the *idée fixe* of the *Fantastique* and the *Harold* theme as other demonstrations of Berlioz's melodic methods. Except for the *Romeo* "solo" (Part II), he does not use a single one of the sublime examples; by proving with the lesser he proves twice over.

And what he proves has two aspects; one, that Berlioz's melody is stylized and decorative as well as passionate and expressive; the other, that "in Berlioz's music there is no valid distinction between intelligence and feeling, form and material." To the clear-cut argument one might add that the analyst could have found further evidence from a comparison between the *idée fixe* that he cites, the theme of the Introduction that it incorporates, and its original form in the prize cantata *Herminie* of 1828, where (among other details) the force now given by the leap of a seventh in the second phrase was absent by reason of a bland octave.

It would be giving away the plot to tell here what discoveries Mr. Primmer brings us in his chapters on tonality (central and longest) and on harmony, and what definition he proposes in his concise, three-page conclusion on "the Berlioz style." Besides, since Mr. Primmer confirms every informed listener's belief that the generative principle of Berlioz's music is melody (in its fundamental, "Gregorian" sense), it seemed appropriate to concentrate here on that part of the inquiry, and leave room for a few words about the author's no doubt deliberate omissions.

First, though Mr. Primmer stresses the great importance of rhythm in Berlioz, he does not treat of it as a constituent of style. That the subject calls for study is evident, not only from what Berlioz said in his essay of 1837, but also from what musicians have said since Saint-Saëns and Romain Rolland and keep saying down to Messiaen and Boulez. As Robert Craft put it in a review of the complete *Benvenuto Cellini* on discs, with his rhythm Berlioz "invades the twentieth century."

Second, sufficient as is Mr. Primmer's treatment of harmony (thereby completing Koechlin and Wotton's fragmentary evidence), there is still another facet of it to be taken into account, namely, its relation to Berlioz's virtuoso mastery of the guitar. Fortunately, *this* subject has been studied and written up by Mr. Paul J. Dallman, of the University of Maryland music department. His detailed explanation of the idiomatic methods underlying Berlioz's "inexplicable" progressions removes all doubt that in ignoring the piano and what it dictates through the layout of its fingering, Berlioz was not haphazard or perverse: his ear was trained by the dictates of a different "keyboard," no less legitimate— perhaps more legitimate in adhering to true intervals and avoiding the piano's asymmetrical distribution of accidentals. Mr. Dallman's book introduces some new concepts and terms (such as "moving chord formation") which should answer questions of the kind Mr. Primmer mentions in passing, for example, Berlioz's habit of harmonizing from the top down, rather than from the bass.

Finally, the Berlioz style presupposes a theory of acoustics about which science has not yet made up its mind. It is set forth in the *Treatise on Orchestration* (page 293 of the Lemoine edition in French) and it is acted upon in the "monumental" works, notably the *Requiem* and *Te Deum.* Colin Davis conducting them in Saint Paul's is to the best of my knowledge the only student of the scores who has paid artistic attention to this (literal) dimension of their form. There are passages in the less voluminous works too (e.g., *L'Enfance du Christ*), where the same regard for what one acoustician calls "the Berlioz cavity," with its enhancement of the bass, would contribute yet one more element of structure. Berlioz's grand orchestra of 466 players and 360 choristers is obviously the prototype of the synthesizer used by our electronic composers, but it retains the advantage of more numerous and more flexible spatial relations as modifiers of sound.

The other two books on Berlioz appearing within a few months of Mr. Primmer's are worth having, but do not match his in originality and power.[2] M. Bailbé's is an ingenious piece of stylistic criticism, bent on the *Memoirs* exclusively. It shows that despite his frequent disclaimers Berlioz was an accomplished writer, and not simply as a critic and theorist of music, but as a storyteller, observer of nature, composer of dialogue and dramatic scenes, psychologist, parodist, and prose poet. The thousands who read the *Memoirs* surely respond to him in all these roles and their modulations, but without noting them. Here the techniques and their lineage are set out, together with an "anthropology" of choice passages. The commentator's conclusion would be massively reconfirmed if he took in the other dozen volumes of prose, including the letters. The conclusion itself is in perfect accord with Mr. Primmer's about the music: it is that Berlioz, solidly grounded in the French tradition, is the most comprehensive of Romantic artists, embracing and fusing all genres and materials in the Berlioz style.

Mr. A. E. F. Dickinson's discursive quarto picture book also aims at comprehensiveness—nothing short of "the works." The author is a veteran of the program-note school of criticism, and in this volume his wayward facility is not held down by a system, as it was in his exemplary little work of almost fifty years ago, *The Musical Design of "The Ring."* In consequence one is jolted rather than led from description to valuation to comparison. Apropos of the *Requiem*, for instance, we hear about Bach, Beethoven, Britten, Verdi, and Wilfred Owen, to land at last upon a short paragraph extolling Stravinsky's *Requiem Canticles* as more compressed than Berlioz's corresponding sections. This extreme Toveyism also produces frequent enigmas, as in the remark about "the sub-acid absorptions of the homesick Hylas" (in the *Trojans*).

2. Joseph-Marc Bailbé, *Berlioz, Artiste et Ecrivain dans les Mémoires* (Paris, 1972). A. E. F. Dickinson, *The Music of Berlioz* (New York, 1972).

Throughout, the text is spiked with bits of history and biography which ill comport with the organization of chapters by scoring ("Voices and Orchestra: Cantatas and Scenes"). Flanking the eleven chapters of that type come two essays: "Berlioz the Progressive" and "Berlioz's Methods." Both are well-intentioned; Mr. Dickinson fairly tries to show off the best points of his balky steed, but rider and beast are not at one. The expositor's ultimate verdict, despite many handsome compliments, boils down to the word used to characterize Berlioz's harmony: opportunism. The joke behind this rather wide discrepancy from Mr. Primmer's conclusion is that both critics are connected with the University of Durham: they should hold a symposium in tête-à-tête.

One word more on art of another sort: Mr. Dickinson's volume has on the jacket and as frontispiece one of Mr. Michael Ayrton's all-too-numerous likenesses of Berlioz. Like the others, this one betrays a strange and damnable preconception, which gives the master's stoical patrician countenance the marks of a weak will and sullen self-pity. Happily, every line of Mr. Ayrton's work is refuted by every line of Mr. Primmer's.

1974

15

The Misbehavior of Lélio

Though he came to Paris aged not quite eighteen, an untraveled provincial from a very small village, young Berlioz quickly learned what was needed to make the Parisian audiences take notice of the new in music, art, or literature: it was done by assault. But by nature Berlioz was sensitive and reserved, bursting with genius—to be sure—but also prudent and fundamentally respectable in the sense in which his "county-family" upbringing understood these terms. If he was to make himself aggressive and self-promoting, he must first overcome the handicap of an aristocratic temper and the self-critical spirit of a superior intellect.

But there it was—Paris expected the young unknowns, with or without a patron, to *lancer un bateau, pincer une guitare*. These pieces of art jargon mean: do something arresting and distinctive in a milieu already full of gifted individualists and of *poseurs* presenting a similar façade. It was perhaps a disadvantage to have a real "boat" to launch, and (as it happened) to be in the literal sense an accomplished guitarist. So like the heroes of Balzac's novels who were contemporary with him, Berlioz must find the appropriate mask and suitable form of scandal with which to draw attention to himself. I mean by scandal a public act that would get him talked about in the right circles. He was, in short, a Julien Sorel or a Rastignac with the eternal problem to solve: how to make one's way.

Now the generation of Romanticists to which Berlioz belonged shared certain beliefs which, when carried into action, seemed to stir the public out of its stodgy philistine habits. One point in this new creed was that the artist is a hero and the true leader of culture and society. He is a genius, which means one who engenders, and he may be recognized by his standing out from the mass in ways that seem egotistical and eccentric.

A related point was that the genius is passionate, demonic, and sacrifices everything to his love and his art. Considerations of caution, fear of failure, and regard for what others will say, which move the ordinary man, do not move him. Outwardly he is beset by his enemies and the vicissitudes of life, but he triumphs in the end even if all the forces of society and of hell should conspire against him.

These ideas make up the cultural background against which we should read the two pieces of prose that Berlioz provided as the listener's guide to his first great work, the *Symphonie fantastique* and to its so-called sequel, *Lélio, or the Return to Life.*

The five situations indicated in the text that accompanies the symphony are too well-known to repeat here.[1] But they constitute the precedent, so to speak, for the farrago that introduces the five sections of *Lélio*. In both narratives the hero is an artist and in love; in both he is at grips with elements of the social world and the nether world. The second piece is called "The Return to Life," because in the first the hero has been executed and properly consigned to hell.

But all this, which with a little rearrangement might make a conventional opera libretto that people would memorize, is now of no particular consequence. Berlioz admitted so much himself when he said that, once known, the *Symphonie fantastique* needed nothing more than the short titles of each movement as indications of their setting.

He was right, as current practice proves. But he had also

1. Dreams and Passions; At a Ball; Scenes in the Country; March to the Scaffold; Dream of a Witches' Revel. (Ed.)

been right, earlier, to make up his cock-and-bull story of the artist-hero in love and wandering about. For it was this pseudo-autobiographical sketch that drew Paris to the premiere of his epoch-making work and excited talk and notoriety as Berlioz intended.

I call it pseudo-autobiographical because in spite of all that has been written to the contrary, the "program" of the *Fantastique* does not record Berlioz's own love affair with the actress Harriet Smithson. For one thing—easily verified—he was never guillotined. Nor did he take opium and consort with witches; he did not even take Harriet to a ball as the Waltz movement is supposed to imply. In short, the program was a successful promotional piece, for a public that was used to opera but not to dramatic music for orchestra alone in the manner of Beethoven. When the *Symphonie fantastique* was first performed, Beethoven had been dead only three years, and his characteristic works were still fought over as being "extreme" and often impossible to follow.

Now we are in a position to take up *Lélio*. The date of its presentation to the Paris crowd is two years after the *Fantastique*, six months after Berlioz's sojourn as prize-winner at the Academy in Rome. Those two years had been emotionally trying. Harriet Smithson had proved unattainable and Berlioz had fallen in love again, this time much less intellectually, with the beautiful young pianist Camille Moke. They were formally engaged just before he left for his three-year fellowship. He naturally hated such a long separation, and knowing how ambitious she was he must have feared the worst. His apprehensions were justified. He had one more year to stay abroad when, without notice to Berlioz, she married the prosperous piano manufacturer Pleyel. Berlioz gave up his last term of Roman residence and came back to re-establish himself in the public eye.

Unfortunately, his time in Italy had not been outwardly fruitful. He had composed some songs, he had revised his symphony with minute care, and he had tramped with his guitar over the campagna and the Abruzzi hills, playing dances and songs for the peasants he met and lived with. He had stored up impressions and musical ideas in abundance, as appeared later. But at the moment he had little to show for the time spent, unless one could count as accomplishments the firm friendships with Mendelssohn and Glinka.

All the same, to re-enter Paris as a laureate-composer yet empty-handed was an unthinkable paradox. It was to resolve this predicament that *Lélio* was put together. Berlioz had on hand a number of pieces of music which he knew to be first-rate and most of which had, strictly speaking, never been performed. Among these were the several examination papers he had written in his four attempts at the Rome Prize. He had heard them played only in a piano reduction (and unrehearsed) on the day the judges rendered their decision.

From these cantatas, set like passages of translation at sight and composed in isolation from all aids, Berlioz chose for *Lélio* what are now nos. 2 and 3 and its echo. He added two songs from his early student days (nos. 1 and 4) and concluded with the Fantasia on Shakespeare's *Tempest*, which had been played in 1830 to a handful of people at the Opera during an evening of torrential rain. How to make an "attraction" out of this material was the problem. It would be absurd to imagine that a mere announcement of these pieces—or of any other similar collection he might make—would bring out those blasé boulevardiers, ruthless self-seekers, and pitiless critics who make up the *Tout-Paris* of any period and whom Berlioz at twenty-nine knew like his own kith and kin.

Hence the recourse to a second quasi-libretto, energized by a link with the still-remembered self-dramatization of the *Symphonie fantastique* "program" and by the idea of using Shakespeare to carry the critical war of Romanticism into the enemy territory of conventional opinion. The result is a piece of rodomontade that once again drew the curious and the influential; passages of the spoken text were taken as references to living persons and loudly applauded: Berlioz had effected his return to Paris by means of his *Return to Life*. Incidentally, it should be remembered that the "monodrama" or "melologue" form was not uncommon. Beethoven had used it in *Egmont*, Weber and Méhul had contributed to the genre, and the notion of it had prompted Mozart to say: "I have always wished to write a drama of this kind." So Berlioz had precedents and was not a mad inventor of an unworkable form.

Today, the contrivance is felt to be artificial, and in *Lélio* the speaking part is much too long. The text has moments of terse effectiveness and humor in which we get a glimpse of Berlioz the virtuoso prose writer and critic; but many more moments are pure bombast in the vein of the stage plays of the time. Indeed, in 1832, the *Lélio* speaker was a leading actor named Bocage, who made the most of those moments, to the delight of listeners able to take it "straight," as we cannot. What must be said of this early nineteenth-century "happening" in two segments performed two years apart is that they enclose the only offerings of Berlioz music that found favor with the Parisians.

Nor should we laugh at them and at him too heartily. To this day, the "story" of the *Fantastique* exerts a fascination upon many who seem, in spite of great learning, unsure of their way through the music; and the verbal hodgepodge of *Lélio* exerts a kind of nagging appeal to conductors, actors, and audiences (witness today's revival), in spite of the quaint nonsense of a bygone age.

The wit and the nonsense do not make *Lélio* "one work," though even in this patch-quilt one sees Berlioz's sure hand both within the musical numbers and within the whole. His opening is a song with piano accompaniment, because the closing number uses the piano (in original fashion) as timbre and percussion. To balance the *Fantastique*, the "scenes" are also five in number, and to honor his idols Berlioz begins with Goethe and ends with Shakespeare. He deploys the sequence of key relationships agreeably, like the contrasts in mood and in the disposition of forces, and he works up a true climax in the vigorous fantasia, with its anticipation of Stravinsky and the *Sacre* in the Caliban and storm motifs. The ultimate sounding of the *idée fixe* from the earlier symphony is a trick to catch the groundlings and the only thing to say about it is that it worked.

But knowing Berlioz as we do now, through his music as well as through his critical and theoretical writings, we may be sure that only two things in *Lélio* really interested him: the music, first, and the spoken remarks about esthetics, second. For the rest, he had exhibited to the public, not himself, but the mask behind which he shielded his reserve and what the French call *pudeur*—the moral quality compounded of self-respect, considerateness, and modesty. Read the *Memoirs* to see how it is possible to show oneself truly without exhibitionism or unsolicited confession.

If it is thought that this reserve is belied by the master's evident striving to have his music played and to play it himself whenever possible, it must be remembered that composing—or better, sculpturing—in timbre as Berlioz did, he had to test his works by hearing, if he were to add to the expressive powers of his medium. All his scores were held back for repeated revision before he let them be published. Hearing meant confirming or modifying inspirations, and thus stimulating his peculiar genius, the genius that enabled him to organize large movements on the bases of tone-color and rhythmic patterns, in addition to melody and harmony. Listen to the first fruits of this innovative art in the music of *Lélio*.

1955/1979

16

Romeo and Juliet in Music

Besides the inspiration radiating from Shakespeare's play and the musical inspiration native to the composer, we owe the *Romeo and Juliet* Symphony to the inspired act of a third genius, Niccoló Paganini. It was in 1833, during one of the Paris visits of the great violin virtuoso, that he came to know Berlioz's music and commissioned from him a viola concerto—the later *Harold in Italy*. The publicity thus afforded was all to the good, but it was not enough to end the young composer's struggles. Four years later the battle was not yet won. The official *Requiem* had been a success but the opera *Benvenuto Cellini* had been killed by ill luck and intrigues. It was then that Paganini, coming forward at the close of a Berlioz concert, testified by a public demonstration of homage that here was a new master. This was astonishing enough but the the sequel was still more so: two days later Berlioz received from Paganini a note requesting him in flattering terms to accept a gift of 20,000 francs.

All kinds of devious motives have been ascribed to Paganini for this stroke of generosity, which was in fact the first fellowship in creative arts awarded in modern times. But the giver's own explanation is the best: "I saw a young man full of genius, whose strength and courage might have ultimately broken down under the strain . . . . I said to myself, 'It is my duty to help him.' When my claims to musical renown are reckoned up, it will not be the least that I was the first to recognize a genius and draw public attention to him."

Thanks to the violinist's other discovery, namely, that even a genius must eat, Berlioz was freed for half a year from the drudgery of journalism and the necessity of giving concerts. He knew at once what he wanted to compose and dedicate to his benefactor. Ten years before, at the height of the Romantic revolution in poetry, he and his friend Emile Deschamps had reveled in the then new-found works of Shakespeare. Deschamps' translation of *Romeo and Juliet* was passed from hand to hand in manuscript, and Berlioz came to know the play by heart. A little later, his stay in Italy as winner of the Rome Prize so kindled his musical interest in the same drama that he sketched a plan for the work. Thus its general form and character were fixed by the time he set about composing with a free mind in the spring of 1839.

The plan involved his friend Deschamps once more, for Berlioz had designed a choral symphony and needed verses for the vocal parts. He knew it was impossible to set Shakespeare word for word. Rather, the example of Beethoven's Ninth was before his eye, but he did not presume either to imitate or improve upon it. Berlioz's genius tended naturally to the dramatic, to sharp characterization, and his sense of form sought for a different kind of architectural balance from Beethoven's. Moreover, he wanted the human voice to play a role early in his work and to recur at intervals, instead of bursting forth only at the climax; he wanted to diversify its uses—now a single voice, now a few, now many; and lastly, he wanted to follow Shakespeare in the only way appropriate to a musician, that of dramatizing discontinuous scenes—enough scenes to recall the progress of the tragedy and no more. In short, the dramatic symphony was to be neither an opera nor an instrumental paraphrase in four conventional movements (though we still find in it an allegro, an adagio, a scherzo and a finale). It was to be *sui generis*, a new form. Seen in historical perspective, Berlioz's form looks like the thing musicians have always striven for, whether it is Handel crossing oratorio and opera, or Stravinsky designing *Oedipus* and *Persephone*.

There is perhaps no obligation to like what composers show a fancy for doing, but the fact that many have felt the attraction of a free and dramatic vocal-instrumental form at least shows the unimportance of one facile objection to *Romeo and Juliet*—that we never know whether it is a solo, a chorus, or an instrumental movement that we are to hear next. Dramatic music is not like railroading, in which it is essential to know at any moment what is going on in the next section. And of course the listener with a memory can, by hearing the work a second time, steel himself against the shock of surprise, turning it into the pleasurable shock of recognition.

The Symphony is in four parts, the first and last of which are subdivided into four distinct movements. It is these opening and concluding portions of the work which, requiring voices as they do, are not familiar to the concert-going public.[1] Yet they are essential to a true appreciation of the well-known sequence of Romeo's reverie, the Love scene, and the Queen Mab Scherzo, for the themes of these orchestral sections are announced and articulated in the Prologue. And what is equally important, the passionate drama culminating in the Love scene can hardly satisfy us if it turns short and ends in the ensuing Scherzo. In the plan of the work as the whole, the Mab music is in fact an interlude, a breathing space afforded us between the episode of love and the contemplation of death to follow.

Berlioz declared in his memoirs that his musical drama resembled the Shakespearean tragedy very little. This statement no one will care to dispute, for it is at once accurate and modest. But one ought to add that the two creations correspond in genre and in spirit, despite all obvious differences.

1. This essay was first published in 1953. (Ed.)

True, Berlioz uses the so-called "Garrick ending," which prevailed in his day and according to which the lovers witness each other's death in the burial vault. Again, Berlioz directed his librettist to enlarge the close of the drama into an expression of mass emotion: two peoples rather than two chieftains are reconciled over the gaping tomb. All this is in the interests of music, which is not content to end on a brisk handshake; the finale of a choral symphony must have the impact of the universal—as in Beethoven.

For the same musical reason, Berlioz seizes on the fact of Juliet's feigned death to fashion a sublime funeral march in fugal style, instrumental in the first half, vocal in the second. Similarly, Mercutio's abundant poetic fancies justify the fairy music of the Scherzo. In short, at every point the composer exploits the occasions that can be *sung*, whether by instruments or by the human voice, at the same time as he wishes to create in the listener a succession of moods that will parallel the action of the well-known love story. Finally, to warrant the term symphonic, the character of the music must be elevated and its coherence manifest.

Toward coherence, Shakespeare's prologue furnished a hint which Berlioz turned to account by inventing a device often followed since—e.g. in Wagner's *Ring*—the device of stating compactly and in the desired context the themes that will be developed later. Closely studied, Berlioz's Prologue will show with what minute care he anticipated all the significant turns of his musico-dramatic plot. To give but one instance, the last lines of the Prologue, which come so naturally out of what precedes, are sung to a fragment of the Funeral March. For a like reason, the "strife" theme of the orchestral Introduction is heard again when in the Finale, Montagues and Capulets foregather and reject Friar Laurence's peacemaking.

But Berlioz's art is never a "system" and we are not bound to memorize tags in notes or words. The unity of the plan will establish itself with familiar knowledge of its parts. The kinship will then appear between relevant moments of the Scherzo and the Scherzetto; between the Ball music and the simple yet hauntingly nostalgic chorus of young Capulets scattering homewards in the darkness; between the close of the Death scene and the music of at least three earlier movements. It can be said without fear of contradiction—indeed it has been said by no less a musician than Saint-Saëns—that the *Romeo and Juliet* Symphony is a tour de force of formal organization and inner consistency. For my part, it is the only large work of Berlioz's that I consider flawless—that is, the only work which makes me feel—self-centered customer as I am—that I want nothing different, nothing removed, nothing shorter, longer, or in another place. One can perhaps attribute to Berlioz's half year of freedom this organic beauty, this perfect health in all the members. Berlioz had enjoyed himself and spared no pains: the pianist Moscheles, who visited Berlioz and saw the score shortly after its completion, remarked on the probable din of the Ball scene but conceded that the manuscript was "exquisitely penned."

Dedicated to Paganini, the work was put into rehearsal as soon as it was finished and it was produced at the Paris Conservatoire on November 24, 1839. Berlioz conducted and the audience (which included the twenty-six-year-old Richard Wagner) was extraordinarily responsive, considering the novelty of the music and the form. As usual, Berlioz listened to his own work with a critical ear and was dissatisfied with certain parts, which he promptly altered. Significantly, he saw the error of having followed Shakespeare too slavishly in using a second prologue halfway through. It upset the balance of voice and orchestra which, as we have it now, is so delicately poised: we never quite forget that human beings are near, no matter how deep our enchantment in the feelings that lie too deep for words and speak to us in purer tones. Of these instrumental scenes of melancholy, love, and death, Berlioz was later to write:

"If in the famous balcony scene and in the funeral vault the dialogue between the lovers, Juliet's asides, and the passionate pleading of Romeo are not sung; if, in a word, the duets are entrusted to the orchestra, the reasons are several and easily grasped. The first—and this would suffice by itself—is that the work is not an opera but a symphony. Secondly, duets of this character have been composed for voices a thousand times before and by the greatest masters. It was therefore the part of prudence, as well as a challenge, to atempt a new mode of expression. Lastly, since the very sublimity of the love story made it a perilous task for the composer to depict it, he chose to give his imagination a wider latitude than the positive meaning of words would have allowed; he resorted instead to the instrumental idiom, a richer, more varied, less fixed language, which by reason of its very indefiniteness, is incomparably more powerful for the present purpose."

This statement makes it clear that Berlioz did not for a moment suppose his symphony to be a piece of story-telling. Those who have heard in the Love scene Juliet's Nurse knocking on the door must take the responsibility, no less than the credit, for such an interpretation. They will get no backing from Berlioz nor from his knowledgeable listeners. Yet a doubt may remain about one of the fourteen scenes, that of the lovers' death in the vault of the Capulets. So good a judge as Felix Weingartner, writing half a century ago, deemed this section the only piece of program music Berlioz ever wrote. And the reason for this judgment was that while listening to the music he, Weingartner, could virtually see the tragic sequence of events.

One may wonder whether today the famous conductor would advance the same objection. It is in fact the objection advanced long before against the dramatic symphony as such, namely, that it is neither drama nor symphony because drama requires visible action and distinct persons, and symphonies must suggest nothing outside themselves. In this view opera is justified because it combines sound and signs in exact parallelism. But nowadays, thanks in part to the enormous extension of the audience for discs, and in part to our educated musical responses, opera itself is becoming a species of dramatic symphony. Millions of listeners are familiar with *Orphée* or *Otello*, who never saw these works staged. More and more concert groups are giving operas without trappings—and Berlioz's conception of drama-in-the-music is thereby vindicated.

It is relevant to Weingartner's comment on the Tomb scene that our getting used to opera from discs has not meant learning to visualize the invisible, but just the reverse: listeners have got over any inclination to form mental images, or to ask for visual aids when truly dramatic music speaks to them directly about what is involved in the given situation. In other words, in opera itself music has never really referred to what occurred on the stage; it has referred to the same hidden reality which words and actions point to—like music—that is, to the *meaning*.

In the present symphony, the Tomb scene does not differ from the rest. Nowhere is there anything to see. How indeed form any image whatsoever of the sublime Invocation with its gripping sonorities—the song of horns, bassoons, and English horn rising out of the somber rhythm of the deep but muted strings? And in the agitation and silences that follow, why not simply recognize the distortion of the love themes? In life and death and in this symphony, Romeo and Juliet are the exact opposite of good boys and girls: they should be heard and not seen.

Perhaps in the Finale the hardened operagoer will not be able to keep from imagining the skirmish between the clans and fixing with the mind's eye the figure of the Friar who gradually compels a reconciliation. This is drama in the simplest sense, intentionally so. But one should be thankful that it is conveyed in the broad strokes of a musical imagination, rather than with the standardized gestures and rocking-horse tactics of an opera troupe. Nothing should mar the intensity of the feeling, which is here of a different order from that generated by the Love scenes, though no less elevated in its kind, since the relative crudeness of a popular emotion (as compared with individual passion) is made up for by its sweeping, flood-like quality. And in this Finale, moreover, we ascend from the musical expression of a popular assembly to its transformation into a hymn of brotherly love. The words do not matter; Deschamps' verses are for the most part inept—this being one clear sign that the work does not resemble Shakespeare—and Berlioz had to repeat a few dull lines when he decided to discard the excess that his librettist had thrust on him. Yet the musical pulse does not falter, and the end is as strong as the beginning.

Starting from Shakespeare and Beethoven to shape his own creation, Berlioz trod his undeviating path with a clear consciousness of his innovation. In the words of Bernard van Dieren, he "sucked all the hidden music" in *Romeo and Juliet* and "revealed it in a musical structure." As for the progeny of that new form, the Dramatic Symphony, it has been numerous and variegated, occupying the attention of composers and listeners almost from the day when Paganini's largesse was repaid by the first audition of (as Berlioz put it) *"his* score."

1953/1962

Culture and History

17

Romanticism: Definition of an Age

Romanticism is a part of the great revolution which drew the intellect of Europe from a monarchical into a popular state, from the court and the fashionable capitals into the open country and the five continents, from the expectation and desire of fixity into the desire and expectation of change.

No such enlargement of mental and physical horizons had been felt since the previous romantic era, that of the expansion of Europe in the sixteenth century. Both were ages of exuberance and exploration, and both yielded comparable fruits: men of "universal" scope, and works of art whose conception likens them to complete worlds. Nineteenth century romanticism would accept nothing less than the universe as a naked fact because it witnessed—or foresaw—the wreck of a society. At the same time, romanticism faced the cultural task of primitive men without the relaxed responsibilities of primitives. Romanticism had to reabsorb the realities which the preceding two centuries had quite literally put out of court—wild nature, passion, superstition, myth, history, and "foreign parts." It was consequently not "exoticism" but discovery when Chateaubriand or Byron sought out the Near East or the Far West, when De Quincey or Nerval explored the world of dreams, when Delacroix or Scott depicted the Middle Ages, when Rousseau or Wordsworth looked within themselves for sentiments hitherto concealed, when Pushkin and Balzac imported the commonplace and the extraordinary into fiction: romanticism was a comprehensive realism.

There is no doubt that romanticism accepted an enormous challenge and made an enormous claim. But to begin with, it inherited an enormous fortune, which had been accumulating since the fall of Rome. The Middle Ages, the Renaissance, and the Enlightenment were an open treasure house; when the twenty-five years of revolution had cleared the ground for a new start, the romantics could build like first settlers who had not only brought with them perfected tools but who could also boast of abundant technical talent. In sheer amount of intellectual gifts, few epochs can match that which stretches from the birth of Goethe in 1749 to the death of Berlioz one hundred and twenty years later. This span embraces, but does not coincide with, the period usually identified with pictorial romanticism, the manifestations of which are rooted in tendencies appearing much earlier. Within this span lie the birth years of eminent men still living,[1] thus making the romantic era the parent century of our own times. This is the major difficulty in seeing it steadily and whole. We have grown up within our father's house and our striving for independence makes us abhor the language spoken there. Until recently our best critics used every means to dissociate us from romanticism. It is they who have kept repeating that by the mid-nineteenth century the movement had failed and that all the monuments of romanticist art are "flawed masterpieces." The flattering inference is that after 1850 a new cultural start was made, from whose finer strain we are sprung.

Correctly interpreted, this double protection against the original romanticism might be acceptable, but it is not likely that the anti-romanticists would accept the necessary clauses of interpretation. Romanticism "failed" because, like all movements, it was the work of men. Cultural history is a succession of failures in which are embedded great achieve-

1. This essay was first published in 1949 in *The Magazine of Art*. Hence the emphasis on the graphic arts. (Ed.)

ments or, alternatively, it is a succession of achievements which end in failure. The work of an age is like a glacier, which strews the ground with debris, but also marks its passage with great terminal moraines. Greece, Rome, the Middle Ages, the Renaissance, the Reformation, the Enlightenment—all failed to usher in the millennium or to exhaust the possibilities of the human spirit. Death, fatigue, accidents of all sorts put an end to whatever is "working" or has worked. Berlioz's vision of music festivals commensurate with the needs of a great modern nation failed because the elements he sought in the social order were mutually antagonistic, and no doubt also because he had not at his command the political power of a Louis XIV or Napoleon—who in their spheres also failed.

Hence those works of Berlioz which were conceived for the nation's use lack the adventitious yet necessary merit of having been assimilated by his living compatriots. This is also true of innumerable other works sprung from kindred conceptions in the other arts, for example, the panels in high relief that François Rude designed for the Arc de Triomphe, of which only the *Call to Arms* was commissioned and executed. Does this mean that the great sketches of the romantic cultural edifice are on that account worthless? They are accurately termed "flawed masterpieces," for no human work is flawless, and sketches are all we have of any period. In time our love and desire fill them in, which creates the pleasing illusion of perfection in the distance: the Mozart symphony seems lucid and perfect because it no longer strives to speak, as it once did, of a life at hand, and so no longer provokes outraged comparisons. Habit, moreover, has given us an indulgent taste for the style's characteristic weakness or the form's inevitable padding. But to good contemporary judges, the work seems rough and full of flaws. Horace may tell us that sometimes Homer nods, but we palliate the dullness with jargon or sentimental attitudes entirely of our own making. It is proper that we should do so, but it follows that what we rightly value and call perfect is enjoyed at the cost of a wise and magnanimous overlooking of flaws. After a time —as Shakespeare's reputation proves—this becomes automatic and unconscious. The pressure of a relentless modernism which keeps offending us helps to develop this receptivity for the work of thirty or fifty or seventy years ago, all *its* modernism spent.

Even after making allowance for a changing perspective, there remains to be made the broad distinction between what may be called gothic and classic principles of art. Romanticism is "gothic"; its aim is to bring into a tense equilibrium many radical diversities, and it consequently produces work that shows rough texture, discontinuities, distortions—antitheses in structure as well as in meaning. From the classical point of view these are flaws; but they are consented to by the romanticist—indeed sought after—for the sake of drama. They are not oversights on the artist's part, but planned concessions to the medium and the aim it subserves, as in engineering one finds gaps, vents, or holes to balance the effects of expansion by heat or stress. Far from lacking a sense of form or neglecting its claims, the romanticist abandons the ready-made formula because its excessive generality affords too loose a fit. He constantly alters or invents formal devices in order that the work of art may satisfy the several requirements of subject, substance, and meaning, rather than simply fulfil a routine expectation. Delacroix in his *Journal* admonishes himself: "Do not run after a vain perfection. There are certain faults—or deemed such by the vulgar— which often are what gives life." And again, "To make a wholly new kind of painting . . . by the extreme variety in the foreshortened parts." The result is a characteristic distortion or asymmetry, which may be observed equally in gothic and romantic work, in Shakespeare, Goethe, Berlioz, Hugo, Delacroix or Stendhal. Hence the folly of applying a classic or symmetrical "stencil" over a romanticist conception: the parts that come through to the observer are bound to seem incoherent and to violate "the" form. A comparison of such mistaken attempts in several arts yields another historical proof of unity in romantic principles and serves to exonerate any great artist taken singly. Here is Delacroix being taken to task by a critic of our own day: "By the aid of brilliant color he partly conceals his uncertain draughtsmanship; but the drawing is ragged, and the segments composing his picture are broken by gaps and fissures. He obtains vividness by his sketchy technique, but the agonized faces, the swirling naked bodies, the faked ramping chargers, the theatrical Medea . . . are too unsubstantial, too obviously put together by dextrous invention to convey the dramatic truth which Delacroix imagined he brushed into them" (Thomas Craven, *Men of Art*).

This might be called the standard accusation, in general and in detail. Change only the technical terms and titles of subjects and you have the usual denunciation of Berlioz, the colorist who lacked draftsmanship; of Balzac, the melodramatic contriver of empty effects; of Stendhal, the injudicious artist who was led astray by love of the picturesque and who neglected motive to the detriment of clear design. But the constructive power of the great romanticists cannot be measured by casual or hostile inspection. Study is needed in order to find the deep premeditation of structure within a work which at first seems all improvisation and surface effects. Thus did Van Gogh and Emile Bernard study Delacroix, of whom the latter says, "No one more than Delacroix took greater care to establish his shadows with earths, ochres and blacks in order to weld together all the parts of his compositions." Van Gogh, more interested in color, finds that Delacroix's composition also owes something to that supposedly adventitious element: "he proceeds by color as Rembrandt by values, but one is as good as the other." Berlioz too, whose form can be vindicated on traditional grounds, similarly made tone-color an element of structure, and in a like manner he too incurred the charge of using it as a cloak.

Beyond technique and the justification of technique is the provocative question of subject matter. Although critics often pretend to disregard the subject of a work of art, they respond to it and, if repelled, attempt to rationalize their impression by impugning the form. It was very justly said by Paul Bourget, one of Stendhal's first admirers in the 1880s, that recognition had been denied the novelist because "he had taken the dangerous privilege of inventing for himself unique feelings and writing of them in an unexampled style." The objections to Berlioz's subjects are familiar: violent, fantastic, extravagantly emotional. Craven, the impugner of Delacroix already cited, speaks of the painter's state of mind as "Byronism," which is "an extinct malady" and takes it for granted that because "Greece is of less significance than Persian oil fields," the *Massacre at Scio* depicts unreal "hollow forms." (Yet three pages farther on he adds, "I have no fault to find with his subject matter.") This was written before the last World War, during which it was curious to observe the quick resurrection of these various "Byronic" and "romantic" subjects under the stern teaching of European events.

The lesson of course is not merely that we must refrain from asking romanticist work to show a classical surface; it is also that we cannot appreciate the art of any age without first acquiring an equivalent of the experience it depicts. Since we cannot return to the past in person, we must immerse ourselves in the literature, the history, and the speech of the period and observe its recurrent features, as we might try to decode a cipher without a key: the longer the text in the unknown tongue, the sooner we unriddle it. But just as in ciphers or in cognate languages resemblances may lead to serious misconceptions, so between the speech of romanticism and ours some confusions are bound to occur, unless this overlapping is recognized and the separate meanings finely distinguished. Being born at a given time and with a given temperament defines the idiom of any creator, and conversely that idiom lives only in the works by which we still judge the time. To recapture the exact meaning of the romanticist revolution and thus come to enjoy its products independently of the associations of subsequent art forms, it is obviously necessary to understand the precise relation of earlier to later, of romanticism to its sequels.

The clue here proposed is that the initial Romanticism or first phase—from 1790 to 1850—put forth all the themes and ideas used in Western culture until our own times. Romanticism was encyclopedic. The next three phases, commonly called Realism, Impressionism (or Symbolism) and Naturalism worked separate veins of the original deposit; they were periods of specialization. None of these four phases stops neatly in order to let the next begin. They orchestrate their tendencies as best they may and project themselves into the present age—hence the problem of sorting out. After 1840, moreover, one discerns a steady resistance to both Romanticism and its various offshoots; this dissent once again calls itself Classicism. The neoclassic impulse is the same whether it moves Puvis de Chavannes, Brahms in mid-career, or Stravinsky in his postwar restlessness seeking "authority, order and discipline." The crisscrossing of styles, movements, and opinions becomes wonderfully complicated but not beyond profitable analysis.

The first transformation is that of the inclusive realism (with a small *r*) of the romantics into the specialized restricted, and embittered realism of the Realists with a capital *R*. The change came from a desire to simplify in order to grasp the real more surely and closely. The Realists carved themselves a path down the center of experience, taking as real what mankind shares in common, what is ordinary, tangible, recurrent—Courbet's workaday subjects and "photographic" technique. Realism corresponded to the materialistic science of the fifties,which displaced romantic vitalism. Soon realism came to mean not simply the common but the sordid; it began not alone to "correct" romanticism by reduction but to reproach it for failing to make its extraordinary visions an everyday occurrence.

In the eighties a new generation of artists, after seeking the real but dissatisfied with a limited definition of it, discovered that the true haunts of the real were no longer in the factual and the commonplace but in the subjective and the mysterious, in "impressions" and "symbols." This was phase three, clearly related to romanticism and sometimes called "neoromanticism." Artists seeking new symbols to convey fresh impressions frequently adopt names and slogans suggesting that the work of their predecessors was totally lacking in symbols and impressions; thus the first romanticists, whose clamor about "truth" and "drama" meant *new* truth and *more vivid* drama, were oddly enough called naturalistic and symbolic, as well as being accused of cultivating art for art's sake.

In the later decades (eighties and nineties) still other men dealt with the decay of realism by reacting against the reaction; they strengthened the dose of concreteness in their art by borrowings from science and sociology which they called naturalism. That symbolism and naturalism can coexist in one man or one work is evidenced by Huysmans, the Goncourt brothers, George Moore, and several impressionist painters.

The schema given is necessarily abstract, but what it states as a generality is what everyone admits in detail. Studying Balzac, the "impressionist" Henry James says, "all roads lead back to him." Delacroix, says the historian, is the fountainhead of modern painting. Courbet, Signac, Van Gogh, Odilon Redon, and Renoir looked back to him and in one way or another proceed from him. Yet not everyone whose eye can spot an impressionist canvas would see its "descent with modification" from any given Delacroix. The reasons for this are two: according to our schema, there is bound to be *more* impressionism in an impressionist than in a Delacroix, for the impressionist element is but one of Delacroix's many perceptions, whereas it is the whole stock in trade of the impressionist. The romanticist is inclusive, his descendants exclusive. It cannot be too often repeated: technically and philosophically, the romantic is an encyclopedist while his successors are by contrast specialists. In art, as in science, historiography, philosophy, and economics, they refine, extend, and multiply what the romantic has found and made. The second reason is corollary to the first: you must know where to go in Delacroix to find the clearest foreshadowing of later methods. You must, for example, turn to his canvas *Christ on Lake Genesareth* and find in it what Signac and Van Gogh found. If you seek instead Delacroix's meaning for the realists, study the *Algerian Women*; for his naturalism, the *Jewish Wedding* or the *Massacre at Scio*. His romanticism is the sum total of these styles, made into *his* style by fusion with the less definable elements of an individual sensibility.

This hypothesis may easily be tested upon Berlioz, and even by using evidence from an opponent: "There is not one Berlioz," says the English critic Elliot, "there are half a dozen; and they are as different from one another as they are different from all other composers. The Berlioz of the *Requiem* and the *Te Deum* is poles apart from the Berlioz of *Benvenuto Cellini*. What have either of these in common . . . with the composer of *Romeo et Juliette* . . .? What of him who penned *Les Troyens*—or that unique middle section of *L'Enfance du Christ?*" Berlioz answered this ahead of time: "A change of subject requires a change of style," and this explanation is endorsed by those who have made it their business to trace the development of nineteeth-century music and who find in

Berlioz the germs of musical realism, impressionism, and naturalism down to Strauss and Stravinsky. The connection, it goes without saying, leaves the respective merits and originality of the several artists absolutely intact.

The only reason, apart from its interest, for investigating this general kinship of periods and styles is that it spells Open Sesame to dozens of historical riddles, while preventing the confusion of individual sensibility with *Zeitgeist*. Sensibility is the artist's personal touch—the tone or temper which no one is bound to like. *Zeitgeist* is the predominant temper, the tone of time. An epoch obviously selects or brings out those who can do its proper work. Romanticism faced the work of reconstruction and rehabilitation of total experience after desiccation and decay. It follows that romantic accomplishment appears more incomplete, less equipoised than work done in the spirit of exclusion, of elimination of opposites, of unwillingness to take risks, of refusal to acknowledge the second horn of each dilemma. Romantic work is the work of self-reliance, tension, and perpetual innovation. It leads to the creation of the unique form for each conception and thus to the regard for individual tone, nuance, local color, and what modernism calls "experiment." Hence in romanticism one finds the constituent parts of numerous styles down to the present, and in these styles a ballasting of original romanticism. Only its amount seems minimal, because of the later-comers' historic necessity to do something other and neater than their great and "gothic" predecessors.

1949

18

Liberalism and the Religion of Art

*The spirit of poetry is in itself favorable to humanity and
liberty; but, we suspect, not in times like these . . . . The spirit
of poetry is not the spirit of mortification or of martyrdom.
Poetry dwells in a perpetual Utopia of its own, and is, for that
reason, very ill calculated to make a paradise upon earth, by
encountering the shocks and disappointments of the world.*

Hazlitt (1816)

No matter how elaborate and interesting the play, the actors
have to be got off the stage somehow. We may regret their
demise, because we have learned to like or to tolerate them
through a long evening, but the forces of removal claim our
allegiance too, and they are, in the current cant of social
discussion, healthy. That is why, when we speak of the traditions underlying modern culture—culture in the old sense of
high art and letters—and again when we speak of Liberalism
as a movement of ideas and a form of behavior, we should not
repine at the evidences that both are beginning to share a
common oblivion. The consciousness of these two endings
occurring together is of course painful. It is largely the cause
of our vagrant disquiet, our anxiety, self-reproach, and
scapegoat-hunting, to which we give such emphatic and ob-
sessive utterance, as if they were permanent necessities. But
why such torments at the passing of Liberalism and the
post-Renaissance ideals of art?

By "Liberalism" I do not of course mean Liberal politics
merely, but the great design of emancipation that burst forth

in the eighteenth century, after many obscure beginnings stretching back as far as the Protestant Reformation. Liberalism in this sense is an assertion of the primacy of Man: Man must be free to fashion his life and his institutions in the light of his ever-expanding intellect. Hence all the old repressive arrangements must be destroyed—kings and priests, inherited traditions and unexamined creeds. Custom law must be recast by reason into a code, parliaments must be set up as the arena of free discussion; in theory, nothing is sacred, nothing beyond the reach of questioning and remaking. Liberalism makes Man his own master. It soon finds out, at the hands of the Romantic psychologists and poets, that Man is an abstraction; there are only men. So it follows that individual men in their multitude must be freed. Equal in status, they must be given the opportunity to develop, to strive, to make prevail their particular truths. The right to speak, to print, to assemble, to vote, to criticize, to appeal against authority, to organize for every conceivable good cause—all derive from the original dream of liberty.

In this conception, economic liberalism is a by-product, not a main object. Free trade is but one part of the general hope of being without chains. It is by their own cumbrousness and dwindling practicality that the old mercantile restrictions became the natural targets of those who planned to make all things new. Similarly, liberal parties and liberal politics were the result and not the source of Liberalism. Finally, the link between Liberalism and the bourgeoisie is historical, not imperative. There were bourgeois for centuries before Liberalism was thought of, and if one traces with care the progress of Liberalism during the last 150 years, one finds that its practical advances by propaganda and gunfire were in each generation the work of *some* bourgeois, mostly young, rather than the bourgeoisie as a whole and as such.

I speak of gunfire, but in essence Liberalism is a conception that relies on the spoken and written word, rather than the sword. Liberalism is argumentative and self-conscious, not dictatorial and awe-inspiring; it is a thing of written constitutions, lawbooks, and journalism, rather than fiats and symbolic appeals. The editorial, the placard, and the elementary school have been its instruments, instead of the scepter, the cross, the pilgrimage, the pageant, and the churchhouse. In a word, Liberalism is secular and simple— one man, one vote, and the voice of the people is the voice of God. Accordingly, when Liberalism had reached its farthest goal, at some point after World War I, its stamp on civilization was that of agnosticism and democracy.

What had happened, meanwhile, to the religious impulses of mankind—to the love of mystery and the capacity for superstition? When life has been stripped and sanitized by reason—or at least by discourse that sounds like reason—the unsatisfied desires that are left over must find some outlet. The tenets of the few rearguard reactionaries are by definition not acceptable to the majority. What happened was that the thoughtful, the cultivated, the restless and disaffected made a religion of art. As early as the beginning of the nineteenth century, the combined effect of the French Revolution and of the repression that followed was to thrust upon art the duty of affording salvation. The artist, renamed genius, became a hero; and for all those who could not recapture their lost faith in the ecclesiastical revivals of the period, the devotion to art became a passion.

Now, as soon as art assumes the role of redeeming life, it must take on the task of criticizing it. Like the church, it must moralize mankind, denounce sin, and threaten the City of Man with destruction. Throughout the nineteenth century that is what poets and novelists and painters and musicians are busy doing. When their subject or technique does not permit the lesson to shine forth, their essays and polemics come to the rescue. Wordsworth and Hugo, Baudelaire and

Dostoevsky are poets *and* prophets. Theirs is a perpetual
sursum corda. By the nineties, the enlightened part of Europe
is convinced that virtue has fled from common existence and
common men and resides in art and artists alone. Artists and
their followers are by then dedicated to the cult of contempt
for whatever is not art. Society, government, business, the
professions, common tastes and manners, ambition, faith,
morals, and indeed anything savoring of the norm are con-
demned with as fierce animus as ever moved nihilists to
throw bombs at emperors and kings. All this, art was able to
do in the free air of Liberalism. Only, by a fine but necessary
irony, it was not the world of ancient privilege that Western
art was denouncing, it was the new world of Liberalism, the
world of freedom, practical reason, and common sense, of
industrial production and all-exploring science, the world
that artists came to call bourgeois, like the Marxists, the
world pictured in the daily paper.

If this is roughly the story of Liberalism and Culture, then it
becomes a puzzle for us in 1967 to explain our present predicament: why should the dying throes of Liberalism depress
us equally with the tent-sulking of our culture-makers? One
would naturally suppose that the public worship of the arts, a
victory so obvious and so unexpected, would fill everybody,
including the artists, with joy. Yet it is precisely joy that is
lacking. Certainly the most heeded artists are the most joy-
less beings alive. They could all adopt as a motto Samuel
Beckett's theme of a bloody today following a bloody yesterday, with no expectation but another bloody today when
tomorrow comes. And the development of that theme is
short and unvaried: society is no good; people are no good;
the conditions of life are no good. Only innocence—that is,
childhood or the primitive—escapes total rejection and
thereby becomes the measure of all things. Baudelaire had
told us long ago that genius was the recapture of childhood,

but by now genius is no good; to play the genius now is nothing but a bourgeois affectation; it too is institutionalized and has no further point to make. The point has been made, over and over, by Flaubert and Melville and Yeats and Joyce and the rest. The bourgeois themselves feel and acknowledge that they are no good. They go and applaud the repetitious onslaughts on their lives and ways like the nobles before the French Revolution. The upshot is that there is no enemy left, hence there is no reason for the artist's cursing and prophesying.

Perhaps we find here a clue to the now-standardized virulence of the artistic temper, the desperate violence of expression resorted to as a matter of course: it has become virtually impossible to stir up the animals in the pit, because most of them have already been knocked senseless. What is left for a bourgeois audience to feel when it is shown on the stage, in a play called *Saved*, some young louts torturing a baby in a perambulator, rolling it in its own excrement, then killing it with stones? The producer has boasted of the "triumph" of having got such a scene staged, but it is an empty triumph, one of a series, latterly mass-produced. For the spectator, clearly, there is nothing more to do but to re-enact the scene in real life. We let the young do it for us, as gratuitous acts, for kicks, and we are then forced to "understand" and condone the results of this train of images and deeds, in which individual responsibility is lost.

For our purely reflective moods, we are offered fiction which either makes a feature of sadistic fantasy or which implies the proposition that madness is the central truth of our being. Man is alone and apart, says the French writer Le Clézio. "Yet at moments of curious concentration—madness—he can merge with his world." And Sartre praises him for a story about a toothache, in which, according to the philosopher, "there is more than a man's rejection of pain as unacceptable." There is "a kind of basic questioning of

Christian acceptance." To have discovered the unaccept-
ability of pain is a feat of the artistic imagination evidently
reserved for our century.

But we are entitled to ask, What about the Liberal dogma
of the dignity of man and the sacredness of the individual?
How are we saved by seeing a baby stoned to death or,
glorifying man's madness? Where is justice now, and what
significance can we attach to justice when anyone has the
right to operate on his neighbor's sensibility or living body in
the name of art and desirable madness?

To answer this indecent question is to say what happened
when Liberalism no longer found barriers to break down and
prisoners to liberate. That situation, which is ours, may seem
a paradox when we think of the ignorance, bigotry, and pov-
erty that remain. But we should remember that in history a
cause has life and unifying effect only so long as it is on the
rise, fighting and moving from goal to goal—the franchise for
men, rights for women, prison reform, an end to all the
slaveries, black and white, human and animal. With the
triumph of progressive education for children, a relaxed sexual code, and the abolition of capital punishment, there
were—there are—no more theoretical bounds to freedom.
Permissiveness, as we call it in society, flexibility as it is
known in the schools, is everywhere the dominant tendency.
Indeed, it is fast becoming a new commandment: "Thou shalt
not prefer one thing to another." No wonder the last ounce
of energy in emancipation has gone. Speaking of her early
maturity, Simone de Beauvoir reports the resulting sensation
very accurately: "We had no external limitations, no over-
riding authority, no imposed pattern of existence. We
created our own links with the world, and freedom was the
very essence of our existence." When this can be said, it is
clear that there is nothing to push against but the empty air, a
feeling which is at first agreeable, then is disconcerting, and

ends by causing the anguish of pointlessness—the horror of the absurd.

Of course, there remained as an arena for the fast-deflating spirit of liberty the contradictory society created by Liberalism in its closing phase; I mean the industrial urban system, which begins to take shape in the 1870s and which in a hundred years has become the welfare state. It is a contradictory system because it is once again a network of rules and constraints risen from liberal desires and coexisting with the loosest liberal attitudes. For the liberty of the worker there are unions, for the democratizing of health and prosperity there are prohibitions and taxes. Each new philanthropic purpose is carried out at the cost of preventing, directing, interfering with some impulse that might be harmful. Western civilization is now more tightly feudal and mercantilist than it has ever been, and every liberal mind can see the rightness of the reasoning that has redefined liberty into a jungle of laws and hindrances.

It is suggestive that the growth of regulation started in the Germany of Bismarck as the concomitant of a superior industrial plant. For the generalized use of machines which we miscall "technology" brought an abundance that had to be consumed, and industrial life required something that would compensate the toilers for their loss of individuality, of self-will and self-regard, of free movement and dramatic effort. Something, I say, had to be done to palliate their nervous fatigue, their self-contempt, and their boredom, which is only vital energy unused. The tedium (if I may further improve a phrase) is the massage. And the compensation is the culture of cities, rooted in the newspaper and rising by degrees to spectator sports, organized betting, and panoptical sexuality. At the same time, through paid vacations and unemployment insurance ad lib, foreign travel and the fringes of artistic enjoyment are coming within the reach of the masses who, by the force of their numbers, are establishing the standards of the whole society.

This society, the institutions that serve it, and the state that regiments the mass, are easy targets for the hostility of the liberal and the artistic spirits conjoined. Near the beginning of the American republic, John Adams, bred in the eighteenth-century culture, could say in his diary that he and his sons must abstain from the cultivation of the fine arts and fight for liberty instead, so that his grandchildren could enjoy the arts in peace. But now it is the very institutions of a sophisticated liberty that everybody wants to fight for being stupid, hostile, and absurd. The attack comes from the revolted artist, and he speaks for every conscious individual.

That individual has indeed been moralized by the Liberal dogma and estheticized by the artistic dogma until every occurrence of life reduces him to frustration and despair. So, like the avant-garde playwright, he resorts to one or another form of violence as the common medium of expression. For example, a critic who theorizes best about the black and blue arts of the day relieves political feelings by informing the world that "America was founded on a genocide" and that "the white race is the cancer of human history," even though the "desperateness of things is obscured by the comforts and liberties that America does offer."

The position is indeed desperate, for it is that of the moral person, obliged to right every wrong and yet paralyzed by the magnitude of evil itself. It is this predicament that makes our American undergraduates so wretched. In their confidences to teachers, much more than in their public protests, they show their sense of sin and of helplessness. They are sure that they have a duty to depose the President, stop the war in Vietnam, and make Negroes immediately happy and powerful. In order to take these few imperative measures, society must be destroyed—or at least its most hateful institutions, such as the CIA, the stock exchange, and the university.

Then the good—who are the young—can make a fresh start with clean hands. But they find that they are not strong enough. There are too many people about, too much native corruption. All the rebels can do is obstruct what is going on and demand "participation" in the name of "the democratic process" and unspecified "rights."

The heartbreak and sympathy one may feel at this sight does not change the fact that here is the deliquescence of the liberal and artistic ideals. For in these manifestations of unrest only fantasy is at work. Just as the short-story writer finds pain unacceptable and rejects it, so the young social rebel finds mankind unacceptable and wants it whisked away. The acceptance of a rule to mitigate inevitable conflicts seems to him a betrayal of virtue, and when the institution he deems evil does not yield to his protest, he stages a social tantrum. Permissiveness in turn accepts what should be still less acceptable than pain—the dissolution of society.

It is no doubt the religion of art, the strength and perfection of art, that have taught modern men to expect a unity and coherence which life does not show. And the desire for reproducing that same order and beauty in the world, without rule, yet amid endless rules, is driving more and more people mad. The contempt for politics, the hatred of the state, the self-righteousness not only of students but also of adult intellectuals are by-products of anger at the fact that Idea and Will outrun execution and hope. The greatness of Liberalism was its determination to harbor dissent and test conviction by debate. But a bewildered and anonymous mass can do neither, and our dissenters scorn the canons of behavior that debate requires. Today, whoever dissents from dissent is outside the pale; no mere dispute, but a religious war. For dissent in its exasperation should now be called secession—which is but a way for a minority to excommunicate the majority.

To the strength of this attitude many elements of our

peculiar state of civilization contribute. The paradox, for example, that mass media impede communication induces cynicism about debate and armor-plates the rigidities of sectarian opinion. Again, the perpetual reminder of diversity and change scatters the wits and diminishes the power to attend, decide, and conclude. Too often the so-called democratic process leaves the conscientious mind baffled and hopeless. The overblown committee system shows a general incapacity for transacting business, which ends by an unwillingness to see it transacted; just as in the spread of casual manners, what looks like ease at first becomes at last a selfish indifference to the wants of others. In other terms, Western man's technical powers of contact and response have brought him close to that sense of overcrowding which has long made Eastern man self-centered and callous to all but his own clan. Finally, the surrealism of recent scientific thought has removed the last ground of common judgment. Anything can happen. Anything you hear is possibly true. Anything can be used to achieve what you fancy you might like. Our so-called planning is made up of these disparate elements; it is Utopian and apocalyptic talk, and although its predictions rarely come true and seldom enslave the imaginations of those without machinery to sell, they have the effect of augmenting the self-conscious suspicion that we are being worked upon, not so much living as being engineered to live; the obverse being, of course, the haunting thought that if we could find the right means—whether early conditioning, or electrodes planted in the brain, or a subtle use of drugs—we could control men and better the world. As one humorless sociologist put it: "Human attitudes must be changed in order to put into effect what we know."

The upshot of this manipulation by both material and mental forces is that the citizen of the modern state sees and feels and talks of endless change while profoundly aware that nothing he cares for makes headway. In the Liberal lexicon change without progress is mad, and that is one reason why madness seems so appropriate to the arts of Liberalism in extremis.

Madness, I suppose, needs no definition. In its most general—I might even say its most sociable—meaning, it implies a comic or tragic discrepancy between profession and performance. The madness of the man who thinks he is Napoleon consists in the fact that he does not do Napoleonic things. Today's madness is of the same sort. We boast of rapid transport and crawl in traffic jams at three miles an hour. We thunder about justice and equal rights and develop systems of sentencing and paroling that defy analysis and let loose the sane or insane homicide upon the public in the name of philanthropy and science. We suddenly find it difficult to keep prisoners from breaking jail—but we shall shortly put a man on the moon. We think we have discovered in puritanism about love the cause of painful inner conflict, so we celebrate sexuality, only to find it fraudulent in life but flourishing in books, where it consorts with repetitious cruelty. We are so infatuated with experiment that invoking the word validates all manner of horror and stupidity, both foolish and criminal. For example, to dose small children with a little fluoride, we propose to put tons of it at great expense in the water supply and wash the streets and flush the toilets with it. Or, again, if, as in the so-called Martin case in Connecticut, a dubious doctor practices sexual perversions on the emotionally unstable boys placed in his care by unknowing parents, the attempt to stop his "therapy" encounters resistance from the combined force of the local citizens, the press, the experts, and the law courts. What is more, that sordid case once judged, its merits are put as an open question to university students by a respected textbook on the criminal law. Whatever is, is right in the worst of all possible worlds.

It is undoubtedly to escape these contradictions that so many people are frantic to flee the actual world into one based on a simpler geometry, or one of partial nescience, such as is given by drugs, fasting, and umbilical contemplation. How can a sane mind choose in a dilemma such as that of measles in Nigeria? In that country the disease is virulent and kills. Inoculation would save many. But the inhabitants refuse inoculation. Should they be forced to undergo it? If they were, and many thereby survived, the population would increase and starve. This is a good example of what we pleasantly call Control over Nature. Out of individual frustration and imaginative horror comes the nihilism reflected in our art, which thus acts as both a safety valve and a call to destruction. The circle is complete; it whirls faster and faster. Out of such collective frustration comes the new separatism and new nationalisms. Every group wants to cut loose from its trammels, usually personified as some colonial or other oppressor. But the motive at work springs from the dream of total, frictionless autonomy. Else why should Scotland and Wales seek separation from England, Brittany and the Basques from France? The aim is quite literally dis-integration, and the word accurately describes our time. There is not one of us who would not change places with Robinson Crusoe *before* he found the footprint.

This is to say in effect that we live in one of the typical eras of our tradition. Let me call it the era of Montaigne—disordered, introspective, dogmatic, unprincipled, and murderous; an era in which the best are cultured but not educated, intensely moral but not honorable; an era, obviously, in which to philosophize is to learn to die.

This much we can borrow from Montaigne. But we can, if we wish, reinterpret his maxim. We need not, unless we choose, do this dying in our own persons. We can let our habits, our assumptions, and our expectations die, and what we can learn from philosophy is to let them die without fuss. The experience we dread may be new to ourselves, but it is not new to our tradition. There have been such great endings before—in the thirteenth century, at the close of the Protestant Reformation, at the turn from the eighteenth to the nineteenth century. Much earlier, in the age of St. Augustine, we discern in the record many of the symptoms now familiar to us at first hand. Great cadences of this kind do not necessarily spell the final quietus—on the contrary. There is a certain zest in massive removals and in turning large corners. This fact of stopping and turning is in truth the root idea of the word *epoch*, which we often misuse and should reserve for this phenomenon. Naming it would take away half its terror.

And what should strengthen equanimity in the face of destruction all around is the quality and intention in the work of our artists, who are as a group the best indicators of the cultural weather. Our artists are soured, destructive, nihilistic, but they are these things with enormous vigor and independence. While making rubble of all that we hold dear, they force our noses into the fresh raw material of sensation. The poets throw at us words and images without frills of feeling or freight of thought. The painters make our eyes pop—and that may be the ultimate meaning of Pop Art; others are content to let color vibrate before us. The musicians produce new sounds with the aid of machines and open our ears perforce. The novelists create unimaginable scenes and damn the consequences. As I showed earlier, the price is high, but that is because we are ourselves enfeebled characters whom the old militant Liberalism no longer invigorates. We vainly try to hedge, as most of our jargon reveals—we say *handicapped* for crippled, *underprivileged* for *poor*, *disturbed* for *crazy*, and *developing* for *undeveloped*. We dare not call things by their right names, not so much because we are kindly as because we want to obtain kindness for ourselves. We are permissive, not from love of liberty, but because we lack self-control and fear restraint as such. We praise innocence because we want the license to behave like an infant.

These are defects, not virtues or misfortunes. They are not eternal but can be overcome by a philosophy appropriate to such an age as ours. We may be too lazy or too blind to cooperate in the elimination of our era, but the great comfort is that even if we do not learn the right steps for ending gracefully we shall be reborn just the same. The wave of the future is in the hair of our young men. I say "we," but I mean our spirit, which starting from boredom will feed on sensation till it recreates idea, emotion, and belief in forms which we cannot imagine but which will make our descendants cry out that it is bliss to be alive in the new dawn and that to be young is very heaven.

1967

19

Truth in Biography: Leonardo and Freud

Now that Freud belongs to the ages, we shall probably witness a double shift in the public attitude towards his work. On the one hand, scholarship will examine with increasing care and interest the worth of his ideas; and on the other, the layman will forget all but a few of his own misconceptions and allow his animus to die out. Freud will be both absorbed and neglected, in accordance with our usual way of dealing with dead philosophers.

While this process is setting in, it may not be out of place to hazard a word or two about that application of Freudian theory which is perhaps the most important after the directly clinical. I refer to psychoanalytic biography and art criticism. Much of what passes currently under that name is no more than a vague coloring of common facts with a sexual interpretation.[1] It often boils down to the word "impotent" as an explanation for whatever seems odd in the life or work of an artist. Certain writers, who adopt a non-Freudian form of psychoanalysis, merely replace sex by self-assertion, or some such expression of the ego, and it is remarkable how simple in their handling the nature of a complex becomes. All these "interpretations" are of course verbalisms, and it is almost needless to say that Freud's own work in this field gives them no countenance.

Since Freud professed, however, to have laid the bases of a general psychology, there is nothing to prevent the use of its principles in writing the lives of the great. The statement one

1. This was written in 1940. (Ed.)

often sees, that Freud's ideas belong exclusively in the psy-
chiatric chamber—not to say the padded cell—is a mistake at
the other extreme. Freud dealt with art and biography both
theoretically and practically, and the sooner we assess his
contributions the better for all the disciplines concerned.

And first the practice. Before Leonardo da Vinci had become, for some unknown reason, a popular hero of biography, Freud had written his famous essay on him, the point
of which is indicated by the subtitle: *A Psychosexual Study of
an Infantile Reminiscence.* The book is short and deliberate.
One is given from the start a sense of confidence, and
throughout, a feeling that a man who writes so judicially
cannot but be judicious. The thesis is that Leonardo was all
his life a potential invert who turned all his sexual energies
into the channels of observation and research. Freud thus
explains why Leonardo generally failed to finish his pictures,
why his personality was "removed from the understanding of
his contemporaries," and why he painted by preference
enigmatic smiling women and beautiful youths. The chief clue
consists in Leonardo's recorded reminiscence of a vulture
having flapped with his tail the lips of the infant in his cradle.
Use is also made of Leonardo's illegitimacy and of his relation
to his mother, step-mother, and father, as further proofs of
his arrested sexual development. All this, together with the
written and painted works of the master, is supposed to explain the kind of artist and thinker he was. As for the sources
of the facts themselves, they are Leonardo's notebooks, contemporary documents, and later traditions.

The heterogeneity of Freud's proofs is in fact the most
embarrassing thing in his analysis. He takes entries in
Leonardo's journals, casual hints in old biographies, reported
hearsay, guesses in modern historical novels, and his own
rather conventional view of medieval science, as all equally
relevant and convincing. His notion of evidence is not steady.
He appeals to "probability" for establishing the fact that

Leonardo's "reminiscence" was a fantasy and not an actual event, though there is an equal probability that childhood reminiscences come from being told of an event so often or so vividly that it is mistaken for a personal memory. Probability is in any case a dangerous oracle, and elsewhere Freud wisely asks us to disregard it when he has some unusual interpretation to offer.

Meantime, he makes everything grist to his mill, regardless of what a lawyer or historian might consider unwarranted inference. For example, it is enough that Leonardo was, as a young man, accused of homosexual practice. That he was exonerated does not seem to matter: suspicion implies grounds for suspicion. This is the old fallacy of "where there's smoke, there's fire" and it is disturbing to find it here. But Freud not only accepts, he also rejects, with excessive partiality: Leonardo's interest in smiling women and youths as subjects to depict was matched by his interest in ugly old men and women, deformed creatures, and "characters" of all sorts, as well as the common and uncommon aspects of Nature. Yet we hear little or nothing from Freud about these things which are also to be found in the notebooks.

With regard to Leonardo's artistic personality—his slowness in working and his abandonment of half-finished projects—Freud never gives us any comparative measure that would clearly bring out Leonardo's peculiarity. We are merely told that in such matters Leonardo is "more so" than any other artist, or that "the difference is apparent." In truth, Freud has failed to take a control case as the technique of comparison requires. The interpretation of an entry in the diaries having to do with Caterina's funeral expenses, for example, should be matched with similar financial entries in Delacroix's journal. The reluctance to finish what he started should be compared with the same trouble in Goethe, who was, as everyone knows, anything but sexually abnormal.

Other, less ambiguous entries are actually twisted by Freud

from their obvious meaning: for example, that given by Solmi (page 14 of Freud's book) supposedly shows Leonardo's frigidity, when all it states is a platitude, which has been repeated hundreds of times by others, about the disgusting indignity of the sexual act. Freud's reasoning is equally inadmissible when he argues from the negative fact that Leonardo left no erotic or obscene drawings as have other artists. Has Freud really found that most painters are like Turner, who did leave such sketches? No, and even if he had, what could he prove by it? The argument runs in a circle: Leonardo was frigid because he left no erotic pictures, and he left none because he was frigid.

So far, it is but fair to say, Freud has only committed the same faults as dozens of other biographers who have no psychoanalytic pretensions. He has made the most of what he found without caring much about its origin or sifting out its exact bearing. He may even be more readily excused than others one could name, in that he nowhere tries to capitalize on this laxity to create sensation or arouse derisiveness at the expense of his subject. At this distance of time it matters very little what Leonardo's sex life was like. Its only interest lies in the possibility of our learning from it something of general application. That is why it remains a pity that Freud's biographical technique should be so open to criticism before we even get to the interpretation of the main clue.

Let us now see how this interpretation really works. What is interpreted is the reminiscence recorded by Leonardo himself, of the vulture's tail flapping his infant lips. Apparently the bird's tail has a well-known symbolic significance, both as a word in many languages and pictorially. Consequently Leonardo must have used it in that sense, namely, to represent male sexuality. The *ipse dixit* is reinforced by Freud's discovery that the Egyptians worshipped a goddess called *Mut*, one of whose heads was that of a vulture. After further details, the inference is made that when Leonardo was thinking of his mother (*Mutter*) he translated her into a vulture. This assumes on Leonardo's part a knowledge of Egyptian religion ("quite possible," says Freud, because Leonardo owned so many old books) and likewise a knowledge of German roots, for *madre* and *Mutter*, though related, are hardly identical. Yet Freud ends with "certainty" when he finds that the Church Fathers knew the whole Egyptian vulture fable; that Leonardo was widely read in the Church Fathers; and that Milan was the place where such books most often appeared in the early days of printing.

The real content of the fantasy, then, is that the child missed his father and felt himself abandoned with his mother. This explanation undoubtedly fits in with the social facts as we know them, but a good deal more of Egyptian religion has to be explained to us before we understand the interrelations of the phallic symbol, the mother suckling her child, and the social loneliness of that child. And when we have taken in all this, together with some undoubtedly sound clinical remarks on homosexuality, we again reach the artist who is alleged to have chosen as apprentices handsome boys rather than talented ones. Once more on pure biographical ground, where he can claim no exemption from common logic, Freud argues thus: Leonardo's apprentices were not talented, since none of them became famous. Therefore he chose them for their looks; therefore he was sexually attracted to them. This is of course another series of uncontrolled arguments which implies that the pupils of a great painter must turn out geniuses. As for the fact of these apprentices being handsome, "it has always been emphasized" that they were so, and furthermore, Leonardo was "kind and considerate" to them. The completed interpretation now reads: "Through the erotic relations to my mother I became a homosexual."

At this point it is easy to dismiss the whole thing with a contemptuous shrug; but that will not tell us precisely what is

wrong with this particular piece of Freudian analysis. We
must first set aside as all-too-common frailties the lapses of
logic in the use of historical materials. We are then left with
two major difficulties. First, Freud assumes a connection,
which he never proves, between Leonardo's homosexuality
and his work. He says that Leonardo was a great observer of
nature, painted enigmatic-looking females, and undertook
more than he could finish *because* he was homosexually inclined. How does this cause operate and what other element
coexists with it to make it productive in Leonardo and useless
in thousands of others? If we really want to know more about
art and artists, it is surely this forgotten ingredient that we
should look for. The homosexuality may simply be an un-
specialized driving force. Secondly, what clinches the fact
that Leonardo was what Freud alleges, is the symbolic meaning of the reminiscence and of the paintings and sketches.
Hence we must ask how symbolism works in art and how we
can make sure of its correct interpretation.

The first difficulty could very likely be settled by an extension of the historical method, a comparative study of artistic
lives that would clear up many points for the ordinary biographer as well. We all harbor fantastic ideas about the way
artists think and work, about the formative influences in their
lives, the nature of inspiration and effort, the development of
technique, and the evolution of feelings, virtues, and vices in
relation to the work of art. All the superstitions on these
points, which masquerade in our minds as common knowledge, it would be a boon to replace by verified and generalized data constituting as it were a Comparative Anatomy of
Art. To such a study the psychoanalyst could contribute the
etiology of clearly pathological cases. If Leonardo is considered one, it would be interesting, for example, to examine
the parallel instance of Sir Isaac Newton. His unusual attachment to his mother, his aloofness from common feelings
and passions, his nervous breakdown, and the quarrel with

Locke over a seemingly imaginary "embroilment with women," would furnish important points of similarity and difference, particularly when we note Freud's idea that Leonardo's intense curiosity about Nature is somehow connected with arrested sexual development.

The second difficulty, to wit, Freud's method of symbol analysis, is much more exclusively his own province; but if the method is to be widely used in general biography, the historian and critic must be allowed a questioning voice and an occasional veto—if only for the sake of preventing the inferior practitioners from fobbing off their hocus-pocus as new psychological discoveries.

Freud himself gives us the means of questioning him when he explains in various parts of his writings how he arrived at what he calls depth-psychology. His earlier theory of dreams is its starting point and we are therefore plunged at once into the sea of symbolism. What is a symbol? It is a sign for a thing—be it abstraction or concrete object. In the Leonardo study we are presumably enlightened by seeing that his childhood reminiscence is a symbol—a sign of something else—and interpreting it correctly. This assumption rests in turn on the psychological fact that we all use symbols in our capacities of dreamers, speakers, and conscious thinkers. The artist is the symbol-maker par excellence, from which it follows that in art as in dreams, there is a key to be found.

Freud's key is his theory of dreams. Briefly stated, it posits that sleep is a turning away from the real external world, and that dreams in sleep are the fulfillment of instinctive wishes. Freud distinguishes between the "manifest dream"—the story or picture that the patient describes to the analyst; and the "latent dream," or meaning extracted by the analyst. In a sense, the manifest dream is a work of art made up of personal or general symbols, and the latent dream is its message or purport.

But here we strike a snag. The analyst discovers the

meaning of his patient's dreams by studying their symbolism during a long and intimate association. In the course of an ordinary analysis, thousands of facts and fancies and symbols are described and discussed. It is by empirical judgment, based on past and present experience, that the analyst discovers the hidden meaning of a symbol. This being so, the difficulty of analyzing art by the same process is obvious. There are not enough symbols in the printed or painted work, and the author of them does not participate in their interpretation. To be sure, certain symbols do crop up again and again in the human mind, as comparative mythology amply proves. But even granting to the advocates of art-criticism-by-mythology that symbols fall into patterns and carry a general meaning, the excuse for psychoanalyzing the artist is to discover in the work of art more precise associations and more deeply hidden relations, in short more meaning, than an ordinary inspection reveals. This the small number of symbols does not permit, and Freud's unsatisfactory treatment of Leonardo shows on the contrary that the attempt ends in the further confusion of biographical truth.

There is an additional objection. The parallel between symbols in art and symbols in dreams brings Freud to the conclusion that art is, like sleep, "a turning away from the real external world." For him as for so many superficial critics, art is an "escape." He says: "Art is almost always harmless and beneficent; it does not seek to be anything else but illusion. Save in the case of a few people who are, one might say, obsessed with art, it never dares to make any attacks on reality." Consequently, in his psychoanalytic study of a German novelette called *Gradiva*, Freud passes from the "real" events of the story to the dreams of its hero and to the person of its author as if they were on a continuous plane, and the whole essay is fittingly entitled "Delusion and Dream." Delusion and dream and art become synonymous unrealities opposed to the "real" thought of the scientist or businessman.

This extraordinary sequence of errors is almost beyond belief. In the first place, the parallel originally made for purposes of symbol analysis was between art and dreams, not art and sleep. The fact that sleep may be a turning away from reality therefore states nothing whatever about the relation of *art* to reality. Even if it did, the dreaming in sleep, according to Freud, expresses in symbols the tendency of perfectly real instincts and wishes. So, on his own showing, art has a right to be considered an expression in symbols of perfectly real emotions and ideals.

Moreover, in any art, but particularly in painting, it is a far more delicate question than Freud seems to think, to determine what is a symbol and what meaning it hides. Suppose Leonardo to have drawn a sketch of his reminiscence of the vulture, what evidence have we except Freud's say-so for supposing that it signifies more than we actually see? To put it another way, if a vulture invariably means Leonardo's mother, what symbol must Leonardo use when he means just a plain vulture? This dilemma states in a new form the old biographical fallacy of imputing motives, also known in everyday life as "putting two and two together." The commonplace biographer writes: "Jonathan Swift was bitter against the human race because he was not made a bishop." Imputed motive for bitterness: disappointment. But is every case of bitterness also one of disappointment? Can there be no wider reason, perhaps in the observation of mankind? Psychoanalytic biography now enters the fray: Swift did not marry Stella and some of Swift's poems are obscene. Therefore Swift was impotent. No wonder he assailed mankind! Swift's opinon seems to be "explained" and by the same stroke, Swift's secret nature.

The thing is really too easy. Biography can learn much from Freud's depth-psychology insofar as it corrects our *general* ideas of human motive and behavior, and insists on a treatment of the whole man as against the fiction of a dis-

embodied intellect. But it cannot give us a magic key to
unlock the inner character of artists whose uncommon complexity is the chief reason for our interest in their lives. The
trick of psychoanalyzing the dead cannot be done by reduc-
ing every living fact to some lower mechanical cause and
every artistic or philosophic statement to some hidden and
universal impulse. What is wanted is a more exact analysis of
individual cases, not merely more spectacular guessing.
Lastly, it will not do to forget that art deals with the reality
outside as well as the emotions within. Hence the ordinary
rules of evidence and inference must apply. The notion of art
as escape is sterile, and is indeed itself an escape from the
necessity of dealing with social facts by invoking the caprices
of the subconscious. Freud's fiasco with Leonardo should
stand as a warning to possible imitators and also as an encouragement for his disciples to chart the artistic soul along new
meridians.

1940

Delacroix: Sketch of the Artist in Words

Whether or not he was the son of his ostensible father or of Talleyrand is one of those questions that must be left to those who nibble at the arts for gossip's sake. The interesting fact is that like Berlioz and Balzac and Hugo, Delacroix is a cultural product of Revolutionary and Napoleonic France. His father was at his death in 1805 an Imperial official in southern France, and the remembered tumult and glory of the years of Delacroix's childhood and youth inform the painter's work to the very end.

An orphan at sixteen, Delacroix left the lycée a year later, to enter the studio of Guérin. His first published drawings also date from that same year of Waterloo, 1815. Precocious, taciturn, and shy, Delacroix worked with fierce concentration, though not without the solace of friendship: he lived with his sister and found among his fellow students three friends who remained his intimates for life. Overwork brought on a serious illness in 1820. Then comes another friendship with Géricault, soon cut short by the latter's death. In 1822 Delacroix prepares his first salon exhibition: *Dante and Virgil*. This work may seem equally remote from the French Revolution and from Delacroix's later dramatic distortions of form, but his temperament is already in evidence. Indeed, it might be said that all his life Delacroix depicted only one subject in many forms—the menace and mystery of the universe. In the *Dante and Virgil*, the glowing walls of the fortress of Dis in the background and the limbs of the damned clutching at the boat in which the poets cross the infernal waters render the characteristic Delacrucian mood.

Soon the expression of that mood was to undergo technical development, thanks to a new artistic contact, with the young English painter Bonington. Delacroix was preparing his second salon, due in 1824, with a subject taken from current events in the manner of Géricault, the Turkish massacre of Greeks at Chios. A sight of Bonington's work led Delacroix to remake his own scheme. There follow portraits of friends and historical, literary, and religious scenes, culminating in the *Marino Faliero*, exhibited with nine others at the Salon of 1827.

By then Delacroix had begun to keep his famous Journal, in which he records his technical observations, his friendships, his relations with women, and his meditations on style and on the great masters. Delacroix firmly believed that his taste and his art were alike austere, classical, anti-Romantic. He disliked the new literature of Hugo and Balzac and preferred Racine to Corneille. True, he let himself become friends with George Sand, but it was probably because of Chopin, whose music he relished, while abominating that of Berlioz.

The paradox here is visible, but not inexplicable. To those who did not analyze but only tasted, it might seem as if the new literature and new music of the 1830s made a point of looseness and extravagance. The truth is that the geniuses among the crowd—Hugo, Berlioz, and Balzac—were deliberate craftsmen, whose main principle was exactly Delacroix's: the expression of the highest passion in the most controlled form. Only, the form need not be set form: it was to be original form, and used only for the one unique purpose; whereat the critics complained that all was lost. Delacroix, whether he liked it or not, was (correctly) lumped in with his great contemporaries as a Romanticist. Did he not paint *Liberty on the Barricades* after 1830? The artist

nevertheless suffered from what he considered a deep misunderstanding, though he vented his spleen only occasionally
in the Journal. Publicly, he was stoical, enduring until nearly
his sixtieth year the contumely of the newspapers and the
"right-thinking" bourgeois. Indeed, it took the World's Fair
of 1855 in Paris before that all-knowing city was really aware
of the great creator it had harbored for a third of a century.

At the beginning of that span, in 1832, Delacroix, aged
thirty-four, underwent the last of his formative experiences:
invited by a cousin in the government he went to Morocco,
then a new and "exotic" land. Those seven months under a
burning sky were the revelation of a new world of color.
Delacroix discovered that shadows are not necessarily black
but can be purple or reflect other deep colors. His mind
(and some wonderful notebooks) was filled with new shapes,
costumes, animals, and architecture. He returned, dazzled, to
begin the works of his maturity, starting with the great decorative compositions of the Chamber of Deputies and City
Hall—commissions obtained, once again, through official
connections.

About this time also began his first serious liaison, with
Mme de Forget. All his ladies, until the end, when he came
under the ascendancy of his housekeeper, were women of
taste, position, and discernment. This last they must have
had, to appreciate the haughty and penetrating intellect that
one finds in the letters and the Journal and again in the hypnotizing *Self-Portrait*. It is a remarkable coincidence that Delacroix and Berlioz should have been, contrary to the norm,
masters of the word as well as of their respective arts, and
that Victor Hugo the poet should have been an extraordinary
draftsman. The synesthesia of the arts, which we hear so much
of nowadays, begins earlier than we think.

Out of the Moroccan trip came, in 1834, that seminal work
Algerian Women at Home, which pulled like a magnet at nearly

every great nineteenth-century painter. Then in 1838 comes the first of the two *Medeas*, each a diagnostic work in its period. By 1839, Delacroix had three times offered himself for membership in the Institute and been rejected. Illness, casual love affairs, heavy work on the ceilings and walls of public buildings fill out the years until the consecration of 1855. Only at the ninth trial, in 1857, did the Institute catch up with public opinion and elect him a member.

In the wonderful variety of Delacroix's works, some stand out as not merely characteristic but unique in the history of art for the expression of ideas and feelings in a form no other artist could have conceived. Such are those already mentioned—the *Dante*, the two *Medeas*, the self-portrait, and the *Algerian Women*. To these must be added as summits of his art: the *Crusaders Entering Constantinople,* the *Execution of Marino Faliero*, the *Death of Sardanapalus*, the *Battle of Poitiers*, and—to name only one of the stupendous murals, the Apollo ceiling in the Louvre. By their titles all these suggest the historical and mythological subjects typical of the time; but Delacroix does not illustrate incidents any more than Berlioz fits sounds to programs. Each renders in his medium his vision of existence and communicates the thrill of recognition to thousands who know neither history nor literature but have some awareness of the multiform enigma of life.

By the time of his election to the Institute, Delacroix was chronically ill, worn out by a kind of warfare that the twentieth century scarcely understands: he had won innumerable battles; painted, drawn, or engraved nearly a thousand important works; lived in physical comfort and close friendships worthy of his genius—and yet the crown of true fame as it was then understood was wanting: to be an academician, even if nonacademic. By 1858, he had just enough strength and willpower left to undertake the chapels of St.-Sulpice, with which he closed his career as painter in 1861. Between that year and his death two years later, we have—a symbolic touch—a fine essay on the work of a neglected contemporary and a painting on an Arab subject.

1971

21

Biography and Criticism: A Misalliance?

As a youth, years ago, I enjoyed the frequent hospitality of an older couple whose children were of my own age. The father, who was a scientist of some note, liked talking with the young on many subjects, and several times drew me out on what he called "this business of art." He was anything but insensitive to color and line and tone; what he resisted was the view which he saw gaining ground, that art was a solemn affair, an oracle to be trusted. Poetry, now—was it anything but a string of false or doubtful propositions dressed up to prevent close analysis?

I have no memory of what I said or whether I made any lasting impression on an otherwise receptive mind. But I do remember one source—or at least one reinforcement—of the rooted prejudice. When an undergraduate at a great eastern university in the nineties, my fatherly friend had taken a course on the English lyric. The readings were from Palgrave's *Golden Treasury*, and the lectures, by a well-known scholar, consisted of careful accounts of the lives of the poets. The schools they went to, the patrons and wives they had, the journeys they made, the books they read and published were minutely chronicled, with thoughtful discussions of moot points and rival theories. Then, after two or three hours thus spent, the lecturer would come to the assigned lyric: "And now, gentlemen, what shall we say of this exquisite work? There is only one thing to say—a gem, a gem!"

These details remain vivid in my mind, because that last ritual phrase had become a family catchword that had to be explained to every newcomer. When something was approved of in a general way, but not really known or warmly liked, it was a "ajemmajem." The girls themselves, when asked about a new young man who had proved pleasant but not entrancing, would reply casually: "Oh, ajemmajem."

Bored by the "lives" and unassisted to the readings, my friend and his classmates had been in no danger of becoming esthetes. If literature must be a study in college, this so-called historical criticism was worse than futile; it was prophylactic. The revolt against it came, as everybody knows, in the 1920s. By the New Critics the dogma was laid down that history and biography have nothing to contribute to criticism, have nothing to do with art. The only thing that exists for the critic is The Work. Whoever made it was mortal and unimportant, but the work is *aes triplex* cast in a unique and inevitable form, for the creative act is not self-expression but mastery. The personality and emotions of the artist are as irrelevant to the achievement as the color of his hair; the work is as autonomous as a pillar of stone in the desert. Hence, to grasp the merit and meaning of a work, the critical mind must direct itself to its logic and structure—internal relations, not external.

No one will want to deny the superiority of this teaching over the treatment of the English lyric in the college course of 1890. The new criticism swept like a salubrious wind over the miasma of pseudohistorical academic study, and there is little danger of its return. The enterprise of sanitation went even further. It branded as also irrelevant the temperament of the critic. *His* "biography," in the form of moods and tastes, could yield only an impression of the work, quite without validity. Typical of a school—though no doubt more sensitive than the academic lecturer—Anatole France might seek to justify his four volumes of literary criticism as the adventures of a soul among masterpieces, but this confession of narcissism proved only that he was not a critic.

In short, the new, self-sacrificial mode of interpreting art was to be objective in a double sense: the work under scrutiny is an autonomous object; the critic strips himself of personality in order to dissect. Both principles imply the use of method. The critical reformation in effect fulfilled the wish of my scientist friend, who could not believe in the seriousness of art until a close analysis of the propositions of poetry was possible.

This state of mind was in time modified by a "theory of literature" which tried to bring into play a restricted form of history. By a kind of analogy with zoological evolution, the theory strung successive works of art on a line and noted the formal changes leading to the perfected type at the end. That type served both as a means of organizing the sequence and as a measure with which to judge the merits of each specimen. In this scheme the autonomy of the single work is reduced, of course, but collectively autonomy is saved; for the cause of change in successive types lies in their predecessors, not in outside influences. This exclusive attention to the intrinsic makes the description and analysis of the works singly or together a true *literary* history, pure and free from the miscellany of life.

Modern critics have with few exceptions observed these self-imposed limits, whether in their original or modified form. The diversity of "methods" and "approaches" applied to the several arts does not contradict the principle of exclusion they hold in common. Rather, it confirms the generality that, despite a marked indifference or opposition to science, the critics in highest repute have adopted the primary rule of scientific work, which is to withdraw selfhood from both object and beholder. The critical activity thus becomes a methodical, quasi scientific process.

This redirecting of the critical mind has strong appeal and high plausibility. The interpreter's concentration on form seems warranted by the artist's similar preoccupation. Nothing in art "stands up" until the right form is found, and many artists have described their work as a search for pure form, as the making of absolute structures. Yet on reflection it proves impossible to take such remarks literally, as if the making or discovery of forms in art were an unconditioned effort. The right form for what? There is not one but many answers—right for the material chosen; for the space or use to be suited; for the moral, social, or emotional ends to be served; for keeping the audience awake and interested; for rebellion's sake and doing something new; and—more generally —for exercising and stretching one's peculiar talents.

These and other common motives constitute a notable part of intention, which does inform the work, however elusive and unrepeating intention turns out to be. And motive and intention alike imply the possibility of gauging their realization. It is the essential feat of criticism to judge artistic success by ascertaining whether intention is fulfilled, while intention can be ascertained only from the work itself, the fulfillment. But in this bootstrap operation the part of intention that is made up of common motives can be subjected to the test of artistic practicality at least. Beethoven wanted to write a choral symphony, a thing never before attempted. The form had to be created. How does it prove itself, in the making and the hearing? As in architecture, the finished work must be usable (playable, readable, listenable, graspable). In a hundred places form has to fit local purpose or obstacle, and the evidence of these needs is often found nowhere but in sources external to the work. No "method" limited to "intrinsic" elements will discover the contingencies amid which all art is produced: that is not only a truth but a truism, a tautology.[1]

Starting from this axiom, one who rejects the claims of

1. Among contingent motives are some that have "nothing to do with art" yet are often found close to it—the love of fame or money, the desire to impose one's will or impress others. These powerful urges cannot be treated as if nonexistent; their effect, if any, must be assessed. When Gide tells us that up to *The Counterfeiters* all his work had but one intention, to "convince and carry away" his unresponsive wife Madeleine, we must discover, if we can, whether this purpose modified Gide's other intentions, moral and esthetic. In short, the desire to please (including the artist's desire to please himself) is no negligible part of intention, and like all human impulses its quality varies from the fastidious to the indifferent and the shameless.

method and autonomy may choose to pursue the argument on theoretical grounds. Logic and psychology raise doubts about the possibility of so much "rigor" and detachment, as I shall try to make clear later. But I prefer to begin with the conditions of the critical task as they typically present themselves, and to show the emptiness of the claims by examples of historical and biographical criticism that lead the mind to The Work itself and supply an understanding of it not otherwise obtainable.

But first a word about Understanding. Perhaps no one can define what its criteria are, even for himself; it is much easier to detect what misunderstanding is when one is baffled or when one perceives another's floundering in the presence of a work or idea. These are the situations that justify criticism's existing at all, the second case being the reason or excuse for making any criticism public: it is to counteract conventional opinion, generally false. Noncomprehension is easy because art is difficult, at least in an advanced civilization, which can look back on many schools and embraces many traditions. Out of these come licit and illicit ambiguity, exclusivist vogues, long misrepresentations of plain matters. In such surroundings the work itself becomes more and more changeable, enigmatic. It is no doubt in response to this quaky feeling that the desire for method and objectivity grows so strong. Yet the reliance on method brings no agreement. I have before me a paper by an able young scholar charging that fourteen earlier explanations of Blake's "Tyger" are wrongheaded and proposing a fifteenth. Under the regime of method, it will not do to say the more the merrier, for that is a laissez-faire view which would preclude the finality of any critical findings. If Blake's poem is a problem, it must have one solution and one only, which can be proved like a theorem.

Having long ago expressed my dissent from the prevailing faith in methods,[2] I start from plainer ground and make but

2. In *The Energies of Art* (New York, 1956).

commonsense assumptions—that a work as a whole or in detail is easy to misconceive, that its substance and value are at the mercy of preconceptions which create *pre-perceptions*, and that the main task of criticism is to clear this foreground of obstacles—nothing more. The critic's ultimate hope is that he may facilitate the beholder's pleasure by indicating its kind and by associating it with tenable meanings, emotions, and experiences. Association is what everything lives by in the memory, hence the *data* of the work, right down to points of factual information and right up to images of transcendence, may all be important. The fused cluster of perceptions and associations is The Work in as full a sense as it is given anyone to possess it. Its actual shape and force in a living mind depend on the individual sensorium, which, despite all the journal articles written and to be written, is beyond the *control* of the critic. He wields no scientific club with which to coerce. He can only point and give reasons as he flashes a beam here or there.

The way to the end thus proposed is through the materials of history, including the biographic, since biography—the maker's life—is the mode in which The Work arises in history. The supposition that this matrix can be shucked like the useless rind of a fruit is mere illusion. No critic really discards it. The close reader and all other text analysts make use of etymology, which is a branch of history. Semantics and connotation, like the things and ideas to which words refer, are but fragments of history; and so is the famous "logic" and structure of the work, since much or all of it derives from tradition. As for the meanings and symbols and echoes below the surface, we know it takes an "educated" reader to find them, and his education is only more history distilled. Lastly, the method he applies with such audible effort still leaves him an individual, a temperament, an inevitable Impressionist. His gestures only are methodical.

On these same assumptions one ventures to find in the

author of the work—in his actions and character—possible answers to necessary questions. His circumstances, physical and spiritual, what he knew and intended, can reorient the inquiring mind and afford it farther penetration into the work.

It is time to come to examples. When I began to think of writing about Berlioz, some twenty years before my book appeared in 1950, it was because I saw a discrepancy between all I knew (or thought I knew) and what was said, written, and felt about the man and his music. I saw him and heard his works with a different set of perceiving organs—or else there were two composers of the same name and dates.

If I was right, my task was to replace existing ideas with others closer to the evidence of my senses, and thus modify the pre-perceptions of the common listener and of the critics he trusted. What was needed—to borrow a term from psychology—was a new "apperceptive mass" of beliefs, judgments, and expectations. Now one of the ingredients in the conventional "mass" was that Berlioz was a "literary" composer who was "lost without a program." His music was "scene painting," lacking in musical form and, except for flashes of orchestral color, fundamentally dull. To demonstrate independent musical form in Berlioz required that the supposed instances of his clinging to the alien forms of literature be disproved. *If it had been possible to judge the form direct, without going into "extraneous" matters, its character would have been seen and accepted long since.*

In other words, the disbelief in Berlioz's power to produce "form" lay in the misreading of his biography and had to be uprooted there. Such is one type of critical situation. It had to be shown by reference to history that the use of a written program to attract public interest was a practice antedating Berlioz's beginnings, and that in fact he put an end to it, after yielding to the fashion once, for launching his first symphony, the *Fantastique* of 1830. Even there the program relates to the intervals between the musical movements and not to the movements themselves. So true is this that there are five different versions of the "story," the music remaining unchanged.

Of even more telling effect was a small discovery I made about the "Corsair" overture. It had always been assumed that the music "depicted" the events of Byron's poem. Byron was a romantic; Berlioz, also a romantic, read Byron; so the overture must be "about" the loves and hates of Conrad and Medora. The actual history of the overture is this: it was written in 1831 when Berlioz, having left Rome in the throes of misprized love, was cheerfully recovering by himself in Nice. There he composed his "King Lear" and this other overture, called at first "The Tower of Nice." This title was purely associative, referring to the martello tower where Berlioz had lodgings—there's no program in a tower. The work is a sea piece, like many others down to Debussy's *La mer*.

But Berlioz was not satisfied with his score and put it aside. Twenty years later, while conducting in London, he reworked the draft, calling it "The Red Corsair" overture. Soon afterward the "Red" was dropped, the work remaining exactly as we have it. What sparked my inquiry was: why "Red"? It turned out that Berlioz had recently picked up some novels of James Fenimore Cooper's which he had first enjoyed much earlier. He reread *The Red Rover*. The fact made everything clear: the music had nothing to do with any story; it antedated both its piratical titles by twenty years. Only its generally marine atmosphere and the casual incidents of the composer's life had suggested now one tag, now another by which to designate it.

The knowledge of circumstances as trivial as these removes an error, and it also establishes a truth about a frequent relation between art and life in the maker's career; the act of creation does not take place in a vacuum. By ascertaining Berlioz's habit of retitling, one could dispose of a strictly esthetic misconception, and once the ground was clear it became possible to hear the overture as music. Its remarkable melodic unity, the delightful syncopations that frame the contrasting sections, the filigree harmonic work, and the grand modulation ushering the climax emerged as from a palimpsest. There is no use saying that form and intention ought to be evident at all times to the Careful Critic, or even that the C. C. does discover them if his method is right. The empirical facts of the history of criticism give the lie to both contentions.

Sometimes it is not merely the character of an *oeuvre* that needs biographical elucidation but its very claim to being art. In working out on the small scale of an essay my intuitions about Lincoln as a writer, I found the entire body of critics affirming either that Lincoln had no style in the proper sense or that he developed a style only in his last years, under the agony of civil war. Before then his prose was said to be that of an uneducated midwestern lawyer with a commonplace gift for storytelling. I thought otherwise, but made no headway against conventional opinion by simply quoting from his prose. Its simplicity, dotted with lightning turns of phrase, sounded like inexperience, not art; and—an odd objection from formalists—its largely political or domestic subject matter was felt as disqualifying.

But when I was able to collect evidence of Lincoln's concern with the arrangement of words virtually from his infancy, when I singled out from the record of his life the signs of obsession, moodiness, ruthlessness, consciousness of superiority, then the writer began to emerge from all the other true and false images of the man; and there stood an undeniable artist, whose Gettysburg Address is the most famous but by no means the best of his extraordinary utterances. His styles, in the plural, could then be seen as adapted to a changing purpose and his mastery of language be both felt and accounted for.[3]

3. "Lincoln the Writer," *Writing, Editing, and Publishing* (Chicago, 1971). (Ed.)

It is not a doctrine but a fact that the critic cannot divine by sensibility alone, or even aided by method, what a lecturer who was not listening to his own words once called "this tight-knit-wit of an author." Whether the "wit" is considered to reside wholly in the work's structure or in its entire indefinable purport, the work's situation must also be examined, if only to dispose of the errors that previous readers have wrongly imported from it into their judgments. Right or wrong, judgments are not made by wholly innocent minds; nor can the pure or methodic critic pretend to recover such a mind. If his merit is that of a close reader, he will show it by his sureness and subtlety in the close reading of life; he must be familiar with *its* themes and symbols first. And since even the broadest experience has limits, the competent critic extends it by recourse to other works than his present object, and to history as well.

Without experience, direct and vicarious, how could one detect falseness in art or in criticism? Samuel Butler, who did not like Wordsworth, once wrote an essay in which he showed by a close reading of the second of the poems about Lucy that the reason she "ceased to be" was that Wordsworth had murdered her. The lines fit the thesis, and Wordsworth, says Butler, "was nothing if not accurate." Now suppose the poem and the commentary a fragment from ancient literature. It would be impossible to know whether to call the verses confessional or not: regret and remorse are close kin. Since Butler, criticism has affirmed comparable fancies in dead earnest.

How, again, without knowing more than the work discloses, could one assign degrees of importance to a fiction? Judging by form alone, by coherence, unity, proportion, and mastery of varied tone, one would have to rank *Zuleika Dobson* higher than the novels of Stendhal and Dostoevsky. *The Brothers Karamazov* is not even a finished work. Does the structure visibly tilt? A famous novelist cut out the longueurs in a reissue of Stendhal's two masterpieces: would scanning

the form tell you where the omissions came? Milton shifted
from ten to twelve books as the right division of his epic:
does this structural change destroy the integrity of the poem?

To speak of a work as a world obeying its own laws is high
and fine talk, but in such a world we could never take an
interest—let alone understand it—if we did not know our
own world, with *its* objects and *its* laws, and find these again
in the world made by art. We grasp the solar system because
the elements and their behavior repeat, and likewise the
worlds of, say, Proust and Balzac. In common with each other
and with the real world they contain such elements as: marriage and adultery, the lust for money and for fame, the
bourgeoisie and the aristocracy, music and philosophy, politics and petty jealousy, and—not least significant—the features and street names of one particular city. These are food
for the imagination on a par with the names of Homer's
islands and his catalogue of ships.

One can perhaps condone the overstating of Autonomy on
the ground that the use of "information" in criticism tends to
be crudely literal. After searching for clues in diaries or letters, scholars and publicists alike are led to commit errors
vulgar or perverse. It is then that the censure of the formalist
and internist falls justly, that his strictures deserve full weight
in the very interests of historical criticism. Thus Swift's *Gulliver* and Machiavelli's *The Prince* have both been attributed
to disappointed ambition. Swift was balked in his legitimate
ambitions—and hence the Yahoos; Machiavelli was cast out
by a republic—and hence the murderous Prince. The damage
here is not to the artist's moral character alone; it is to
the work itself, which is read disparagingly: *Gulliver* as mis-
anthropic and *The Prince* as immoral.

Such verdicts are wrapped up in academic language, but
the public strips the wrappings and remembers the clichés.
This in turn is a spur to more sophisticated interpretations
based on the premise of concealed significance, of irony:

Swift and Machiavelli were comic spirits as well as great artists, and art is never literal. So *Gulliver* and *The Prince* must
be elaborate ironies, the one (espeically Book IV on the
Houyhnhnms) a satire not of mankind but of utopias; the
other not a treatise on statecraft but a parody of such
treatises. Like the cry of Fire, the cry of Irony is always
believed, in the interest of one's own safety: one does not
want to get caught. There are, as we shall see, other schemes
than irony for playing about with the concealed intentions
imputed to artists, but one dreads to think what would befall
modern criticism if the idea and the word "ironic" were ex-
punged from the books and forgotten for a space.

Between the crude and the *recherché* notions of artistic
work, then, the legitimate use of external sources is obscured
and its risky but necessary technique neglected. It is risky
because there are no rules, only cautions such as this: acts or
utterances in life are *circumstantial*: they belong to a single
situation. For example, we know that spontaneously or under
goading artists make vivid statements about their work. By
the time these become catchwords they suffer from incurable
ambiguity. What did Milton mean by distinguishing poetry
from prose as "more simple, sensuous, and passionate"? Is
the poetry of *Paradise Lost* simple? If so, what shall we call
Blake's *Songs of Innocence*, which in another sense are anything
but simple? What did Beethoven have in mind when he de-
fended his music as being "not painting, but the expression of
feeling"? Since modern criticism states that feeling and expression are not esthetic categories, do we conclude that
Beethoven (*a*) was no artist or (*b*) did not say anything intelligible?

No short cut will lead to the answers. Only study and
reflection on whole lives and periods will supply the meaning
of critical maxims; they need as much close reading as the
text of a poem. Do they record a mood or a rooted belief?
And if a belief, is it the fruit of experience or of a desire to

oppose another belief, held by a rival, by the crowd, *by the critics?* Most important, how does the thing said in life bear on the question raised by the work? Any slippage here is fatal; the remark may only seem to fit and the artist himself be deceived. I have for convenience of illustration cited only phrases, but what I say applies to whole letters, journal entries, reported conversations, prefaces, essays. No document is exempt from temporality or from the judgment that human motives are always mixed and human perceptions always accented: *interest* in the widest sense is what guides attention, which automatically gives emphasis. These conditions are those of the mind itself. History necessarily reflects the same pattern and thereby gives the searcher hints of order amid the wide confusion.

Mindful of the mixed and the contingent, we can agree that Swift's and Machiavelli's writings owed something to injustice suffered and resented. But *saeva indignatio* is already more than a sense of personal wrong. And by going deeper into biography, by taking all the "hints of order" in conjunction, the critical mind ends by seeing in *Gulliver*, side by side with vengeful thoughts, a wounded love of humanity and in *The Prince* a baffled passion for peace and justice. A stubborn questioner may continue to ask, couldn't similar conclusions be reached by sheer attention to The Work? Apparently not, since after centuries such conclusions still have to be argued against casual and critical readers alike. It is right and easy to blame the "difficulty" of great works, but it would be good to remember also the deceptiveness of the pure esthetic sense and the danger of pre-perceptions fixed nor'nor'west.

The suggestion that critical evidence from biography and history needs thorough surveying before use may give a kind of comfort to the advocates of method—"at least it's hard work too, though a looser type of method." But this consolation must be disallowed. It is *not* method, and modern in-

tellectual systems too readily mistake effort and elaborate-
ness for right reason: they are only devices for playing safe
and equalizing talent. Spending time, counting things, being
ingenious are fundamentally lazy activities. Delegate them to
computers by all means; the results will be as fruitless.

For it is simply not true that facts speak for themselves or
that in a critical inquiry one cannot know too much about a
creator and his work. Judgment is as easily swamped by excess as warped by scarcity of matter. Dickens rejoiced that we
know so little about Shakespeare; modern Shakespeare
scholarship tempts us to agree with Dickens, for other reasons than his. When a search is extensive, evidence repeats;
when it is desperate, pedants make up its bulk by splintering
what there is. In any inquiry much is but superficially relevant, and even what is fresh and to the point is waste unless
judgment interprets the accidental and egregious—though at
times the critic is justified in relying solely upon them: there
are no rules. In a recent book on Diderot may be seen the
effect of raking in all possible items of fact without choice or
assay. A sentence of Aristotle's that Diderot "may have remembered," an engraving "current at the time," a satirical
inscription Diderot wrote for a theater curtain, and other
such crumbs are kneaded into a rationalist account of Plato's
Republic to solve the difficulties of *Rameau's Nephew*, as if the
work were a tract in cipher and not a dramatic masterpiece.
The term that suggests itself for such mishandling is not so
much "improper" as "tactless."

If one is to examine a work through the prism of external
evidence, intuition is as necessary as judgment, and ingenuity
is to be shunned, for the critical task is not to solve but to see.
Readers of scholarly criticism are familiar with the several
kinds of method for "solving"—classifying images, pursuing
thematic words and phrases, disengaging symbols and myths
and psychic patterns from a text seemingly concerned with
other, often mundane things. Reading like a detective will

produce as many conversions of Appearance into Reality as
may be desired. The creator is tracked down and finally
caught and convicted. When an agile mind has once accustomed itself to scan literature or the arts in these ways, it
finds it hard to see things in the light of common day. I
remember one seminar session in which Lionel Trilling and I
vainly urged upon a group of young methodists the idea that
in the nineteenth-century novel the mention of money might
be literal: the characters were poor and needed money, or
they were greedy and wanted more money. Our listeners
declined to believe. Money, some said, was the symbol of the
will to live, unevenly distributed among men, regardless of
merit. Not at all, said others. Money stands for Evil: it cor-
rupts. The poor are good, the moneyed are or become
bad—read the Bible. The two groups came together only in
the conviction that no "great artist" could "study" money in
its own terms as a means of gratification or a cause of despair.
The devotees of method are ripe for all the delusions of
hunting secret messages in Shakespeare or matching the
Book of Revelation with current events.

Most such critics of course content themselves with
findings less scandalous or apocalyptic, but the assumption
remains that all artists go to work in the same way. Just as the
ragman type of interpreter will pick up any fact and find in it a
factor contributing to the masterpiece, the others imagine
that writers bury their true sense as squirrels do nuts, for
unearthing later and feeding the finder. As a matter of history, symbolism in art is not a constant. For us it dates—aptly
enough—from the Symbolist movement. The Victorians,
when faced with its occasional use, had little liking of it.[4]
They relied on plot and character to bind their visions into a
structure; the modern, quasi-musical function of themes they

4. The contemporary dislike of Dickens's *Our Mutual Friend* owed something to his
mixing of symbols with realism; and when he had to defend *Bleak House*, he felt
obliged to give a factual precedent for the fall of the house.

ignored—as Mr. Gordon Ray once had to explain in a critique of several studies that thematicized George Eliot out of recognition: "The three essays differed sharply in their conclusions. What they had in common was a profound misunderstanding of the Victorian novel."

Just like the pointless biographical forays of the academic lecturer in 1890, the modern application of method can be wholly dissevered from the material it works on, thus aggravating irrelevance by anachronisms that a knowledge of history must necessarily discredit. To establish the differences among works or artists, the safeguard against method is biography and common sense. By common sense I mean a mind free from faddishness and self-conceit, and equipped with a nonbookish knowledge of the world. It is clear to common sense that, although artists may find anything grist to the mill, they do not build out of disparate bits and scraps collected from the environment, which the critic can later identify and restore to their owners. These namable sources are at best the occasions that set the artistic imagination going, to reach sometimes startling parallels with actuality.[5]

Common sense tells us also that by staring at a work things may be found in it at the whim or the will of the beholder. Anybody brought up in a lycée on relentless *explication de texte* (close reading) knows how the fancy sprouts under pressure. The wildest intentions, intricacies, influences can plausibly be shown, a product not of critical genius but of schoolboy ingenuity. In classroom slang it is (or was) called "torturing" (a text). "Have you done your torture yet?" For the critical Torquemada, the two opposite views of the artist as unconscious or as superconscious are equally convenient. If like M. Jean-Paul Weber one defines creation in art as the

---

5. The great instance is that of Boileau's mock epic *Le lutrin*, which turned out to depict with fine accuracy a monastic house-feud the poet had only heard of.

infinite modulation of a single theme which was traumatically impressed on the artist's unconscious in childhood, the field of conjecture is limitless.[6] Every word or act acquires a meaning, directly or by suitable torture, for the analysis posits an inescapable determinism. In thus exploiting the work one is of course dabbling in biography: the method is not "pure" or restricted in its inquisition. And it is biography on two disjoined levels, that of evidence open to all and that of deduction from analytic theory known to few. I have given elsewhere the reasons why I think the results of that mixture are illicit and unconvincing.[7] If they are so as to men and their motives, they are so *a fortiori* about the shyer intention and meaning of works of art.

By making the contrary assumption that everything in a product of the mind is consciously meant, a whole other realm of evidence is flouted. Individual habit, influence by language and tradition, inattention and magnanimous disregard of trifles—all suffice to account for the presence of details seized on by criticism—for example, the repetition of words or imagery. And of course sheer accident plays its part, at least for all but doctrinaire determinists, who (consistently enough) seem determined to find significance. It is a faith like another, but a man who will philosophize about Time in Cervantes or Goethe because the events in *Don Quixote* and *Faust* violate the order of the seasons, or who will make Shakespeare insinuate dark tidings about the womb because Lady Macbeth declares herself barren and also a suckler of children is a man lost to the sense of probability: let him cling to method.

The methods that "analyze" in the conscious and unconscious modes not only contradict each other but also undermine the modern critic's first principle, that the work of art is a self-enclosed object. For what are these "meanings" that are

6. See his *Domaines thématiques* (Paris, 1963).
7. In *Clio and the Doctors* (Chicago, 1974).

dug out of the work? Has it not been axiomatic since the 1880s that art is a pure creation? Its meaning, if one must answer the bourgeois questions about it, is only what the object is in itself, ideal and transcendent. "A poem must not mean but be." A painting is "the realization of an independent organism on a flat surface." "Every art tends to approximate the condition of music, which is pure form." This refrain has sounded patronizingly in our ears for nearly a century; it is the creed of most artists and connoisseurs. What is puzzling about this consensus on meaninglessness is that during that same lapse of time it has been found necessary to produce the largest output of commentary since Alexandria. Every new journal testifies to the richness of this explanatory literature which theory declares superfluous.

This paradox is but another example of the tendency toward absolutist thought in persons of more sensibility than reflective habit. Anyone will readily grant that art is for the most part not the direct imitation of nature, or the mere expression of a self, or the vehicle of explicit moral and social doctrine, or anything like a medium of information. But the fabric of art has again and again included these elements or served these purposes, vulgar as they may be. History and biography show when and why it has been so, and no one is in fact reluctant to accept as art the sculpture of a Gothic cathedral or a Bach cantata, *Pilgrim's Progress* or the novels of Balzac.

In beholding complex or abstract objects, we draw on correspondingly developed perceptions, which enable us to bring to each encounter minds flexible enough to respond differently to stylistic (that is to say, historical or biographical) variations. We do not listen to Bach as we do to Webern: we shift gears. Now when it is clear that a work of art does not impose even its surface appearance—let alone its effective form—like a waffle iron on soft batter, it must also be clear that the attempt to disconnect art and life, insight and temperament, imagination and vicarious experience is self-deception.

Art itself is indeed the strongest part of our vicarious experience. It merges with the direct whether we like it or not, as is shown by the thoughts, linked with some present active concern, that arise unbidden from the buried memory of a play or concert, a poem or painting. On those occasions a matter of deep interest is to discover how all the threads of one's experience are interwoven. One contemplates, for example, the indefinable connection between the figure of Rubens as courtier and diplomat and the art of the stupendous panels for the marriage of Marie de Medici in the Louvre. Viewers who lack the imagination of what the State is find these works merely virtuoso bombast. The born statist is, on the contrary, moved almost to tears. Only afterward, when reading some passage of Hobbes's *Leviathan*, will he discover the same pathos that stirred him in plastic form, independently of any symbolism or "story" or private interest in the historic king and queen.

This allusive freedom accounts for two of the facts before us—the variability of art over time (related to its ambiguity now) and the willfulness, so to speak, with which a period ordains what its art and criticism shall be. Although artistic enthusiasm likes to believe that the ages have conspired to bring about the right and perfect Art of Today, candor suggests that it is right and perfect only because we will have it so. We want to make room for our peculiar spirit—shove aside Shakespeare to let in Donne; we want change; we want to vindicate the neglected talents and virtues akin to ours. This is altogether proper. We have wanted poetry cryptic, witty, metaphysical, and painting nonobjective, witty, and metaphysical. We have given up storytelling over the whole range of art, including the novel (and, I would add, architecture, which now loves the noncommittal or enigmatic), all this so that we could freely make up our own stories, myths, symbols—or deny them all, as the mood takes us. Our witty music also eschews feeling and drama, and films may be made of a flux of indeterminate shapes. These are our meanings and intentions. We are enamored of il-literalism, which is why the critics have to work overtime to fill in the great silences of our "autonomous worlds."

A vested interest of this sort, a bias determining the signs we wish to respond to, is an historical constant. Each such bias has a beginning, a middle, and an end. History shows the rationality of its phases, exemplified in certain works and in one or more successive clusters of artists. The great works would then seem to be crystallizations of thought at an historical moment, which is also of necessity a biographical moment. It is this brand on the shoulder by Time which forever prevents, say, Schubert's Unfinished Symphony from being finished by somebody else. Yet the persistent feeling of independence from Time, though misstated by the critics, corresponds to a real perception. The pearl is utterly unlike the oyster. And the work is certainly not the mechanical product, nor yet the representation of the historical moment—any more than "the moment" is one year or ten, one climax of tradition or one stroke of new genius. All one-to-one correlations falsify, all linear and spherical analogies mislead. As in the evolution of language, the number of variables affecting art and springing from it is indefinitely great.

What then can criticism do? What has it got to work with? Obviously with the smaller portion of the numberless variables. Solid evidence from history and biography that bears on the character of the work or artist may, if handled with tact, light up dark places and remove blinders. The truism is worth repeating: if The Work raises questions, it is not self-sufficient, and whatever is not to be found within it must come from outside. Most often the addition is made not to the work but to the critic's organs of perception and system of reasoning. A new fact causes him to rearrange his mental furniture or screen out the rubbish. In establishing the text itself (in any art), history and biography do the main work. An opus number is a piece of history but may need biography to correct it, for it may follow the date of publication, not composition, and do so irregularly at that.

For ultimate enjoyment, to be sure, in the concert hall or library, The Work has to stand by itself. It pleases or not by its own means alone. But it is in fact rarely so isolated. There are Introductions and Program Notes, and we are informed with good reason that this sonata by the great Mozart was written at fifteen. Perhaps a thorough and accurate "placing" of what we care about in art would enlarge our individual sympathies and modify our tastes. The new configurations might well do more for enjoyment than all the competing "analyses." Many years ago Degas said "*Il faut décourager les arts*." I am far from agreeing, but I am ready to say that critics of a certain kind are in need of active discouragement. Too much is written about matters that should be taken in by the beholder as he hears or scans the work. It is not desirable that his conscious mind should entertain—or be prepared to entertain—clear statements of what he experiences under the spell of a masterpiece. The very reason why art is finer when it shows rather than tells is that comprehension is then immediate, not discursive. Ideally, the spectator must absorb—in order to be absorbed; and this means that the critic should shut up until he is wanted.

Against the view that the critic's task is chiefly facilitation and that for this purpose biography and history are his chief resources, there remain two common and related objections that can be quickly disposed of. The first should be called a danger rather than a difficulty. It is that the critic will turn his assignment upside down and use The Work as a document to explain the life, times, or character of the maker. Of such a performance one need only say that it is an individual error as well as a piece of bad historiography. To quote from poems or cite paintings to *illustrate* facts or attitudes discovered in historical and biographical research is legitimate; but no account based wholly or largely on excerpts from art can satisfy the historian. The fragility and ambiguity of such evidence is what makes some archaeological reconstructions more wonderful than convincing.

The second objection is a more serious form of this same inversion. Pascal was open to it when he said that in a book he wanted to find a man, not an author. All our modern instincts go the other way: the man is *haïssable*—and we don't care much for the author either. Wanting the work and nothing but the work, we make sure that no knowledge of these two fellows will shock us in our esthetic contemplation, like a dead face rising from the bottom of a pond.

To this threat from biography I would oppose the fact that we all know too much already about our favored artists to pretend an esthetic virginity. At the same time, by not pretending to it and developing our historical sense instead, we can become masters of our attention. Though we cannot help having a definite idea about John Donne as man and author, we can keep any irrelevant knowledge subliminal in rereading "The Second Anniversary." When listening to *Don Giovanni* we may even think once or twice: "That's just like Mozart!" without spoiling our pleasure or his art. It *is* like Mozart. And to dwell on "a daring modulation" or "an expressive scale on the flute" would be just as "wrong" as thinking of the composer, man and boy, by name and date.

True, one may be so constituted that the association of one's ideas always gets the better of consecutive thought. Alas, a listener whose mind is always flying tangents is rightly suspect; he will not make a good critic. But it is the conformation of his brain and the instability of his interest that divert him from The Work. It is not the knowledge *as such* that Mozart was a freemason and a bankrupt, loved champagne and the sound of the clarinet. The duty of the critic or connoisseur is to fuse his knowledge with his perceptions and dismiss what is not apposite. If he succeeds, he will find that nothing he knows in this fashion is "extraneous."

1975

22

Let the Artists Decide: An Interview

In one of your recent articles, you state, "Literature is the art which makes out of commonplace words a new substance that is expressive in the same manner as music: it does not tell, it shows." It strikes me that there has been a great deal of attempt at persuasion in the arts of the modern age. It hasn't continued to "show" in the old sense any more, has it?

That's a tough question as you very well know. The modern arts, I think, have taken on an additional duty—that of destroying our artistic expectations and perceptions, based on the last 500 years of high art. I think many modern artists have been purposeful destroyers. Through jokes and parodies and shocks—the whole surrealist movement in painting is a good example, or John Cage in music—the arts tell us: "You don't listen, you don't see, you're full of notions, you want nothing but copies of the great masterpieces, or derivatives from them. Well, we're going to teach you better than that—by fooling you, by shocking you, by making fun of you as audience." At least that accounts for a great deal of the art produced since 1920. I look upon this tendency as a kind of historical obligation the artists have felt, coming as they did at the end of a long period crowded with masterpieces—masterpieces which cannot be copied and ought not to produce still more derivatives. So the artist had little else to do but remind us of the importance of the senses in appreciating art, and at the same time making us self-conscious about what we call Art. That's how we arrive at anti-art, minimal art, art that is to be disposed of, found on the beaches, or made of a discarded refrigerator door. All those things are fiercely pedagogical: they're trying to teach the modern world something. I think the lesson has been learned, and we're sick of it, but now there seems not much else to do. At least this leveling of the ground for future creation has gone on, and will go on until somebody says the ground *is* level and we can put a new edifice of art on it, along lines that nobody can now predict or imagine.

Your comments in the chapter entitled "The Modern Ego"[1] suggest to me that the twentieth century has effectively denied its capacity to have genuine feelings. Do you still hold this view? What will artists of today have to do to reverse this trend?

I think self-consciousness in the bad sense is the disease of the age, and it's been brought on by bad experiences, beginning with the First World War, reinforced by the analytic method borrowed from science and applied to everything that is thought and felt. The general principle is, "It isn't as you think it is, it's something else." That idea undermines courage in people faster than anything else. That's why we have an age of anti-heroes, because the hero must have self-confidence, and the follower or admirer of the hero must in doing so be willing to take a chance.

There seems to be a nascent revival of Romanticism in the air these days, Romanticism being defined as a reaching out for the infinite capacities of individual man. Doesn't this reaching out for more tried forms of artistic expression offer us some hope that art will do better in the important matters?

I think the reaching out *is* there. The question is whether it is genuine, in the sense of being grounded in strong impulses

1. *Classic, Romantic, and Modern* (Chicago: University of Chicago Press, 1975). (Ed.)

and convictions, and not solely in the desire for a kind of restfulness, which modern art and modern life do not provide. What I'm asssuming is that good art, great art, is a strong affirmation. It isn't a search for a lotus-eaters' land. Then, I am also prepared for the fact that new tendencies in the arts always begin as affectation. Take, for example the return of the liking for Gothic architecture. It began during the mid-1700s with people picking up a few fragments and having artificial ruins in their back yards. We laugh at that, but they were doing the work of *re-recognition*. Later on, the thing becomes genuine. The same goes with the so-called revival of learning in the fourteenth and fifteenth centuries in Italy: valuing every scrap of the ancient classics and trying to put up buildings like theirs, thinking that everything contemporary was no good and that everything ancient was perfect. I call that affectation. Perhaps it's the only way in which people can move from one position to another. It's something which literally is "put on," to see if it fits.

Have you picked up any manifestations of new, strong impulses?

I can't think of any, except one that happens to be a peculiar interest of mine: I should like to see electronic music develop forms and attach them in some purely musical way to the pattern of human feeling and perception. If it did that, if the composers managed it in a natural way, then we would have a new art, an unexampled kind of art. I see very little else in the other arts that holds out the same promise of genuine freshness. Because for quite a while now, novelty in the arts has simply been doing the opposite of the usual, doing the topsy-turvy, the offbeat, both to attract attention in a market glutted with artists and to bypass the need for inspiration in the face of the flood of masterpieces which are now more and more on top of us—through museums, reproductions, the long-playing record, and paperback books—in a way the artist in past ages never knew. He never had to contend with so much glaring and obvious competition from the art which preceded him.

People in bygone times had the ability to put aside, as they needed to, the impositions of the masters around and before them, while at the same time as they desired, within limits, they could and would study them and learn much from imitating them. Whereas today, there is a lack of the sense of history, although at the same time we are awed (to a pathologic degree) by what's come before. And we seek to exploit shock as a reaction to that.

Yes. You can say it simply in a false syllogism: Great new art in the past has been shocking. Therefore, if I shock, I am producing great new art now. Also, shock attracts attention, and attention is what the artist needs. You can't blame him for wanting to be seen or heard or published. And if he writes something apparently mild, however strong in fact, the performance does not single him out.

The place of art in the past, in the present, and in human feeling, is so complex that no matter how conscientious one is in searching out the facts and comparing them, one ends convinced that every statement one makes about art, culture, and society is a guess, a very tentative hypothesis. History, if we may personify it for a moment, has a way of turning corners very sharply and facing the world with entirely new and—sometimes—attractive things.

Is art a mirror of its generation, or can its energies transmute its surroundings, the times which produce it?

It's not a mirror in the sense of being a perfectly faithful account of what went on or what people were like. What art shows is an inescapable relation which needs interpreting. For example, there have been artists who went counter to everything that surrounded them, but they too were influenced by the age, for when you're fighting something it leaves its imprint, and it records what occasions your resistance or rejection just as much as if one were a faithful mirror. And then there's always the individual distortion. Students who think they can read the novels of the 1840s and have some idea of how women and children were treated then are making a great mistake. There's no way of telling whether the particular novels on which they base their conclusions idealize, or were purely fanciful, or reflected a conventional position which very few people actually acted out. Such conclusions are laid upon quicksand.

One of the most popular questions asked about art is whether or not it has failed to mirror, or to change, its surroundings.

Yes. I'm not sure we ought to say that art has such-and-such functions and is doing well, or is barely passing with a C-minus grade. Art isn't something like a responsible public institution that we can criticize for not doing what we want. We've got to leave it to the artists; they have a hard enough time as it is, finding themselves, finding subjects, patrons— *feeding* themselves.

But the state of the art does concern the artists themselves. In a way, they are fish swimming in a stream that could be more, or less, polluted.

Yes, but individually they filter out what doesn't concern them. After all, the complete works of Jane Austen do not contain any reference to the French Revolution or its violent consequences in England. It's an isolated world, and yet critics find moral issues of the time very deftly handled in them. So, as I've said, "mirror" is a very ambiguous word which every user will interpret differently. The simple-minded will want the event and the record, either on canvas or in a book. As for music, the connection is there just as much. But it's not definable—you can't point to it or command it. You can't say, "Mr. Beethoven, I want something about Napoleon in one of your next symphonies."

Yet, and still, many feel this to be a burning issue: what modern art says to man, and what he says about himself.

Temperamentally I dislike the idea of expecting art to produce something for our good. Where did we get this notion that art was our servant in an institutional manner? I can criticize the post office because it doesn't deliver letters, or delivers them to the wrong place, or costs too much; but I am not disposed to say to art, wherever "it" might be found, "See here, you haven't been fulfilling your contract and I'm going to sue."

But isn't the artistic experience something like a contract?

True, but only after the fact. I want artists to do and produce what they want, and let them take the brickbats or the praise once they've done it. That differs from another system which is no longer ours—*commissioning* an artist, sitting on top of him and making him justify his ideas from the point of view of our needs. But with an unknown artist, I can neither direct him nor any of his *confrères* to give me something. I have only the right of rejection.

Precisely. But isn't art supposed to endeavor to show us something about ourselves, that we may not have thought of before?

I don't know that it has any such obligation. I think that it generally *does* show that—and it *will.*

Instead of "obligation," perhaps we can use the word "function," and back up to describe what function art really has. Or perhaps "function" is too didactic a word; maybe "effect" is more in order.

We can always complain of the effect. When art and religion were related, as I think in the best periods they have been, then the function could be more or less defined and even dictated. But today we are secular and pluralistic. You can have a portrait of your young daughter with golden curls, looking "just like life" if you want, or you can have an Albers series of squares within squares, called "Young Daughter." So pluralism, like the supermarket, gives us every brand, every kind, size, color. We go and shop.

I didn't have anything so specific in mind as "intervention."

I know, but that would be the only device by which you could exert a demand. Nowadays, perhaps our exercise of the right of rejection ought to be greater than it is. We've been hypnotized by the importance of art with a capital "A." But, even saying that it should mirror, or that it should show us something, teach us something about ourselves—that's as bad, or as futile, as saying that it should please and entertain us. We've given up the latter, by the way: we don't want to be pleased, and people *suspect* entertainment.

Shall we ever see a good cross-pollinated vocabulary of the arts? Are there enough real cognates among the arts that could be hooked up so that, when we talk, we say what we truly mean when calling a symphony "literary," a sculpture "full of movement," a painting "musical"?

It's the job of the critic to set his house in order, beginning with the vocabulary. In a highly literary age like the nineteenth century, it was perfectly natural that musicians and painters should take what they called "literary subjects," subjects which, as I've tried to show, do not remove their work from the realm of music or painting. Rodin was interested in history. All right, he took historical subjects, biographical subjects. Choice has to be natural and spontaneous. I don't think we can teach a painter to read if he doesn't feel like it. The essence of what he does remains, whether he reads or not.

This desire is very strong among artists, to communicate across the boundaries of their arts.

It's difficult. Painters tend to be inarticulate, because they think in shapes and colors, and they've never paid attention to words. Though some of them talk a great deal, unaware that what they say contradicts what they do, or is impossible to believe.

I was reading a statement recently by Henry Moore which in effect advised the artist never to talk about what he was doing because this would contaminate the artistic impulse and take his thoughts away from the nonverbal things going through his head. It's fascinating, because there are some artists who seem to have the need for chattering on at great length about what they're doing.

The modern world wants an explanation of everything, usually in quasi-technical terms. Earlier artists did their jobs and went on to the next ones without writing paragraphs of blather in the exhibition catalogs. Often there were none. The prose in our latter-day catalogs is an exhibit in itself—of mistaken intention, of "notions." The painter who paints a good picture should leave it at that. It's sometimes interesting to know what an artist has meant to do, or is looking for, but even that has to be interpreted, because when artists, including literary artists, are often unpracticed in the craft of systematizing ideas, you have to read what they say as clues and hints rather than as literal statements.

Robert Schumann was a very good music critic, and so were Bernard Shaw and Berlioz; Delacroix was in painting; and a good many literary men, beginning with Dante. But, generally speaking, art is a different mode of thought; as you say Moore points out, it's nonverbal creation. Let others rattle on, and let the creator create.

I've been touched by what you have written about the Modern movement and its stoppage by the First World War.

Yes, I think that's being confirmed day by day—that we go back to that prewar decade or to nothing. We need the honesty of that time in modern art, its example of health, genuineness, and affirmation in every innovative gesture of art. It contains in germ form everything we've done since. We've elaborated, we've teased out and analyzed, but it's still the seminal period in all the modern arts.

1980

23

The Case for Cultural History

Every reader today understands the meaning of the term Cultural History and could indicate its bearing. The idea of culture has not only been popularized by History's sister disciplines, Sociology and Anthropology, but men of letters have also made use of the word and the idea to explain the literature and the temper of recent times. "Our culture" is an entity to reckon with.

But in the mid-twenties, when I began my training in history, cultural history meant little or nothing outside professional circles. And there the phrase, taken as a literal translation of the German *Kulturgeschichte*, carried a taint of fraud. Good men sincerely doubted whether the thing denoted by it could be history at all. With a few exceptions, solid historians feared that a dangerous kind of philosophy lurked behind any professed history of culture. How could it deal with tested and tangible facts? And if it did not, it must dabble in ideas and "forms"; it must talk of the spirit of an age; it must reduce the past to essences and pursue the *Zeitgeist* by means which, strictly considered, would prove incommunicable.

The recognized traditions of historiography in the period I speak of were few. The oldest was the political. It dated from the beginning of the nineteenth century and took its motto from Edward Freeman, who had said in the later "scientific" phase of the tradition that history was "past politics." Buttressing political history was diplomatic and military history. But a second, newer tradition proclaimed the shallowness of these state-ridden histories and regarded its events as being but the surface manifestation of underlying economic forces. The influence of Karl Marx was at work in this departure from "standard" history, but he himself had in fact been jolted out of his Hegelian historical philosophy by the writings of the Saint-Simonians and other socialists, as well as by the histories of Sismondi, Guizot, and Louis Blanc; so that he was not the sole cause of the new departure. It had taken a century for the acknowledged economic element in human affairs to generate a specialized form of research and writing. We can judge of its unfamiliarity to American readers when we remember the hostile reception given Beard's *An Economic Interpretation of the Constitution* in 1913.

The First World War, coming soon afterwards, brought about a great change in public opinion. The war itself was visibly an industrial effort and the postwar generation was led by writers of note to believe that such catastrophes were the work of bankers, cartels, and munition makers. Historians who could not be dismissed as popularizers wrote as if men and nations were "pawns" in a perpetual struggle of "interests." Imperialism, which so regularly brought about wars, was the product of that same capitalist greed to which every other movement in society was but a "cloak." In the Europe of the twenties the historical assumptions roughly summed up here seemed to be verified by the success of socialism and communism, which renewed the vogue of Marx and Engels' writings and prepared the Great Depression cult of "Marxist Science."

But although the economic interpretation made earlier histories seem narrow, it did not prevail for long. To be sure, it left a valuable residue of economic studies free from doctrine. But other considerations made the tendentious view seem narrow in its turn, and more than narrow—mechanical and dogmatic in ways alien to the very method of history. In the first place, the war had brought many Americans to

Europe, of whom an influential part returned there as soon as they could after demobilization. Amid the pleasures of Paris or Capri they began that elementary cultural criticism which consisted in satirizing their native land through novels and plays; and in doing this they consciously or unconsciously denied the first premise of economic causation: the capitalist systems of Europe and America might be identical in form and purpose. but the two cultures *felt* very different.

When the Great Depression came, repatriating the exiles and luring them into Marxist study groups, their awareness of cultural fact was doubtless obscured, but it was replaced by a new concern which is still with us, the preoccupation with ideas that we call ideology. Though Marxist in origin, this concern also worked against the materialist conception of history. For in both immersions, in foreign culture and in ideology, the mind is led away from the tangible elements of society expressible in laws, battles, statistics, and toward the imponderable influence of habits, assumptions, and beliefs.

In the late twenties, the interest in these last was made systematic through the flowering of new disciplines that had been founded or reconceived by great innovators around 1900: the cultural anthropology of Franz Boas, the sociology of Durkheim, and the psychiatry of Freud. The culture pattern, the social group, the unconscious mind were beginning to be talked of as real forces—almost as independent beings—which made election returns and the price of wheat seem futilities by comparison. Indeed, a revulsion of feeling against the practical and business life took place in the United States in the thirties which quite transcended the resentment against an economic system that had broken down. It was as if the articulate had made over the image of modern industrial man. Hard work and the emblems of success were no longer civilized goals; they were replaced by the aims and rewards of the artist—leisure for sensation and the fine arts.

This recurrence of a mood which had swept Western

Europe during the nineties was accompanied by ponderings on the fate of civilizations. Spengler's *Decline of the West* appeared in 1918 and inspired critics and imitators, from Egon Friedell to Arnold Toynbee. Thoughtful readers were taken back to earlier prophets of doom or decay—Tocqueville, Gobineau, Nietzsche, Burckhardt, Flinders Petrie—and without abandoning their own interest in the local and contemporary, came to feel that mere events, however great or striking, were trivial compared with the rise and fall of whole cultures. As the Second World War swept over the entire world, it seemed as if we were witnessing at once the fulfillment of nineteenth-century prophecy and the spectacle of our new historical interest: old cultures sinking in the West and new ones rising in the East.

Today, therefore, anyone who thinks at all is something of a cultural historian. He thinks with the notions of cultural force, cultural crisis, cultural trend perpetually in mind. Newspapers and magazines are one mass of cultural "analysis," and books of every kind, not excepting fiction, make a large place for "the cultural context" as something far more intimate and compelling than the old economic base, the physical environment, or the still older "manners and morals."

These very remarks of mine are an act of cultural retrospect testifying to the receptivity which can be assumed in the modern reader: the ground has been prepared and the demand is there. But a general and fragmentary resumé of this sort differs from cultural history in the scholarly or professional sense. In that domain, the difficulties foreseen by the earlier skeptics subsist, and always will, though the skepticism itself has been gradually overcome by a combination of boldness with intelligent trial-and-error. The chief obstacles are: the indefiniteness of "ideas" when considered as historical agents and the apparent remoteness of the arts from the main stream of history. Clearly, if cultural history cannot

embrace art and thought, it makes an empty claim; without
them, we might as well content ourselves with politico-
economic history, seasoned with a dash of "social history"
whenever some powerful movement of feeling disturbs
familiar customs.

I remember being counseled, when I began in my graduate
studies to show a taste for cultural affairs, to keep such things
as an avocation. Fortunately, there existed in the Columbia
University History Department a tradition that counte-
nanced specializing in the history of thought. James Harvey
Robinson, then retired, had made his reputation by a course
and a textbook on the intellectual development of modern
Europe, and some of his successors—notably David Muzzey
and Carlton J. H. Hayes—continued to teach such kindred
subjects as the history of ancient thought and culture and the
rise of modern nationalism. It was on these foundations that
Hayes built to prepare his students for the doctorate, and it
was under his guidance and protection that my eccentric determination grew.

My purpose was of course not original or unique but reflected another tendency then expressing itself in the movement that was to be known later as General Education. In the
twenties this meant chiefly the possibility of uniting some
parts at least of philosophy, history, and the arts in an intelligible account of our past as thinking beings. In this endeavor George Edward Woodberry, Frederick J. E. Wood-
bridge, and John Erskine had played leading roles, and their
success could be measured a decade later, when Hayes in
1932–34 transformed his *Political and Social History of Modern Europe* into a *Political and Cultural History*. Students and
teachers across the country were evidently ready for the full
sections on art and the numerous, admirably chosen illustrations, which proved wordlessly to the eye that culture does
change in determinate ways. When about the same time the

Harper series on modern history was being planned under the editorship of William L. Langer, a versatile diplomatic historian, each volume was designed to contain at least one chapter on thought and culture.

These innovations were in fact a return. At the critical period when American universities were being fashioned around or out of the former colleges, that is to say in the 1880s, the proponents of specialized graduate study assumed that undergraduate education would remain untouched. They did not foresee that by their very success in scholarship all subject matters would split, after which every fragment would enlarge into a specialty, so that in time the unity of knowledge would disappear. We have the words of a representative university builder, John W. Burgess, to show how unsuspecting of future harm that generation was: we may assume, says Burgess in effect, that every young man who comes to our graduate school will have previously acquired the elements of *general literature and universal history.*

Whether the old classical education did in fact impart this knowledge of cultural history is of no moment here. It was an ideal which could no longer be followed when men gave up omnicompetence for specialization and resigned professorial chairs carved out of half a dozen branches of learning in order to become masters of one subbranch or period. For fifty years, as we saw, it seemed both undesirable and impossible to reconstruct the fabric of cultural history. But it was not for want of warnings. Philosophical minds saw the danger of atomized knowledge, however exact, and none expressed it more clearly than William James when he said:

> You can given humanistic value to almost anything by teaching it historically. Geology, economics, mechanics, are humanities when taught with reference to the successive achievements of the geniuses to which these

sciences owe their being. Not taught thus, literature remains grammar, art a catalogue, and natural science a sheet of formulas and weights and measures.

But for the reasons noted earlier, the sponsorship of philosophy was still suspect. Hegel was a menace and Buckle a solemn caution. History having painfully achieved the status of science must not fall back into the incertitude of ideas, even if it was occasionally forced to take account of such ideas as patriotism, nationalism, and imperialism. These must be reduced to causes that were facts, or history lost its virtue. Thus matters stood, until changes working within history itself, within culture, brought the public and the profession face to face with a desire and a capacity for cultural history.

To say that now we all more or less take cultural history for granted does not, of course, mean that we all understand it in the same way. Its wide acceptance is less a common intellectual conclusion than a sign of the self-consciousness which characterizes our times: we love to talk about our culture as we do about our psyches. The genre also records a shift from the last century's individualism to the collective awareness imposed on ours. Everything inclines us to believe that no man and no part of a man exists independently of the rest, and that consequently in history no single element is a prime mover, no single kind of clue an explanation of everything else.

But for the reader of cultural history or criticism—and all the more for the writer—many fundamental questions remain, questions that must be clearly put even if no hope exists of final answers. To begin with, which "culture"? It is not for the historian what it is for the anthropologist. For the last-named culture is an all-inclusive term covering everything from pots and pans to religion. But the historian writing about his own culture obviously need not describe for his readers what they know from daily use. Indeed he must not, or he will swamp his valuable new thoughts under tedious detail. Yet the historian cannot, either, take culture in its purely honorific sense of "things of the mind." The highbrow's culture is too likely to be a very thin slice of life—all butter and no bread—and as such incapable of standing by itself. It requires what we call background and might better be called underpinning. Given the task of appreciating all that is historically wrapped up in a Cavalier lyric, one must know what a Cavalier was, how he looked, whence he drew his ideas of honor and to what wars he was going when he bade farewell to Lucasta. Immediately, the historian is face to face with King Charles's head, the ritual of knighthood, Puritanism, and the origin of the fashion for men to wear long hair in curls. All this and more is necessary for an *historical* understanding of the unique cultural product from which we quote "I could not love thee, dear, so much . . . ." Conversely, the poem preserves an historical moment and may help reconstruct the cultural, that is to say at once the factual and emotional, past.

The cultural historian, in other words, must steer a middle course between total description (which is possible only to the anthropologist working on a limited tribal culture) and circumscribed narrative (which is the task of the specialist in the institutionalized products of culture: poetry or metaphysics or old silver). No one can say, not even the cultural historian himself, what class of facts he may be called on to bring into his narrative in order to make it intelligible. For example, writing of the 1840s in England or the 1860s in the United States, he would surely have to say a good deal about railroads, for they were new and influential in the culture. In a history of the 1940s or 60s he might neglect railroads altogether. The intelligibility of the whole, the relevance of the part are his sole criteria. This means that the cultural historian selects his material not by fixed rule but by the *esprit de finesse* that Pascal speaks of, the gift, namely, of seeing a quantity of fine points in a given relation without ever being able to demonstrate it. The historian in general can only show, not prove; persuade, not convince; and the cultural historian more than any other occupies that characteristic position.

In his private, shifting definition of culture the historian must moreover have regard to his audience. A cultural history of Japan for Western readers must include much that is useless to the Japanese; and even a cultural history of England written for the English will need supplementing for Americans. This is as much as to say that cultural facts do not unmistakably exist as such—a corollary from our elastic understanding of culture. Unlike a political, diplomatic, or economic fact, a cultural fact is generally not singled out for us by gross visible consequences. The publication of *The Origin of Species* in 1859 may resemble a political fact in the uproar it provoked, but we know that evolutionary theory and the belief in it do not date from 1859. This imposes on the cultural historian the delicate task of telling us where and how Evolution existed as a cultural fact for a century before 1859.

Contrast again the clear-cut overturn of a dynasty or the defeat of a government at the polls with the gradual destruction of a moral order such as Victorianism. When does it take place? It begins in the mind, in many minds, but how do we date and measure its progress? Is it from Samuel Butler's conception of *The Way of All Flesh*, finished in 1885, but not published till 1903? Or earlier, from the time when Dr. Clifford Allbutt began to give private lectures on sexual hygiene and Swinburne shocked all decent people with the sensuality of *Poems and Ballads*? In short how does the moral atmosphere change so that Fitzgerald's *Omar Khayyam*, a complete failure in the 1860s, is everybody's bedside book in 1900, by which time almost all the respectable beards and stovepipe hats have disappeared, decadence is fashionable, and woman is emancipated? And to add some material factors, how do the bicycle, the typewriter, and the automobile fit into this great cultural revolution? Has the vogue of outdoor sports anything to do with it? And what of the Boy Scout movement and the prevalence of appendicitis?

All the questions that might be asked raise the one great problem of assessing connectedness and strength of influence—again a task for the *esprit de finesse* and often a grievance to the student. The beginner is impatient and wants "the facts"; he contrasts unfavorably what he calls "straight history" with the apparently crooked ways of cultural history; and in a certain sense he is right. The ways of cultural history are devious and uncertain to the degree that there can never be a handbook which will list all the valuable facts, and no short cut to arrive at an understanding of relationships. Political and diplomatic history may be intricate in detail but they are emotionally simple—just like war, which they replace and resemble. But cultural life is both intricate and emotionally complex. One must be steeped in the trivialities of a period, one must be a virtual intimate of its principal figures, to pass judgment on who knew what, who influenced whom, how far an idea was strange or commonplace, or so fundamental and obvious as to pass unnoticed.

This kind of expertise does not of course exclude the use of statistics when these are available—the numbers of people who attended the Handel festivals in the eighteenth century, who welcomed Jenny Lind to the United States in 1850, or who visited the Crystal Palace the following year. But most often counting merely confirms; or else—as in the record of a book's sales—the figures themselves need confirmation. When, for example, we refer quantitatively to the great dissemination of Toynbee's *Study of History* in full and abridged forms, we must look elsewhere to make sure of what we are asserting: is it the acceptance of the author's thesis, and if so is it assent to the whole or to some part? Is it a generalized understanding of his tendency, or do the figures indicate a mere *interest* in the subject, coupled with a vague wish to believe some of the writer's conclusions—conclusions often learned from second hand reports and preceding the purchase of the book? In a word, what is being counted? Whatever report future historians give of the vogue of Toynbee, the fact of mere interest is what a present historian would assert about the comparable diffusion of, say, Herbert Spencer's works. The verdict would then be that his influence was extensive rather than deep, symptomatic rather than creative. Yet large sales do not always signify the same thing. In the success of Byron's *Childe Harold*, for example, real novelty fell in with a public appetite created by the circumstances of English isolation; and the new work, instead of ending with itself, inspired hundreds of artists for the better part of a century.

That these discriminations are not idle should be apparent. They have to be made in assigning magnitudes within the constellations of those who made the past, and they are the very substance of biography. In making such distinctions it is clear that nothing can supersede insight and judgment, neither the sending of questionnaires to the living nor the measuring of radioactivity from the tombs of the dead. And because this is true the skeptic at this point enters a caveat against cultural history. He deems it the most unreliable of historical genres, the farthest removed from the official, literal documents and figures that other kinds of history are directly based on. "You admit," says the skeptic, "that you cannot measure and demonstrate the influence of ideas, the effect of art forms, the impact of social change, yet you expect us to believe that 'the culture' of France or Germany or the American Colonies two centuries ago was as you describe it. Why, the chances are a thousand to one against there being any connection between your so-called evidence—a pitiful heap of books and letters and music and furniture—and the vast reality you pretend to reconstruct. What culture leaves to the historian is but vestiges of the doings of a very few. The more articulate your sources, the less likely that they are representative. You fill in and sketch out with your imagination and in the light of your present-day concerns. How can you honestly set forth the cultural history of so recent a time and so near a place as eighteenth-century Europe and America?"

This looks like a formidable indictment, but there is a sufficient answer to it. In the first place, culture has continuity it lives on as other kinds of facts do not. We have to learn what happened in the election of 1888 but we do not have to learn what is meant by progress, patriotism, natural science, or grand opera. The cultural historian therefore deals in large part with the modifications, the combinations, the rearrangements of ideas, feelings, and sensations familiar to all who lead a conscious existence. This is what enables him to have insight, much in the manner of the anthropologist, who begins to feel the force of minute events once he has gained familiarity with the culture he has been living in. The cultural historian lives imaginatively in his own culture and also in that which he has made his own by study; if at home in both, he is as trustworthy about the one as about the other, no more, no less.

As to the objection that cultural history is restricted to the doings of the highly conscious part of the population, it must be answered that the same objection applies to political and diplomatic history. And if the rejoinder is that the latter activities, led by the few, neverthelss affect the entire people, then the same must be said of cultural affairs. The new ideas of a handful of men in one generation become the fashionable thoughts of the upper class in the next, and the common beliefs of the common man in the third. Everybody now repeats as platitudes what were fresh thoughts in the minds of Jefferson and Franklin; and men of affairs who outside their business seldom give admittance to an idea without a struggle are now convinced that things first said by Adam Smith are self-evident propositions.

Nor is this descent-with-modification limited to opinions. The folk tune is often the art song of an earlier composer, and designs that originate in sophisticated minds and places wind up on wallpaper and chintzes by the yard. In short, regardless of cultural starting points, social groups and classes and nations exist in history through their conscious activities, through the distinctive forms, the characteristic combining of features, by which they strike the observer, contemporary or subsequent. "Exist in history" could be translated "are memorable," for in the definitive words of *1066 and All That*, "history is what you can remember." Just as in biography we take for granted the subject's daily routine of hair-combing and tooth-brushing, so in history we take for granted the great dull uniformities of vegetative behavior.

Hence it is beside the point to argue that millions of our fellow men live and die without bothering their heads about the work of Einstein or Freud or Bernard Shaw. Either the indifferent masses will ultimately feel the impact—the bomb will explode over their heads—or the existence of the masses is demonstrably related to mankind's articulate thought through their acting as background, subject matter, or chief obstacle. For the makers of culture do not make it in a vacuum, and whether they are hindered by the conservative third-hand culture of the mass, or draw the inspiration of their work from pondering over the vast stream of unconscious life, they are part of it, shaped by it. The example of a work such as Hegel's *Philosophy of History* shows how unimportant can be the gap between rarefied thought and its raw material—in this instance the philosopher's difficult vision encompassing the dumb travail of Europe's million's during the Napoleonic wars. It is the same miracle which in Goya's drawings of the same period turns the casual disasters of war—pillage, rape, hanging, and shooting—into spiritual treasure. The unrecordable comes to exist for history through a cultural product of the most deliberate and elevated kind.

It follows from this reciprocal dependence of the articulate and the inarticulate in life that cultural history differs greatly from intellectual history or the history of ideas narrowly defined. Cultural history cannot dwell upon the logic or lack of it in the various conceptions of philosophy, religion, or art without losing its historical character and distorting theirs. The study of these relations has value, but it is historical only in a limited sense, for it rests on exact definitions; and the outstanding characteristic of history as of life is indefiniteness; which is why, again, the *esprit de finesse* is required to grasp it. In communicating his vision the historian does indeed make an apparently hopeless confusion graspable by a certain amount of defining, grouping, and tidying up; but the moment the picture begins to look like a checkerboard, he has overshot the mark; he is no longer on earth but on Mars, where everything is canals.

On earth, for instance, the periods of culture have troublesome historical names—Renaissance, Baroque, Puritan, Classical, Romantic, and the like—which cover multitudinous manifestations of spirit. In using these names to denote men or periods, one cannot avoid trying to disentangle appearance from reality and prejudice from fact. But there is danger to truth in wanting things too clear; in wanting to make the names cover absolutely homogeneous ideas or persons. I for one see no use and great harm in those refined distinctions that profess to sort out eighteen kinds of Romanticism, or Humanism, or Pragmatism. I doubt whether the maker of such distinctions could himself respect them in an extended narrative; and supposing that he could, I fail to see what he would accomplish *as a historian*—unless it were to reduce the battle of ideas to a regulated ballet. To put intellectual order in place of the intelligible disorder of history is to apply the geometrical spirit to a subject that calls for the spirit of finesse.

The very point of tracing an idea to its source is that we then see it at work, meeting a problem or paradox, misunderstood, struggling for life like a newborn infant—not as we shall see it later, washed and dressed up for the photographer. The idea's obscurity or strangeness then has a meaning, and we can all the better gauge its force and do justice to the mind that brought it into the world. We are then not bothered by *his* inconsistency, because for the first time we are in a position to discern what he was thinking of and why he set it forth just so: we see him and it *in history*, pragmatically moving toward an unknown future, instead of as an event already classified—a pioneer, or a sad case, or an imperfect product of his times, now assimilated as one more institution in the body of all institutions we call our cultural heritage.

When we scan that heritage and its growth in any given stretch of time, one of the plainest sights afforded the observer is the extraordinary coherence and striking family likeness among the products of the age. This might in fact be made the test of the cultural historian's knowledge—not how much bibliography he can remember but how infallibly he recognizes a sample of prose, music, or painting, or even a particular deed. For acts too carry their dates engraved upon them, regardless of the motives which, abstractly considered, are eternal.

The historian familiar with the forms will therefore keep all the names of periods and schools as they are given him by history and concentrate on the rationale of their successive *styles*—a term by which he means a good deal more than the outward marks of a fashion. For unless he does mean more, he can hardly encompass the diverse tendencies and warring schools of one age which he knows belong together. Some fifteen years ago, in a series of Lowell Lectures on Romanticism later gathered into a book, I offered as an explanation of the internal unity of cultural periods that it came not from the ideas and forms themselves but from the questions to which these ideas and forms offered answers. On that view it becomes obvious how liberals like Byron and Hazlitt can be Romanticists equally with conservatives like Scott and Joseph de Maistre: they radiate from one center, which is to them no matter of choice but of time's compulsion. And this explanation, if true, also helps to mark off the part in cultural effort that is individual and creative from that which is "given," a product or resultant of anonymous forces.

Having seen my notion accepted as a commonplace in professional circles, I am emboldened to amplify it in hopes of making another lucky hit. As it stands, the source of unity I have suggested is abstract. Retracing it helps us to understand the convergence of opposites in science, philosophy, and political thought. It may even be stretched to cover the technical problems of the fine arts. In either realm, it presupposes the intellectual ability to find and state what these problems are. But what is it that gives to the products of an age their common feel and texture—the quality I have called their family likeness, which has nothing to do with intellect, cuts across genres, and unites things strictly not comparable? We feel, for example, that there is a kinship between the early music of Mozart and the prose of Voltaire—a prose that notoriously does not sing—and we wonder why these twins go so well with Louis XVI furniture. Is it an acquired association of ideas or is there some organizing principle at work? In short, is *style* explicable or arbitrary?

Since we cannot believe in a *Zeitgeist* invisibly at work like Ariel on Prospero's Isle, I submit that style, too, is an answer to a common want; but not so much to formulated problems as to felt difficulties of an emotional kind. Style will vary, of course, with the materials that give it body, but forget the stuff of verse or dress or chairs and an attitude remains: style is fundamentally a pose, a stance, at times a self-delusion, by which the people of any period meet the peculiar dilemmas of their day. In bad times the pose is sheer self-defense. At other moments, being creatures of ambition, men want to "be themselves" by repudiating their fathers—and imitating their grandfathers. Energetic amd insatiable, they want to make the best of both worlds—be gay yet profound, loyal yet canny, heroic yet safe, and so on—resisting choice while strength lasts. In the end they have to adopt the look which affords them the best chance of appearing as they wish to be. They take, as we say, a line; they form a style. Style is the solvent in which incompatibles are meant to merge. If it fits, it catches on and is imitated, to the point of absurdity and paradox—which is why, at least once, every historical style is suddenly seen to be ridiculous. It is then repudiated and a new one devised.

If this genesis of styles is accurate, we can account for a good many curious combinations of human characteristics that are periodic in both senses—time-bound and recurrent; for instance Roman *gravitas* mingled with the satirical spirit, which recurs in England's Augustan age; the boastfulness and gloom of epic heroes from Homer to Beowulf, the elegant frivolity mixed with false tears and real sadness of the late eighteenth century, the demonism and melancholy of the nineteenth, the sentimental toughness and lowbrow pretensions of our own. To ourselves we have no style—we just are—but posterity will smile just the same.

The advantage (and the test) of this hypothesis is that it makes genuine at last the connection between style in cultural products and the oft-invoked "existing conditions." These material elements, forces, states of being, are rightly named: conditions, not sole causes; but they cease to be vague and begin to yield to analysis when we see them as namable facts arousing the emotions reflected in style.

A further corollary is of even more immediate importance to the practitioner. I refer to the present vogue of Revisionism in the history of ideas. It is no doubt excellent to keep delving back into the past for origins. Men and ideas are all too easily overlooked, and our evolving interests also demand that we revalue what earlier workers neglected. It is moreover useful, as time clears the view, to correct over-emphatic distinctions between periods—for example, between the Enlightenment and Romanticism. We should no longer say that the Enlightenment had no sense of history in the face of great researchers like the Benedictines of St. Maur and of great historians such as Voltaire, Gibbon, Hume, and Robertson. In fact, with his *Essay on the Manners and Customs of Nations*, plumb in the middle of the century, Voltaire is the fountainhead of every succeeding movement to create a new and encyclopedic history.

But let us not forget style, and in our zeal to discredit a black-and-white contrast, let us not assume that gray has but one shade. The eighteenth century cultivated history, granted, and Voltaire was a pioneer cultural historian, but there is still a profound difference between the emotion that led him to choose four periods of civilization as alone worthy of record and the emotion behind Ranke's dictum that all periods are immediately before God and equal in his sight. There is an abyss between Gibbon's contempt for the barbarous centuries, his ironic pomp without circumstance, and Michelet's tender, eloquent intimacy with the Middle Ages. They are, we are, all are cultural historians together, but by their styles we may know them apart.

And though by style I explicitly mean more than words, I do not intend to exclude them. They are often the diagnostic signs of "period style" in the sense I have in mind. Depending more on written sources than on any other kind, the modern historian must in all his visions and revisions pay the closest attention to words, making sure that he does not betray them any more than they betray him. This vigilance can

save him from the excesses of the root-and-branch re-
visionists, who would translate all continuity into identity. If
he knows, for example, what "genius" meant to Addison, and
what it meant to Goethe, he will not fall into the error of
supposing that the principles of Romantic literary criticism
were already germinating in *The Tatler*. Or if, again, Tocqueville's claim to having introduced the word "individualism" in 1840 arouses the researcher's skepticism, he may
properly look for the antecedents of the idea. But it must be
that idea, in its concreteness and time-born accidents. It will
not do to go back to the early Renaissance and exhume Pet-
rarch's introspection as a first fact. That will only challenge
others to find in Jacques de Vitry and Robert Sorbon still
earlier proofs of soul-searching. Soon we are reading Abelard
and mustering heretics—all strong individualists before God.
But none—to the candid eye—resemble Tocqueville's model
any more than Fenimore Cooper's heroes of free enterprise
resemble Mr. Herbert Hoover.

Nor should our concentration on like products within a
cultural cycle blind us to the radically unlike which in any age
co-exists with the dominant forms, though submerged or
subdued. Every period has its minority interests, which the
discerning eye must note even when the minority does not
enlarge into the majority of the next generation. The burden
of diagnosis is then to say what the dissonant note contributed to the harmony, how it came to be part of it, and
what fresh, unsuspected, general problem its resolution
would imply. The motions of the whirligig of taste present a
multitude of riddles—why did the geometrical Spinoza lan-
guish in the century of geometry and flourish in the biological
century of Goethe? Why are there so few avowed Prag-
matists today, when pragmatic doctrine oozes out of the
pores of all our straining existentialists and positivists? These
questions, like the rest, will not be evaded by the cultural
historian, present or future, who sees his duty clear. But he

will be able to answer them only by the application of such finesse as he is gifted with. Intelligibility being his goal, he cannot escape the effort to understand; he cannot ask somebody else to explain nor shut his eyes and count. It is insight, after the count has shown a preponderance of old-fashioned dwellings, that makes him say the dominant architecture of New York is modern. The rest is footnotes.

1956; rev. 1972

24

Philosophy and the Arts

The relation between art and philosophy is a subject perenni-
ally attractive—tempting—because it holds out the promise
of a set of rules by which the many minds interested in one or
another of the arts can guide their judgments, classify their
experiences, and prove to themselves and to the world that
art is indeed important. On their side, the great philosophers
who have made systems of the universe have often added an
Esthetics to their Metaphysics, Ethics, and the rest. I say
"added," because in most cases the Esthetics came last, as it
were by an afterthought. Something or somebody reminded
them that art existed, out there in some corner of the visible
world. Or it may be that esthetics came last because the
subject is thorny and it was put off till other questions had
been settled.

In truth, most such esthetics have been rather mechanical
adaptations of formulas and conclusions reached by the philosopher in his previous meditations. It had better fit into the
last cubbyhole or it will have to do without a place. Kant is a
good example of this historical fact. He was as it were the
perfect anesthetic. He had no paintings or sculptures in his
house, and the *Rheinweinlied*, a drinking song by Johann
Andre (1776), was to him "the highest of musical compositions of its kind." John Dewey's fuller awareness of the domain to cover is not more sensuous. Both philosophers—and
many another—give us the impression that their attachment
to art was formal, theoretical, no doubt sympathetic, but
certainly not a passion, as the attachment of the un-

philosophical visibly is. George Santayana is a notable though incomplete exception. In *The Sense of Beauty* he displays his fine sensibility and says many good things. And yet his coolness is not merely philosophical detachment; it is temperamental—as we see in *Reason in Art*, where the man with the cubbyholes again comes forth with intent to have his way.

Other writers have tried to be philosophers of art without first adopting or inventing a general philosophy. They have simply written a Philosophy of Art as their sole contribution to comprehensive inquiry. The defects—or difficulties—one finds in *their* works is that art is usually treated from the point of view of *one* of the arts, that which the author is most familiar with, or finds most congenial and—explicitly or not—takes as representative of the rest. In the reader's mind the thought recurs: "But this doesn't apply to music!"—or painting, or the dance; and the text utters no reply. With the recent expansion of the term "art" to cover film, photography, the popular arts, and the latest avant-garde efforts in "found art," "minimal art," "disposable art," and "aleatory art," it would seem likely that no philosophy of art as such could find its exponent, or could satisfy the diverse connoisseurs, if a thinker attempted the synthetic feat.

In spite of their shortcomings many of the single works by true students of one or more arts are valuable and should be read by anyone who wants to be more than a dilettante partaker or critic. I particularly recommend Louis Arnaud Reid's *Study in Aesthetics* (1931). Not only do such studies bring out aspects of art that will have escaped the beholder, but they also exhibit the variety—the unpredictability—of the responses and judgments that art elicits from thoughtful minds. Or to put it differently, these books show the seemingly infinite number of uses art is made to serve by its devotees. At the same time they show that few people are moved by more than one or two arts. That in itself is an important clue to the nature of the subject.

Indeed, this last fact suggests to me two important truths. One is that temperament must be considered in any philosophy of art. I believe with William James that temperament plays a role in philosophy at large, and not just in theorizing about the arts. But this is another question for another essay. The point here is that detailed psychological knowledge must come early into artistic discussions. We know, for example, that perception and memory show differences among types of individuals; they may be classed as visual, auditory, and motor (or muscular). Who can doubt that the great divergences in judging the classical composers, for example, bear some relation to these marked differences in the habitus of the listeners? And since few things in nature are absolutely clear-cut, it seems probable that the incompatible viewers of Ingres and of Delacroix, though comparably "visual," divide on the degree to which their constitution is "motor."

This supposition is not intended to reduce artistic preference to physical fact and declare it automatic. On the contrary, the psychological truth should enlarge our tolerance of rival schools and incommensurable artists, by showing that the experience they offer is not and cannot be "taken" identically by all beholders.

The second inference I draw from radical diversity is that since temperaments vary and since the several arts differ as they do in their means, their effects, and their power, then a general philosophy—a set of universal statements about Art with a capital A—is an impossible goal, an illusory hope. Such seems to have been the conclusion of the philosopher whom I have already mentioned and whom I trust and admire above all others—William James. Quite apart from my estimate of his mind, he has claims on our confidence in the matter at hand for a number of reasons. He was himself a man of great artistic gifts and rich sensibility. He was a painter by training and almost by profession; his artistry in words makes him one of the masters of American prose. Add his independent judgments in literature and you can be certain that when he said "art" he was not using a mere abstraction.

Equally important, in his epoch-making *Principles of Psychology* he first brought out the fact that the human mind natively and habitually pursues esthetic interests, side by side with the practical. The way sensory experience becomes organized, he tells us, is at once for convenience and for esthetic satisfaction, for the pleasure in design. Form and use go hand in hand. Indeed, it may be said—and I have shown it elsewhere[1]—the mind as James represents it is an artist, not a scientist or manufacturer, as other philosophers have made it out to be.

This Jamesian demonstration is reason enough for anyone interested in the arts as performer, amateur, or critic to read and reread the *Principles of Psychology*. Every chapter, and not just the one on the stream of consciousness, is full of illuminating truths and examples of the ways in which we "take" reality, perceive objects, organize experience, store memories, forge and call up associations. Since art consists of objects—objects made up on purpose to afford peculiar experiences—it is essential to know what goes on when the mind turns its attention to them, for purposes hard to define but most exacting.

James was aware of these several considerations and reflected on them. At times he regretted not having dealt with Esthetics as a topic in itself. Living and writing in the 1890s, he had every inducement to do so: it was the decade when art finally displaced religion in the public mind as the highest expression of spiritual power. Art was social critic, moral prophet, and evangelist of the ideal all in one. It seemed then, and has remained since, the antagonist of a bad world—and its redeemer. So a philosophic account of its essence and function would not have fallen on deaf ears or

1. "William James and the Clue to Art," in *The Energies of Art.* (New York, 1956). (Ed.)

seemed a dispensable appendage to an original system of thought. But James's matured conclusion was the one I appropriated above: the nature of art and the responses to it are too fluid to permit valid generalities. His own words give, as usual, a vivid idea of his understanding: "The difference between the first- and second-best things in art absolutely seems to escape verbal definition. It is a matter of a hair, a shade, an inward quiver of some kind—yet what miles away in point of preciousness! Absolutely the same verbal formula applies to the supreme success and to the thing that just misses it, and yet verbal formulas are all that your aesthetics will give" (*Letters*, 2:87 [1899]).

The phrase "inward quiver" refers, of course, to the feeling-thought of the beholder, the thrill which great art occasions and which has earned such names as "the shock of recognition," "the characteristic shiver"—all akin to the *frisson nouveau* that Victor Hugo found in Baudelaire. All these terms remind us that judgments of art depend in a unique way on feeling and predisposition. We may return to the work and change our opinion, but if we do so it is by virtue of a second "inward quiver"—or its absence. Nobody, in other words, can be reasoned into communion with a given work of art as one can be reasoned into a moral, political, or philosophical position. Take pains to demonstrate the technical skill and formal beauty of a work to a skeptic and he may well say: "I admire it now, yes, but I still don't like it."

The common description of this attitude is "subjectivism," but again, where art is concerned, subjectivity is peculiar. Its most striking feature, perhaps, is the fanaticism that lovers of art show about their likes and dislikes, even though no ulterior interests seem to be involved. The passion is sheer. In politics or religion it can be explained by reference to what victory or defeat will mean to the welfare or future hopes of the individual. But why does an adverse opinion of Brahms or Michelangelo arouse in their admirers a desire to suppress that opinion and muzzle the speaker? In these days of pluralism, differences in morals and religion seem much more easily accepted or endured than in esthetic attachments. No doubt this sectarian fury has something to do with the virtual replacement of traditional religion by art, as I suggested above. But art is not well adapted to conveying the kind of truths out of which theologies are built. And so the indignation, the contempt, the irrevocable damning that go on are frustrated, heightened by the lack of first principles and general formulas.

Thus what we find in the world of the arts is perpetual anarchy. We find it, though it is often unacknowledged. In each clique there is no question that So-and-so are the universally admired masters and Such-and-such their masterpieces. These names and titles differ from clique to clique, from country to country, and from continent to continent; and everywhere those differences are generally ignored. The merest glance at the history of the arts also shows that from generation to generation the masters and masterpieces change, radically. It is hard for us to imagine that for a couple of centuries—long after his death—the greatest literary genius was said to be—Cicero. But the fact is on record. Where is Cicero now? The final judgment of posterity is a myth.

True, periods and places of wide agreement have existed, and they seem to contradict my generality about anarchy being the usual state. The contradiction disappears when one takes into account the working of social pressure. Subjectivity is powerful, but cultural currents are no less so. Many good judges secretly dislike or despise names that conventional minds believe they like and that well-meaning hypocrites pretend to like, for kudos among their friends. This is especially true when some new star is discovered. Thus George III, who was no fool, tried to get Fanny Burney to agree with him about Shakespeare's plays being full of dull stuff, and he added, "Only one mustn't say so, what, what?" It was the beginning of Shakespeare idolatry and the idol dare not be caviled at.

If this is the actual condition of art and the perennial behavior of its devotees—as anyone can see for himself by reading a few histories and a sampling of contemporary critics—we need no longer wonder that Esthetics is an impossible subject for philosophy. It is at once too personal and too social for abstract thought to seize upon any regularities. If the example of history and the historians is invoked—for here too one faces a chaos of facts and beliefs—it is of no avail, for historians succeed in creating order through detachment, which the very nature of art forbids. A philosophy of art on those terms would be but a catalogue of techniques and devices, and even these would be misrepresented, for they have no independent importance, only a functional one as triggers of meaning.

Fortunately, "philosophy" can be understood in at least two senses. It can denote a system, a theory strictly so-called, that is: the most complete and most general view of a subject. It can also mean philosophizing. Not being a philosopher in the first and strict sense, I have taken the liberty, all my life, to philosophize in the second sense—to try to think straight about the subjects that have interested me. What can philosophizing about the arts do for us? The answer I would propose here is not a series of conclusions, even tentative ones, but rather a series of topics or issues about which straight thinking might, in addition to the pleasure of the thing, do some good. What good? Well, such good as this: clearing up the confused vocabulary of criticism for educated minds, and gradually building up a set of commonsense maxims—guidelines—by which sincere people who wish to converse about art could avoid the fumbling and stumbling now caused by what they have been taught—the "ideas" or fashionable cant—thus inducing a wider tolerance through showing how the casual or formal creeds of art-lovers are linked to temperaments and visions of the world.

These endeavors, if they were achieved, would liberate many good souls from the oppression of having to admire what they don't admire and having to repudiate what they secretly love—a net increase in the freedom and happiness of mankind. Even a partial success in this charitable progam would justify the effort. So I proceed to the questions that seem to me to require more or better thinking than they have received.

The first is the psychology of artistic perception: what happens when one is looking at a painting, a ballet, a building; when one is listening to a piece of music or a play; when one is reading poetry, a novel, or any kind of work called literature. Not what ought to happen if you want to boast of your sensibility, but what does happen; and, to begin with, what happens in a perceptual sense.

I. A. Richards in his "practical criticism" of poetry took a step in this direction, but it was not followed up, and his interest was rather in improving response than in ascertaining its elements. His Cambridge colleague P. E. Vernon went farther with music, and his findings should show the way. I suspect that if such inquiries were extended to all the arts, the honest answers would differ markedly from what one thinks is taking place in oneself and in others—let alone differ from the celestial intimations recorded in the works of critics, historians, and artists themselves.

My purpose should not be misunderstood. I am not trying to bring down the enjoyment of art to something simple and commonplace. On the contrary, I think the witnessing of art so complex and comprehensive that *all* its constituents should be brought into awareness, if that is possible, before explanations are contrived. I have in mind such one-sided doctrines as that which holds esthetic experience to be the perception of pure form. I do not know what pure form is and I am not told by the theorists. Nor do I know what others mean when they say that art is for them the gateway to a world of absolute values, or mirrors eternal truths, or transmutes sensation into structure, or creates autonomous worlds obeying their own laws. In fact, I find myself resisting nearly all the honorific remarks that intellectual people make when they are moved under the spell of art to tell the world about it.

Not that I doubt their sincerity or the vividness of the experience that inspires their language; but if we are to have straight thinking we must begin by giving *clear* names to *recognizable* things. And by things I mean not the grammatical parts of technique, but the unpredictable portions of the presented object. Talk and thought about art must conform to the canons of common sense, because art offers itself to the senses and the mind not as an idea or an abstraction, but as a piece of concrete experience. Nor does common sense here mean conventional opinion but thought free of jargon.

Bringing art back to its first condition as experience enables us to frame our question clearly. Art is a special, peculiar kind of experience, yet not radically different from the ordinary kind; the two overlap, more or less. The shapes, colors, sounds, movements, and words that we meet in art begin by resembling the shapes, colors, sounds, movements, and words that we meet when we walk into the kitchen or into the street. Vast as the distance is between the great painter and the house painter, they both strike upon the sensorium by laying pigment on a surface. How do we account for the difference, emotional and other? Red and green on the street mean stop and go, whereas in a painting they have no such suggestion. The two notes of the modern doorbell do not announce a sonata, but a package. Unless we start with this gap in perception—that is, if we compare art only with art—we shall never quite understand what makes art what it is. After more than two thousand years nobody has been able to tell us how the same words that we use to order lunch can be twisted into poetry. To put it abstractly, How does a new, heightened significance come to attach itself to some perceptions apparently identical with those that make up life?

A usual answer is that by their subtle arrangement and their obvious artificiality the sensations, the perceptions—in short, the signals—we receive from art produce in sensitive beings the specifically esthetic experience. Much has been written about the esthetic experience: imitation (mimesis), beauty, harmony, order, systems of relations, Platonic recollection of ideal forms, patterns evoking myths and archetypes, language and logic conveyed through symbols— these and other principles have been put forward as accounting for the difference between Cézanne's apples in paint and the real apples, between the terror in *Oedipus* and *Hamlet* and the terror we read about in the papers.

But none of these abstractions and criteria is adequate. While we are witnessing *Oedipus* we are not really feeling or thinking of pure form, nor does the action imitate anything we have seen—except perhaps in another play. It can also be said that what happens in tragedy is ugly, not beautiful, and much modern art is deliberately un-beautiful. Meanwhile it is equally clear that if we knew nothing of ordinary workaday events and emotions we would not feel terror, even though the stage terror is unlike the terror of being actually held up or kidnapped by a maniac. To which puzzle we should add that the real apples in the bowl must possess some aesthetic quality or Cézanne would not let his eye linger on them. This last point has been reinforced by the principle of "found art": the "artist" shows you a piece of driftwood picked up on the beach and invites you to look upon it esthetically. On 57th Street you pay the gallery for the privilege of gazing at an old spring mattress or—in another gallery and vision of art—at a literal rendering in paint of cans of Campbell soup. Every formula is contradicted by another as well as by a fact, and the whole is a spectacle of anarchy comparable to that which obtains among the judgments of merit and worth.

When one remembers also the doctrinal battles between representationists and so-called abstract artists, between the upholders and the condemners of so-called program music, between the poets who insist on "communicating" and those who insist on puzzling, one must acknowledge that the vocabulary of debate is too primitive to make critical discussion anything but futile.

As for the makers of art, they too are at sixes and sevens, whether they adopt current notions or create their own. This incoherence holds not only in successive generations or schools of art, but simultaneously as well. For example, an American poet gained much praise for a line that said: "A poem must not mean, but be." The disciples favored the notion of art as "autonomous," wholly detached from the real world. They denied that art properly interpreted was meant to convey knowledge or arouse emotion—at least not common emotion, only esthetic emotion. And this, they went on to say, was indefinable: one must experience it, after a long apprenticeship to the best masters. Yet at the very same time, modern practitioners in the plastic arts discovered the merit of African sculpture, Aztec art, Easter Island monuments, and a host of exotic works that we know were made on purpose to convey religious knowledge and arouse plain feeling, not esthetic, in groups and individuals, primitive or highly civilized. In taking these works esthetically, we deny half their value, we only half understand. With not just this one but a whole raft of double standards claiming our distracted observance, the need for philosophizing is more than ever apparent.

If we should start, as I have suggested, with the truths of what happens when a cultivated person goes through the tumultuous experience of taking in a work of art, we might soon reach reach at least a few patches of firm ground. From what we know of psychology at this very moment, it is most unlikely that that experience is in any sense pure. It is not detached from workaday experiences or the dark tangle of our memories. The word "autonomous" does not apply. Again, the associations aroused in each person are not all conscious and not easily controlled, but all are charged with feeling—common emotions of varying kinds and intensities. If Pascal could say that a proposition in geometry becomes a sentiment, then the bearing of a tragedy or symphony, a ballet or a depiction in plastic art, must surely stir and re-shape our viscera. We do say we are "moved" by a work of art. Some modern artists have tried hard to make their works totally aseptic as regards idea, feeling, and purpose; but that has proved a hopeless task. Read the critics and you discover that in a "sculpture" consisting of a double layer of gray building blocks one writer finds "cool serenity" and in a whirl of many-colored lines another sees "intimations of inno-cence." The human mind is so constituted that it finds mean-ings in virtually anything it perceives; the practice is a device for keeping sane.

If that is so, we are (I think) compelled to give up the notion of the esthetic experience as such. Rather, we must see art as an extension of ordinary experience, a man-made extension built of the same materials as life itself, and special in being distilled and intense. That is why we say of art that it is a *creation* and also that is *expressive*. It does not express something already there, as when we say that we "express our gratitude." It is expressive of the nameless and unbound. It shows something new or recasts something old, but always by exploiting our knowledge of life—of a particular type of life at that. If it were not so there would be no need of explana-tions for an understanding of, say, Japanese art, or even of past art, ancient art, in our own culture.

From habit we ignore how much of sheer information we bring to the bare witnessing of any work of art. *Oedipus* would be simply silly to a tribe where incest was not a sin or a crime; *Hamlet* would be incomprehensible to a people ignorant of monarchy, monogamy, play-acting, fencing, soliloquizing, burial in the ground, and the belief in ghosts. It could be shown, I am convinced, that the cliché which turns this play into the spectacle of Hamlet's indecision is due to a type of factual ignorance, namely, of court politics, which Hamlet is as aware of as Shakespeare's audience, whereas academic and theater critics are not. They think Hamlet can do anything he has a mind to because he is a prince, which is a child's view of the state of Denmark. Philosophic criticism should consequently determine what and how much various forms and works of art require us to furnish for their understanding.

What the spectator brings can of course distort the work, or at least give it a peculiar slant. This often happens in periods of strong religious feeling and, in secular times such as ours, of strong ideologies. The Marxist interpretation of Balzac or Theodore Dreiser is a case in point. This danger sets another task for the philosophizing mind: he must try to ascertain the full measure of his emotions and mental associations—impossible, but it must be attempted nonetheless—and then ask himself how far these ingredients of perception and response are consonant with the words or other substance of the work. It is in this self-examination above all that the critic must beware of current formulas and clichés. They are fatally seductive and easy to apply. If candidly considered, most of them will be seen to fit only a portion of the work as actually witnessed, or perhaps not even so much—only a touch here and there. The cant phrase is that myths, symbolic interpretation, theme analysis, biographical facts, depth psychology "throw light." They may, but the manner in which they do and the limits of their purport must be shown, not assumed. Such aids can easily be more plausible than philosophical.

The topics to be philosophized about come down to these: what am I perceiving? what are its possible meanings? what meanings are excluded by other perceptions given earlier or later in the work? what associations are legitimate—that is, not forced, not egotistical, not imported by coterie or convention? Finally, in what fitting words, simple words, can I frame my ordered conclusions for others to compare and verify?

Anyone is free to object that this program kills the excitement appropriate to the experiencing of art. I would reply that it does not kill but postpones the desired fever to the next time. Between experiences, the philosophical spirit analyzes or describes and points out. After all, nobody is compelled to be philosophical. Let the fanatic revel and ejaculate, but let us not take his frenzied phrases for critical terms, any more than the verbalisms of the system-maker or method-monger. It is in any case possible to be passionate and thoughtful, both. There is so much in art that is difficult, obscure, deceptive, that we need to direct upon it all the calm attention we can muster. The great critics have done just that, and they were not insensitive clods, or else they could not have told us the little we can trust about art. It is plain that Aristotle felt, as well as understood, tragedy. For Dryden to restore Chaucer to esteem, he had to be both analytic and involved. When De Quincey wrote the piece on knocking at the gate in *Macbeth* he had been deeply moved, or he would not have discovered the secret of that passage. Likewise, when Lamb explained the apparent fault in Leonardo, or when Hazlitt, as we say, "threw light" on many points of poetry and drama.

What we need, now that art has become common property through a social revolution and diffusion by technology, is to

accumulate the scattered insights into a treasury of philosophical knowledge, couched in clear language. It will not be
universal in scope; it must admit exceptions, variations, and
paradoxes. Different periods and cultures present different
bodies of artistic substance that cannot be reduced to common terms. These differences themselves are, I maintain,
instructive, just as are the irreducible differences in temperament—in sensorium—among individuals. And ultimately reasoning finds its limits. One feels about certain authors, about certain symphonies or paintings, about *Swan
Lake* uncut, that nothing on earth could make one accept
them. They do not merely leave one indifferent as do some
other works; they arouse violent distaste. The cause is not
assignable, and since other good judges bring to those works
and their creators the tribute of reasoned appreciation, one
can only conclude that here is a sign of one's limitations—and
theirs too, since they cannot rescue us from ours. The case
parallels exactly what happens when one meets a stranger
who proves instantly uncongenial. It may be that further acquaintance removes the impression—that may take place
about art, too—but often, too often, the dislike is radical, and
inexplicable.

For artistic pleasure to be felt there must be some correspondence between the secret, speechless, but vivid experience embodied in the work and its counterpart in the beholder. The portion held in common, less than the whole, is
what enables the work gradually to extend the beholder's
awareness to the remainder, to stretch his mind and feelings
and make him believe that he has been in a new world and
seen the ineffable. At that point, if he is not careful, he will
utter a poetic hyperbole. If he is philosophical, he scans his
memory and he notes once again that art is not a homogeneous substance or quality, else he would respond equally
strongly to whatever deserves to be called art. And he concludes with the great critic John Jay Chapman that "we can-

not hope to know what art is." That thought confirms the statement that art is experience extended, for similarly we cannot hope to know what life is. Yet we keep exploring its mysteries and nothing can stop us from philosophizing about it.

1980

Acknowledgments

The editors of the periodicals and publishing houses under whose imprint certain parts of this book first appeared kindly facilitated their reprinting and are hereby thanked for their help.

For this collection, some of the pieces have been retitled and Mr. Barzun has been allowed to make a few minor, non-substantive revisions in the text to gain clarity.

The full bibliographical information appears below, the consecutive numbers corresponding to those of the Table of Contents.

1. Library of Congress lecture, October 23, 1951; reprinted in *The Score* (December 1954).
2. Address to the Society for Music in Liberal Arts Colleges, December 1949; *Juilliard Review* (1954).
3. Reprinted from *High Fidelity* (August 1956). All rights reserved.
4. Review of George Bernard Shaw, *How to Be a Musical Critic,* in *The Mid-Century* (June 1961).
5. Preface to Arthur Loesser, *Men, Women and Pianos* (New York: Simon & Schuster, 1954).
6. Introduction to Joan Peyser, *The New Music: The Sense Behind the Sound* (New York: Delacorte Press, 1971).

Address at Columbia-Princeton Electronic Music Center concerts, McMillin Theatre, Columbia University, May 9 and 10, 1961; expanded into Preface to Herbert Russcol, *The Liberation of Sound* (Englewood Cliffs, N.J.: Prentice-Hall, 1972).

Remarks at Varèse Commemoration at McMillin Theatre, Columbia University, December 1965; revised version in *Columbia University Forum* (Spring 1966).

7. Review of Stendhal, *Life of Rossini,* in *The Nation*, January 24, 1972, under the title "Confounding the Happy Few."

8. *The Musical Quarterly* (January 1980).

9. *The Musical Quarterly* (January 1970).

10. *The Berlioz Society Bulletin* (Summer–Autumn 1977).

11. Exchange of letters with Enid Starkie, published in *The Griffin* (June 1958).

Letter in Book Review section of *The New York Times*, Sunday, January 10, 1972.

12. *Saturday Review* (April 29, 1950).

13. *Atlantic Brief Lives: A Biographical Companion to the Arts*, ed. Louis Kronenberger (Boston: Atlantic–Little, Brown & Company, 1971).

14. Review in *The Musical Quarterly* (January 1974).

15. Typescript reconstructed in 1979 from the original notes for a talk given at a performance of *Lélio* in 1955, at the College of the City of New York.

16. Booklet accompanying the RCA recording of *Romeo and Juliet* by Charles Munch and the Boston Symphony Orchestra, 1953; subsequently excerpted for various concert performances of the same work.

17. *Magazine of Art* (November 1949), under the title "Romanticism: Definition of a Period."

18. *Midway* (Autumn 1967) (published anonymously).

19. *University Review*, Journal of the University of Kansas City, June 1940.

20. *Atlantic Brief Lives* (see No. 13 above).

21. *Critical Inquiry* (March 1975), under the title "Biography and Criticism—a Misalliance Disputed."

22. *Christian Science Monitor*, July 17, 1980. Interview by David Owens, under the title "Looking at Man and His Arts." Reprinted by permission of *The Christian Science*

Monitor, ©1980 The Christian Science Publishing Society. All rights reserved.

23. In *The Varieties of History*, ed. Fritz Stern (New York: Meridian Books, 1956; rev. 1972, under the title "Cultural History: a Synthesis").

24. Lecture at Notre Dame College of Maryland, Baltimore, Md., October 5, 1980.